WILLIAM WALTON: A SOURCE BOOK

WILLIAM WALTON
A SOURCE BOOK

compiled by

STEWART R CRAGGS

Scolar Press

Published by
SCOLAR PRESS
Gower House
Croft Road
Aldershot
Hants GU11 3HR
England

Ashgate Publishing Company
Old Post Road
Brookfield
Vermont 05036
USA

British Library Cataloguing-in-Publication Data.
A catalogue record for this book is available from the British Library.

ISBN 0 85967 934 9

Typeset in 10 point Goudy by Poole Typesetting (Wessex) Ltd., Bournemouth, Dorset
and printed in Britain at the University Press, Cambridge

To

ROY DOUGLAS

Previous Publications

William Walton : a thematic catalogue   OUP, 1977
William Alwyn: a catalogue   Bravura, 1985
Arthur Bliss: a bio-bibliography   Greenwood (USA), 1988
Richard Rodney Bennett: a bio-bibliography   Greenwood, 1989
William Walton: a catalogue   OUP, 1990
John McCabe: a bio-bibliography   Greenwood, 1991

In preparation
Alun Hoddinott: a bio-bibliography   Greenwood
John Ireland: a catalogue   OUP
Arthur Bliss: a source book   Scolar Press
William Mathias: a bio-bibliography   Greenwood
Lennox Berkeley: a source book   Scolar Press
John Ireland: a source book   Scolar Press

Contents

Foreword by Michael Kennedy

Sir William Walton was fortunate in many aspects of his life – in his escape from the Lancashire industrial town of Oldham to Edwardian Oxford; in his generous patrons, from Bishop Strong at Oxford to the Sitwells (who introduced him to Italy), Siegfried Sassoon and Lord Berners; in the women he loved, Imma von Doernberg, Alice Wimborne and his wife Susana. He was fortunate, too, in encountering the man who may be said to be his Köchel, Stewart R Craggs.

With untiring dedication, terrier-like persistence and pertinacity in tracking down facts and manuscripts, and unfailing devotion and enthusiasm for the man and his music, Dr Craggs has for twenty-five years documented the musical facts of Walton's life. Nobody can write about Walton without reference to his researches – or they would be foolhardy if they tried!

His first thematic catalogue of Walton's works appeared in 1977. Its revised version was published thirteen years later, seven years after the composer's death. Now comes this invaluable source-book cataloguing Walton's manuscripts and first editions, tracing and listing collections of his letters and listing his own recordings of his works. There is also a vast bibliography, which includes Walton's own writings. All this amounts to scholarly documentation of a major British composer such as only a few others can boast. Present and future music historians will have every reason to bless the name of Stewart Craggs.

Acknowledgements

I owe a special debt of gratitude to Susana Walton and the Walton Trust, the owners of the Walton copyright, for providing me with information, especially in the form of letters, and giving me permission to reproduce certain items.

I gratefully acknowledge the help of Andrew Potter and his staff at OUP in Oxford, particularly Julian Elloway, Evelyn Hendy and Emma Jane Hutchings; Dr Simon Wright, head of OUP's music hire library and Helen Thompson of OUP's music promotion department.

I also wish to thank Dr William R Aitkin, former Reader in the Department of Librarianship at the University of Strathclyde, Glasgow; Christopher Bornet, Reference Librarian at the Royal College of Music; Kendall Crilly, Public Services Librarian at Yale University; Robert Cross of St. Paul's Bibliographies; Tim Day of the National Sound Archive; Roy Douglas for all kinds of help over the years; Alan Frank, former head of OUP's music department without whose kind help and co-operation much of this initially would not have been possible; Mary Kelly, Assistant Librarian (Special Collections) at Queen's University, Belfast; Michael Kennedy for writing the introduction; Zelda Lawrence-Curran for supplying me with a copy of her thesis; Kevin McBeath for providing much Australian material; Peter Munstedt, Music Librarian at the University of Missouri-Kansas City; Dr Philip Reed of the Britten-Pears Library at Aldeburgh; Arthur Searle of the Manuscripts Collections at the British Library; Diana Sparkes for supplying me with copies of letters from Walton to her father, Hubert Foss; Jeff Walden of the BBC Written Archives Centre at Caversham and H J R Wing, Assistant Librarian at Christ Church, Oxford.

SRC

Chronology

This chronology draws on every available resource from available correspondence to Walton's autograph manuscripts and publication assignments with Oxford University Press. It is hoped thereby to convey an impression of the whole range of activities and commitments of Walton's life.

Walton's original compositions appear on the 'Works' column at the date of completion. All published works appear in italics; unpublished works appear in Roman type. The 'C' numbers refer to the works detailed in my Walton catalogue (OUP, 1990).

Date	Life

1866
11 October   Louisa Maria Turner (mother) born at Herbert Street, Stretford

1867
28 February   Charles Alexander Walton (father) born at Albert Terrace, Hale, Cheshire

1898
10 August   Marriage of Charles Alexander and Louisa Maria at the Macfadyen Memorial Congregational Church, Chorlton-cum-Hardy

1902
29 March   William Turner Walton born at 93 Werneth Hall Road, Oldham, with brothers Noel (b. 1899) and Alexander (b. 1910), and sister Nora (b. 1908)

1912   Enters Christ Church (Oxford) choir school

1916
15 March   Confirmed in Christ Church Cathedral

2 July

16 August

Works	First performances

A *Litany* (C1), Motet for
unaccompanied mixed chorus

Tell me where is fancy bred (C2),
Song for soprano and tenor
voices, 3 violins and piano

Choral prelude on 'Wheatley'
(C3), for organ
    The Forsaken Merman (C4),
Cantata for soprano and tenor
soli, double female chorus and
orchestra

Date	Life
1916 17 September	
26 November	
1917 2 February	
1918	Starts to compose the *Quartet for Piano and Strings* (C7)
11 June	Passes first half of his BMus. examination at New College, Oxford
July	
13 November	Granted an in-College Exhibition for two years by the governing body of Christ Church
1919 February	Meets Osbert Sitwell
12 February	Meets John Masefield and Siegfried Sassoon
June	Fails Responsions
September	Fails Responsions at second attempt
December	Fails Responsions at third attempt
1920 Spring	Visits Italy for the first time with the Sitwells

Works	First performances
	Choral Fantasia for organ: Henry Ley (organ), Cathedral Church of Christ the King, Oxford
For All the Saints	
Valse in C minor (C5), for piano	
Child's Song, for voice and piano. Love laid his sleepless head, for voice and piano. A Lykewake Song, for voice and piano. *The Winds* (C6), for voice and piano	
Quartet for Piano and Strings (C7)	

Date	Life
1920	
8–9 June	Passes second part of his BMus.
20 October	Christ Church governors postpone the renewal of Walton's exhibition
10 November	Governors agree to pay Walton £150 'to clear him from his reasonable liabilities'.
1921	Re-writes the *Piano Quartet* (C7), particularly the Finale
4 March	
September	Has lessons from Ansermet and E. J. Dent
24 September	Walton tells his mother that 'Goossens has Syntax'
November	Starts to compose *Façade* (C12)
1922	
24 January	
7 February	
23 November	
1923	
May–June	Continues to set poems from *Façade*

Works	First performances

Tritons (C8), for voice and piano

The Passionate Shepherd (C9),
for tenor and ten instruments.
  Quartet [No 1] for strings
(C11): first two movements

Two movements of Quartet [No
1] for strings (C11): Pennington
String Quartet, London
Contemporary Music Centre

Dr. Syntax (C10), Pedagogic
overture for orchestra

Façade (C12), Entertainment for   *Façade* (C12)
reciter and chamber ensemble   First private performance at 2
                                         Carlyle Square, London

                                         Façade
                                         Second private performance at
                                         Montague Square, London

Quartet [No 1] for Strings (C11)

Date	Life
1923	
12 June	
5 July	
4 August	Meets Schoenberg and Berg
1924	
1925	
Spring	Visits Spain with the Sitwells
May	Meets George Gershwin
12 May	
12 July	

Works	*First performances*
	Façade (C12): first public performance. Edith Sitwell (reciter) and ensemble, Aeolian Hall, London
	Quartet [No 1] for Strings (C11) – complete: McCullagh String Quartet, Royal College of Music, London
	Quartet [No 1] for Strings (C11): McCullagh String Quartet, Salzburg, Austria (ISCM Festival)
Toccata for Violin and Piano (C13) Fantasia Concertante for two pianos, jazz band and orchestra (C14) Bucolic Comedies (C15), five songs for voice, three with orchestral accompaniment (six instruments)	
	Toccata for Violin and Piano (C13): K Goldsmith (violin) and A Morrison (piano), Queen Square, London
A Son of Heaven (C16), Incidental music to Lytton Strachey's play *Portsmouth Point* (C17), Overture for orchestra	A Son of Heaven (C16): Scala Theatre, London

Date	Life
1925 November	
1926 March–April	
27 April	
4 May	
22 June	
28 June	
29 June	
30 August	Susana Gil Passo (Lady Walton) born
September	Signs a publishing contract for five years with Oxford University Press
November	Orchestrates several numbers of Lord Berners's ballet, The Triumph of Neptune

Works	First performances

Portsmouth Point (C17b), arranged
for piano duet

Lambert's Romeo and Juliet
(C18), orchestrated by Walton

Façade (C12): revised version.
Edith Sitwell (reciter) and
ensemble, New Chenil Galleries,
Chelsea, London

Romeo and Juliet (C18), Monte
Carlo Opera Orchestra,
conducted by C Scotto, Monte
Carlo

Portsmouth Point (C17): The
Tonhalle Orchestra, conducted
by V Andreae (ISCM Festival),
Zurich

Portsmouth Point: Resident
orchestra for the Diaghilev Ballet
Season, conducted by E
Goossens, HM Theatre, London

Siesta (C19) for small orchestra.
Façade (C12c), First suite for
orchestra

Façade (C12): revised version. C
Lambert (reciter) and ensemble,
New Chenil Galleries, Chelsea,
London

Date	Life

1926
24 November

3 December

1927
26 June   Attends an all-Elgar concert. Homage to Elgar

Autumn   Meets Spike Hughes

1928
5 January

14 September

5 December   Works on a *Viola Concerto* (C22), suggested by
                Beecham and designed for Tertis

1929
1 February   Finishes the second movement of the *Viola Concerto*
                (C22)

12 February   Starts the third movement of the *Viola Concerto*
                (C22)

3 July   Hindemith agrees to play the *Viola Concerto* (C22)

Works	First performances
	Siesta (C19) Aeolian Chamber Orchestra, conducted by Walton, Aeolian Hall, London
	The Triumph of Neptune (C20): Resident orchestra, conducted by H Defosse, Lyceum Theatre, London. *Façade: First Suite for Orchestra* (C12c) Orchestra conducted by Walton
Sinfonia Concertante (C21) for orchestra with piano 'continuo'	
	Sinfonia Concertante (C21): York Bowen (piano) and the RPSO, conducted by E Ansermet, Queen's Hall, London
Valse (Façade): concert arrangement for solo piano (C12k)	*Façade* (C12): first European performance: C Lambert (reciter) and ensemble. Rozzi Theatre, Siena (ISCM Festival)
Concerto for Viola and Orchestra (C22)	

Date	Life
1929 21 August	BBC commissions 'the writing of special music for broadcasting' [*Belshazzar's Feast*]
22 September	
3 October	
30 October	
28 November	First recording of *Façade* (C12), Walton conducting, by the Decca Record Company at the Chenil Galleries, London
December	Osbert Sitwell commences the libretto of *Belshazzar's Feast* (C23) in Venice, and Walton the music
1930 January	Hindemith introduces the *Viola Concerto* (C22) to Berlin with Walton conducting
12 January	Confirmation of the commission by the BBC for *Belshazzar's Feast* (C23)

Works	First performances

Façade: ballet based on the first orchestral suite, choreographed by Gunter Hess (C12d A), Hagen, Westphalia

Concerto for Viola and Orchestra (C22): P Hindemith (viola) and the Henry Wood SO, conducted by Walton, Queen's Hall, London

The Winds (C6) and *Tritons* (C8): Odette de Foras and Gordon Bryan, Aeolian Hall, London
Quartet for Piano and Strings (C7): Pierre Tas, James Lockyer, John Gabalfa and Gordon Bryan, Aeolian Hall, London

Date	Life
1930	
March	Approached by C B Cochran for music to one of his revues
3 March	
30 May	A BBC memo states that *Belshazzar's Feast* for two soloists, small chorus and orchestra, has been completed
4 September	Tertis plays the *Viola Concerto* (C22) at the ISCM Festival in Liege
	Agreement between the BBC and Walton that *Belshazzar's Feast* could not be considered for broadcasting because of its size
1931	
March	Chorus parts sent to Leeds for rehearsal of *Belshazzar's Feast*. Chorus begins to rebel against the difficulties in the choral writing
8 March	Walton informs Sassoon that 'I am doing a vast amount of work' [on the orchestration of *Belshazzar's Feast*]
26 April	
Spring	
May	Finishes the orchestration of *Belshazzar's Feast* (C23)

Works	First performances

First complete broadcast
performance of *Façade* (C12)

Façade: ballet based on the first
orchestral suite, choreographed
by Frederick Ashton (C12d B),
Cambridge Theatre, London

Choral Prelude: *Herzlich Thut*
Mich Verlangen – J S Bach:
arranged for piano (C25)

Date	Life

1931
September

8 October

25 November

21 December   Sends *Through Gilded Trellises* (C26) to Dora Foss

22 December

1932
January   Completes *Old Sir Faulk* (C26)
               Walton is left £500 per annum for life in the will
               of Mrs Samuel Courtauld
               Hamilton Harty asks Walton for a symphony, for
               the Hallé Orchestra

February

February–   Works on his symphony at Quidhampton,
March   Wiltshire

March–May   Continues to work on the symphony in Ascona,
               Switzerland

Works	First performances

Belshazzar's Feast (C23), Cantata
for baritone solo, double mixed
chorus and orchestra

Belshazzar's Feast (C23): Dennis
Noble, Leeds Festival Chorus
and LSO, conducted by M
Sargent, Town Hall, Leeds

Belshazzar's Feast (C23): Stuart
Robertson, the National Chorus
and BBC Symphony Orchestra,
conducted by A Boult, Queen's
Hall, London

Make we joy now in this Fest
(C24), Old English carol for
unaccompanied mixed chorus

Three Songs (C26) for voice and
piano

Date	Life
1932	
10 August	Informs Sassoon that he had '. . . collected a number of symphonious bars which promise well'
October	Walton tells Hubert Foss that the symphony shows definite signs of being on the move
10 October	
17 October	
20 December	Confirms (in a letter to Sassoon) that the symphony begins to progress – but with no hope of finishing it for the April performance
1933	
Spring	Shows first movement and scherzo of the *Symphony* (C27) to Angus Morrison
Summer	Works on the slow movement of the *Symphony*, and sketches the opening and coda
September	Working on the last movement of the *Symphony*
1934	
19 March	First performance of the *Symphony* (C27) advertised in the LSO prospectus
Spring	Meets Alice Wimborne
Summer	Asked to compose the music for the film *Escape Me Never* (C28)
Autumn	

Works	First performances

3 *Songs* (C26): D Stevens and H Foss, Wigmore Hall, London

Herzlich Thut Mich Verlangen (C25): H Cohen, Queen's Hall, London

Escape Me Never (C28), Music for the film

Date	Life

1934

5 October   Plans to stage *Belshazzar's Feast* (C23) as a ballet

3 December

1935

1 and 2 April

9 July   Walton writes to Hubert Foss and includes ten bars
               of the finale's main fugue subject (Symphony No 1)

11 August   Mention of a ballet about Bath to a libretto by
               Osbert Sitwell for the de Basil Ballet

30 August

Autumn   Approached for a choral work for the 1936 Norwich
               Festival

October   Moves to 56A South Eaton Place, London
                  Works on The First Shoot, As You Like It and
               The Boy David

14 October

November

6 November

Works	First performances
	Symphony No 1 (C27): first three movements. LSO conducted by H Harty, Queen's Hall, London
	Symphony No 1 (C27): first three movements repeated at Courtauld-Sargent concerts
Symphony No 1 (C27) for orchestra	
	Escape Me Never (C28): film first shown at the London Pavillion
The First Shoot (C29) Ballet The Boy David (C30), Incidental music	
	Symphony No 1 (C27): complete. BBC Symphony Orchestra, conducted by H Harty, Queen's Hall, London

Date	Life
1935 22 November	
10 and 11 December	*Symphony No 1* (C27) recorded by the Decca Record Company
23 December	
1936 24 January	
4 February	
March	Offered contract for a René Clair film
Summer	
3 September	
October	Offered contract for *The Amateur Gentleman* (film)
November	
12 November	

Works	First performances
	Second performance of the *Symphony*: City of Birmingham Orchestra, conducted by L Heward, Town Hall, Birmingham
	The First Shoot (C29): Scene 19 of *Follow the Sun*, Opera House, Manchester
	Siesta: pas de deux (C19c) Pearl Argyle and Robert Helpmann, Sadler's Wells, London
	The First Shoot (C29): Adelphi Theatre, London
As You Like It (C31), Music for the film	
	As You Like It (C31): London Philharmonic Orchestra, conducted by E Kurtz, Carlton Theatre, London
Theme (Adagio) for organ	Organ symphony with themes by Alan Bush, Britten, Walton and Lambert: André Marchal, St John's Church, Red Lion Square, London

Date	Life
1936	
21 November	
27 November	Approached by the BBC for a coronation march
14 December	
1937	
March	
16 April	
11 May	Walton sends 'two more' verses by John Masefield to OUP, with mention of the poet providing words to the music of the trio (*Crown Imperial*)
12 May	
June	Receives an honorary MusDoc degree from the University of Durham
2 July	Receives an honorary Fellowship of the Royal College of Music, London
Summer	
August	Approached for music for the film *The Last Curtain*
16 August	Approached for a test piece for the 1940 National Band Festival at the suggestion of John Ireland

Works	First performances
	The Boy David (C30): King's Theatre, Edinburgh
	The Boy David (C30): H.M. Theatre, London
Crown Imperial (C32), Coronation march for orchestra	
	Crown Imperial (C32): BBC Symphony Orchestra, conducted by A Boult, Kingsway Hall, London (Recording session)
	Crown Imperial (C32): Coronation Orchestra, conducted by A Boult, Westminster Abbey, London (Coronation Service of King George VI)
Dreaming Lips (C34), Music for the film	

Date	Life
1937 28 August	
5 September	
6 October	
11 October	
1 December	
1938 January 30 March	Begins work on the *Violin Concerto* (C37)
Spring	Asked for a work for clarinet and violin by Benny Goodman and Joseph Szigeti
April	Approached for a choral work 'In honour of the City of New York' for the 1939 New York World Fair
	Also asked for music to the film 'Pygmalion'

Works	First performances
	Crown Imperial (C32): BBC Symphony Orchestra, conducted by Walton, Queen's Hall, London
In honour of the City of London (C33): Cantata for mixed chorus and orchestra	
	In honour of the City of London (C33): Leeds Festival Chorus and London Philharmonic Orchestra, conducted by Malcolm Sargent, Town Hall, Leeds
	Dreaming Lips (C34): London Symphony Orchestra, conducted by Boyd Neel, London Pavilion
Façade: Second Suite for Orchestra (C12e)	*In honour of the City of London* (C33): BBC Choral Society and the BBC Symphony Orchestra, conducted by Walton, Queen's Hall, London
	Façade: Second Suite for Orchestra (C12e): New York Philharmonic-Symphony Orchestra, conducted by John Barbirolli, Carnegie Hall, New York

Date	Life
1938	
15 April	Receives a letter from Arthur Bliss asking him to write a violin concerto for the 1939 New York World Fair
28 April	Writes to Arthur Bliss and agrees to the proposals re the violin concerto
June	Completes the first movement of the *Violin Concerto* (C37) Receives an honorary Fellowship of the Royal Academy of Music, London
July	Walton is visited by Frederick Stock to discuss and confirm his proposed commission for the Chicago Symphony Orchestra
10 September	
Autumn	
18 October	Walton writes to Ernest Makower at the British Council and accepts their offer for a violin concerto
November	
22 November	
1939	
18 January	
3 March	Heifetz accepts the *Violin Concerto* (C37)
May	Walton and Alice Wimborne sail to the USA in the *Normandie* to see Heifetz

Works	First performances

Façade: Second Suite for
Orchestra (C12e): BBC Symphony
Orchestra, conducted by Henry
Wood, Queen's Hall, London

Set me as a Seal (C35): Anthem for
unaccompanied mixed chorus

A Stolen Life (C36) Music for the
film

Set me as a Seal (C35) Choir of St
Mary Abbots Church, Kensington

A Stolen Life (C36): BBC TV
Orchestra, conducted by Hyam
Greenbaum, Plaza Theatre,
London

Date	Life
1939 15 May	
2 June	
20 June	Signs a contract to write an orchestral work for the Chicago Symphony Orchestra
3 September	World War II begins
9 September	Considers: a string quartet Amoretti Canti Carnascialeschi Daman and Thyrsis Four Medieval Latin Lyrics Alba, Pastorele et Serena for string orchestra Bartholomew Fair: an overture Varii Capricci: portraits from the Commedia dell'Arte
7 December	
20 December	Considers writing an overture for Chicago about Monsieur Mongo (Nashe)
1940 January	Considers writing an overture 'The Triumph of Silenus' for the Ministry of Information
February–March	Starts works on Major Barbara (C41)
24 April	

Works	*First performances*
Concerto for Violin and Orchestra (C37) – arrangement for violin and piano	
Concerto for Violin and Orchestra (C37) – full orchestral score	
	Concerto for Violin and Orchestra (C37): J Heifetz and the Cleveland Orchestra, conducted by A Rodzinski, Severance Hall, Cleveland (Ohio)
The Wise Virgins (C38): Ballet in one act	
	The Wise Virgins (C38): Sadler's Wells Ballet, Sadler's Wells Theatre, London

Date	Life
1940	
5 May	Receives a letter from George Bernard Shaw about the music for Major Barbara (C41)
15 May	
Summer	Composes some piano pieces for Colette Clark, the daughter of Lord Clark
July	Starts to compose *Scapino* (C40)
Autumn	Asked by the Ministry of Information to arrange a simple overture of popular music to run for about eight minutes
28 December	
1941	
January	
January–February	Considers '. . . the piece for Bridgewater (Leslie), and . . . a clarinet concerto for Benny Goodman'
5 February	
16 February	
21 March	

Works	First performances

Duets for Children (C39): for piano duet

Scapino (C40) Comedy overture for orchestra

Music for Children (C39a) for orchestra
Major Barbara (C41): Music for the film

Concerto for Violin and Orchestra (C37): J Heifetz and the Cleveland Orchestra, conducted by A Rodzinski, Carnegie Hall, New York

Music for Children (C39a): London Philharmonic Orchestra, conducted by B Cameron, Queen's Hall, London

Major Barbara (C41): London Symphony Orchestra, conducted by Muir Mathieson, the Savoy, Nassau (the Bahamas)

Date	Life

1941
3 April

Spring   Receives call up papers from the Ministry of Labour

May   Walton's London home destroyed by enemy bombing

8 May   Considers an opera about Carlo Gesualdo with Cecil
                Gray

Summer   Agrees to write the incidental music for John Gielgud's
                production of Macbeth (C43)

1 November

12 November

2 December   Begins to compose music for The Next of Kin (C42),
                having been attached to the Films Division of the
                Ministry of Information

13 December

22 December

25 December   Begins to compose the incidental music for Macbeth
                (C43)

Works	First performances
	Scapino (C40): Chicago Symphony Orchestra, conducted by F Stock, Orchestra Hall, Chicago
	Concerto for Violin and Orchestra (C37): Henry Holst and the London Philharmonic Orchestra, conducted by Walton, Royal Albert Hall, London
	Scapino (C40): BBC Symphony Orchestra, conducted by W Walton, Corn Exchange, Bedford
	Scapino (C40): London Philharmonic Orchestra, conducted by Walton, Royal Albert Hall, London
The Next of Kin (C42) Music for the film	

Date	Life
1942	
1 January	
16 January	
26 January	Begins to compose the music for the film The Foreman went to France (C44)
	Approached by the BBC for incidental music to Louis MacNeice's play Christopher Columbus (C46)
	Also asked for music for a production of Oedipus Rex in the Royal Albert Hall
12 February	Receives honorary DMus from Oxford University
23 February	
24 March	Arthur Bliss (BBC) commissions Walton for a brass band suite
13 April	
15 May	
29 May	
31 May	Begins to compose the music for the film *The First of the Few* (C45)

Works	*First performances*

Macbeth (C43): Incidental music

Macbeth (C43): London
Philharmonic Orchestra,
conducted by E Irving, Opera
House, Manchester

The Foreman went to France
(C44) Music for the film

The Foreman went to France
(C44): London Philharmonic
Orchestra, conducted by E
Irving, London Pavilion

The Next of Kin (C42): first
public showing; London
Philharmonic Orchestra,
conducted by E Irving, London
Pavilion

Façade (C12): definitive version
C Lambert (speaker) and
ensemble, Aeolian Hall, London

Date	Life
1942 June	
Summer	Approached for choral work for St Matthew's Church, Northampton
6 July	
8 July	
July–August	Composes the incidental music for the radio play Christopher Columbus (C46)
August	
20 August	
September	Composes music for the film Went the Day Well? (C47)
7 October	
12 October	
mid-October	
1 November	
December	

Works	First performances

The First of the Few (C45): Music
for the film

The Next of Kin (C42a):
adaptation for radio
Macbeth (C43): London
Philharmonic Orchestra,
conducted by E Irving, Piccadilly
Theatre, London

Christopher Columbus (C46):
Incidental music

The First of the Few (C45): London
Symphony Orchestra, conducted
by Muir Mathieson, Leicester
Square Theatre, London

Macbeth (C43a): adaptation for
radio
Christopher Columbus (C46):
BBC Chorus and Symphony
Orchestra, conducted by A Boult,
Corn Exchange, Bedford

Went the Day Well? (C47): Music
for the film

Went the Day Well? (C47):
London Philharmonic Orchestra,
conducted by E Irving, London
Pavilion

Prelude and Fugue (The Spitfire)
(C45a)

Date	Life

1943
2 January

3 and 10 January	Records *Belshazzar's Feast* (C23) in Liverpool for the British Council
February	Composes the Fanfares for the Red Army (C48)
	Begins to compose the music for the ballet *The Quest* (C49)
	Offered a contract to write music for the film The Bells go Down

21 February

29 March

6 April

May	Begins to compose *Henry V* (C50)
	Joins the music committee of the British Council
October–November	Re-scores the *Violin Concerto* (C37) and revises the *Sinfonia Concertante* (C21)

Works	First performances
	Prelude and Fugue (The Spitfire) (C45a): The Liverpool Philharmonic Orchestra, conducted by Walton, Philharmonic Hall, Liverpool
	Fanfares for the Red Army (C48): Trumpets and drums of the Life Guards, Royal Horse Guards and the RAF, conducted by M Sargent, Royal Albert Hall, London *Prelude and Fugue (The Spitfire)* (C45a): BBC Symphony Orchestra, conducted by M Sargent, Royal Albert Hall, London
The Quest (C49): Music for the ballet	
	The Quest (C49): Sadler's Wells Ballet, New Theatre, London

Date	Life
1943	
November	The BBC approaches Walton for a victory anthem to celebrate the overthrow of Hitler and a Te Deum for the 50th anniversary of the Promenade Concerts
30 November	
23 December	Walton informs Sir Henry Wood that he is 'safely launched' on a Te Deum for chorus and orchestra
1944	
17 January	
9 February	
May	
15 June	Commissioned for a contribution to the Free French Album
July	Named as one of the committee of five controlling Covent Garden Opera House
9 November	Sends a piano piece (for the Free French Album) to Felix Aprahamian

Works	First performances

Concerto for Violin and Orchestra
(C37): revised version

Concerto for Violin and Orchestra
(C37) – revised version: H Holst
and the Liverpool Philharmonic
Orchestra, conducted by M
Sargent, Civic Hall,
Wolverhampton

Sinfonia Concertante (C21) –
revised version with 'piano
obbligato': C Smith and the
Liverpool Philharmonic
Orchestra, conducted by M
Sargent, Philharmonic Hall,
Liverpool

Henry V (C50): Music for the
film

Lai ⎫ Contributions
Rondet de ⎬ to the Free
Carol ⎭ French Album
(C51)

Date	Life

1944
22 November

1945
30 January   Considers writing a string quartet

5 February

4 March

Summer   Considers writing a choral ballet about Agamemnon
                for the Sadler's Wells Ballet Company

14 September

29 September   Considers setting six verses of John Masefield's
                poetry for the Henry Wood memorial service

29 October   Considers a setting of *Dreamplay* by Strindberg

November   Visits Sweden

1946
January   Considers music for the film of King Lear

12 January   Informs Lady Jessie Wood that he would prefer to
                write a piece for strings

Works	First performances
	Henry V (C50): London Symphony Orchestra, conducted by Muir Mathieson, the Carlton (Haymarket), London
Memorial Fanfare for Henry Wood (C48a) for orchestra	Memorial Fanfare for Henry Wood (C48a): BBC Symphony Orchestra, London Philharmonic Orchestra and London Symphony Orchestra, conducted by A Boult, Royal Albert Hall, London
	Henry V (C50a) – suite from the film music: BBC Choral Society and BBC Symphony Orchestra, conducted by Walton, Royal Albert Hall, London

Date	Life
1946 March	
April	Appointed to the board of the Performing Right Society
26 April	
Summer	Joins the board of the Covent Garden Opera Trust
Autumn	
1947 4 February	The first performance of the *String Quartet* (C53) is postponed
8 February	The BBC commissions an opera from Walton
13 February	Considers an overture to celebrate the first anniversary of the BBC's Third Programme
14 March	Irma Doernberg dies
May	Visits Prague with Alice Wimborne, Alan Bush and Gerald Abraham
4 May	
5 May	
7 June	Meets Christopher Hassall

Works	First performances

Where does the uttered music go?
(C52) Motet for unaccompanied
mixed chorus

> *Where does the uttered music go?*
> (C52): BBC Chorus and Theatre
> Revue Chorus, conducted by L
> Woodgate, St Sepulchre's
> Church, London

Quartet [No 2] for Strings (C53)

> *Quartet [No 2] for Strings* (C53):
> Blech String Quartet,
> Broadcasting House, London
>
> *Quartet [No 2] for Strings* (C53):
> Blech String Quartet, Concert
> Hall, Broadcasting House,
> London

Date	Life

1947

15 July	Decides that *Troilus and Cressida* should be the subject(s) of his opera
12 August	Asked by the BBC to set one of six special poems for broadcasting
September	Commissioned by Diana Menuhin for a *Violin Sonata* (C55)
October	Composes music for the film *Hamlet* (C54)
November	
19 November	Presented with the Gold Medal of the Royal Philharmonic Society

1948

29 January	Announced in the press that the BBC had commissioned an opera from Walton, the theme to be *Troilus and Cressida*
13 March	Libretto sent to Ernest Newman for his opinion and comments
March–April	Revises *Belshazzar's Feast* (C23)
18 April	Newman's 'report' on the libretto
19 April	Alice Wimborne dies
6 May	
June	Resumes work on the *Violin Sonata* (C55)
30 June	Receives an honorary DMus from Trinity College, Dublin
13 September	Sails to Buenos Aires as a delegate to a Performing Right Society conference

Works	First performances

Hamlet (C54): Music for the film

Hamlet (C54): Philharmonia Orchestra, conducted by Muir Mathieson, Odeon Theatre, Leicester Square, London

Date	Life
1948	
13 December	Marries Susana Gil Passo in a civil wedding ceremony
1949	
20 January	Marriage blessed in a church ceremony
29 January	Returns to the UK and completes the *Violin Sonata* (C55)
28 March	Informs Stanford Robinson that the opera libretto is ready
2 June	Asked to be visiting professor at the Yale School of Music for 1949–1950 but declines
5 September	
30 September	
November	
8 November	
1950	
5 February	

Works	First performances

Scapino (C40): Comedy overture
for orchestra: revised version

Sonata for Violin and Piano (C55):
Y Menuhin and L Kentner, the
Tonhalle, Zurich

Sonata for Violin and Piano (C55):
revised version. Devoirs de
Vacances (C39b) – Galop Finale:
unorchestrated

Devoirs de Vacances (C39b):
Ballet des Champs-Elysées,
Theatre des Champs-Elysées,
Paris

Sonata for Violin and Piano (C55):
Y Menuhin and L Kentner,
Theatre Royal, Drury Lane,
London

Date	Life

1950

1 March | Informs the BBC that he is aiming for a Covent Garden performance about June 1952

Summer

27 September

13 November

1951

1 January | Knighted in the New Year's Honours List

March | Considers writing a work for the Festival of Britain celebrations

6 August

21 August | Constant Lambert dies

1952

17 January | Appointed a member of the Swedish Academy of Music

June | Receives an honorary DMus from Manchester University

16 September | Meets Sir William McKie (organist at Westminster Abbey) about music for the forthcoming coronation. Agrees to write a Te Deum for the service – and a March

30 September | Invited officially to contribute a March, a Te Deum and possibly a Psalm for the Coronation Service

Works	*First performances*

Two Pieces for Violin and Piano
(C56)

Two Pieces for Violin and Piano
(C56): F Grinke and E Lush,
Broadcasting House, London

Scapino (C40) – revised version:
Philharmonia Orchestra,
conducted by W Furtwängler,
Royal Albert Hall, London

Happy Birthday to You (C57)

Date	Life

1952

October — Declines a request to contribute a madrigal to *A Garland for the Queen*

31 October — Formal commission from the Arts Council for *Orb and Sceptre* (C59)

November — Begins to compose the *Coronation Te Deum* (C58)

28 November — Agrees with the terms of the Arts Council commission for *Orb and Sceptre* (C59)

December — Begins to compose *Orb and Sceptre* (C59)

1953

5 January — Arrives at the Trio of the March

21 January

late January — Begins work on his variation on Sellinger's Round for Aldeburgh (C61)

February — Finishes the orchestration of the love duet (Act II) and all, to date, of Act III.
Receives a telegram from George Neikrung (California) for a cello concerto

23 March — HM Queen Elizabeth II accepts the dedication of *Orb and Sceptre* (C59)

April — Orchestrates Act I of *Troilus and Cressida* (C62)

Works	First performances

Coronation Te Deum (C58): For
two mixed choruses, two semi-
choruses, boys voices, organ,
orchestra and military brass

Orb and Sceptre (C59)
Coronation March for orchestra

Date	Life

1953

May
Asked to provide music for the film Romeo and Juliet
Attends rehearsals of the *Te Deum* (C58) at
Westminster Abbey Song School

2 June

8 June
Attends the gala performance, at Covent Garden, of
Britten's 'Gloriana'

20 June

August
Sails to the USA and visits the West Coast. First
American appearance as a conductor

December
Completes the orchestration of Act I of *Troilus and
Cressida* (C62)

11 December
Considers writing the music for the film Antony and
Cleopatra

1954

2 January
Works on Act II of *Troilus and Cressida* (C62)
including the Interlude which proves difficult

Works	First performances

The National Anthem (C60)
arranged for orchestra
Variation on Sellinger's Round
(C61) for string orchestra

Orb and Sceptre (C59): Coronation
Orchestra, conducted by A Boult,
Westminster Abbey, London
Coronation Te Deum (C58):
Coronation Choir and Orchestra,
Kneller Hall Trumpets and O
Peasgood (organ), conducted by
W McKie, Westminster Abbey,
London

The National Anthem (C60):
Covent Garden Orchestra,
conducted by J Pritchard, Royal
Opera House, Covent Garden,
London

Variation on Sellinger's Round
(C61): Aldeburgh Festival
Orchestra, conducted by B
Britten, Parish Church of St Peter
and St Paul, Aldeburgh (Suffolk)

Date	Life
1954	
16 January	Hassall sends a new version of the libretto for Act III
19 February	Finishes the Interlude in Act II
4 April	Completes about 15 minutes of Act III of *Troilus and Cressida* (C62) and begins the love scene between Cressida and Diomede
30 April	Decides not to compose a prelude for the opera
July	Works on the last scene of the opera
13 July	Informs Alan Frank at OUP that he is to compose music for the film of *Richard III*
13 September	
November	Rehearsals begin at Covent Garden for *Troilus and Cressida* (C62)
3 December	
1955	
February	Composes music for *Richard III* (C63)
March	
June	Receives an honorary DMus from the University of Cambridge
Summer	Considers writing music for the ballets Macbeth and The Tempest
3 August	Begins to compose a *Cello Concerto* (C65) for Piatigorsky
September	

Works	First performances

Troilus and Cressida (C62): Opera
in 3 acts

> *Troilus and Cressida* (C62): Richard
> Lewis, Magda Lazlo and soloists,
> Covent Garden Opera Chorus
> and Orchestra, conducted by
> Malcolm Sargent, Royal Opera
> House, Covent Garden, London

Richard III (C63): Music for the
film

The Star-Spangled Banner and
National Anthem (C64) arranged
for orchestra

Date	Life
1955	
Autumn	Asked to write a work for the 40th anniversary season of the Cleveland Orchestra
November	Receives an honorary DMus from the University of London
13 December	
1956	
January	Receives a commission for an orchestral work to mark the 70th anniversary of Johannesburg
Spring	Considers a Sinfonietta for the City of Birmingham Symphony Orchestra
31 May	
Summer	Considers a Double Concerto for Heifetz and Piatigorsky
September	Completes the second movement of the *Cello Concerto* (C65)
25 September	
26 October	
6 November	Considers a flute concerto for Elaine Schaffer
13 November	
15 November	The Liverpool Philharmonic Society commissions a second symphony from Walton

Works	First performance

Richard III (C63): Royal
Philharmonic Orchestra,
conducted by Muir Mathieson,
Leicester Square Theatre, London

Johannesburg Festival Overture
(C66) for orchestra

Johannesburg Festival Overture
(C66): South African BC
Symphony Orchestra, conducted
by Malcolm Sargent, City Hall,
Johannesburg, South Africa

Concerto for Cello and Orchestra
(C65)

Johannesburg Festival Overture
(C66): Liverpool Philharmonic
Orchestra, conducted by E Kurtz,
Philharmonic Hall, Liverpool

Date	Life

1957

17 January   Involved in a serious car accident in Italy

23 January

25 January

13 February

March   Invited by Huddersfield Choral Society to write a work for their 125th Anniversary

April   Begins to compose *Partita* (C67)

21 October

November   Begins to compose *Symphony No 2* (C68)
    Considers a choral work about Moses and Pharaoh for Huddersfield Choral Society

1958

30 January

30 April

Works	First performances
	Johannesburg Festival Overture (C66): BBC Symphony Orchestra, conducted by M Sargent, Royal Festival Hall, London
	Concerto for Cello and Orchestra (C65): G Piatigorsky and the Boston Symphony Orchestra, conducted by C Munch, Symphony Hall, Boston (USA)
	Concerto for Cello and Orchestra (C65): G Piatigorsky and the BBC Symphony Orchestra, conducted by M Sargent, Royal Festival Hall, London
Partita (C67) for orchestra	
	Partita for Orchestra (C67): Cleveland Orchestra, conducted by G Szell, Severance Hall, Cleveland (Ohio)
	Partita for Orchestra (C67): The Hallé Orchestra, conducted by Walton, Free Trade Hall, Manchester

Date	Life
1958	
2 May	
Summer	Considers adapting and expanding his music for Macbeth for a film
8 July	Asked by Harry Alan Towers for music for the series The History of the English Speaking Peoples
6 October	Offered a commission by the Serge Koussevitsky Music Foundation for an opera
7 November	Accepts a commission from the Serge Koussevitsky Music Foundation for an unspecified orchestral work
30 December	Projected première of the Second Symphony (C68) postponed
1959	
January	Finishes the first movement of the Second Symphony (C68)
17 January	Signs contract for a March for the series The History of the English Speaking Peoples (C70)
24 January	Original London première of the Second Symphony (C68) postponed
9 March	
9 May	
25 May	

Works	First performances
	Partita for Orchestra (C67): The Hallé Orchestra, conducted by J Barbirolli, Royal Festival Hall, London
March: A History of the English Speaking Peoples (C70) for orchestra	
A Queen's Fanfare (C69)	
	March: A History of the English Speaking Peoples (C70): London Symphony Orchestra, conducted by Walton, ADPC Studios, Elstree

Date	Life

1959
5 June

24 June — Considers a piano concerto for Louis Kentner

14 August — Interest in a possible colour film of *Belshazzar's Feast* for NBC

14 September — Informs Alan Frank at OUP that five poems of *Anon in Love* (C71), a song cycle for Peter Pears and Julian Bream, have been set; however two have proved 'a bit difficult' so will probably be discarded

December

9 December — First movement (later discarded) of the *Second Symphony* (C68) sent to George Szell

1960
February — Visits the USA
Completes the second movement of the *Second Symphony* (C68)
Considers writing music for the film *The Reason Why*
Asked by David Lean for a joint score (with Malcolm Arnold) for his film *Lawrence of Arabia*

28 March — Sends the first (revised) and second movements of the *Second Symphony* (C68) to OUP

April — Mention of an orchestral version of *Anon in Love* (C71) for Richard Lewis

Works	First performances
	A Queen's Fanfare (C69): The State Trumpeters, Westminster Hall, London
Anon in Love (C71): 6 songs for tenor and guitar	

Date	Life
1960 21 June	
22 July	
2 September	
17 October	Considers a Concerto Grosso for George Szell
23 November	Asked by OUP to contribute to *Carols for Choirs I* (*What Cheer?* (C73))
24 November	Mention of the Koussevitsky Foundation pieces which '. . . could be a Suite Concertante for five solo wind and orchestra'
23 December	
1961 16 March	
April	Visits Ulster and conducts the *Second Symphony*
18 April	Becomes the 14th honorary Freeman of the Borough of Oldham

Works	First performances
	Anon in Love (C71): Peter Pears and Julian Bream, Shrubland Park Hall, Claydon (Ipswich)
Symphony No 2 (C68) for orchestra	
	Symphony No 2 (C68): Royal Liverpool Philharmonic Orchestra, conducted by J Pritchard, Usher Hall, Edinburgh
	Symphony No 2 (C68): Royal Liverpool Philharmonic Orchestra, conducted by J Pritchard, Royal Festival Hall, London
Gloria (C72): for contralto, tenor and bass soli, double mixed chorus and orchestra	
	Façade: ballet based on the first orchestral suite, choreographed by John Cranko (C12d C), States Theatre, Stuttgart

Date	Life
1961 26 April	
June	Commissioned by Granada TV for his Prelude, Call Signs and End Music (C75)
3 June	
2 August	Invited to write a new work for the special 150th Anniversary Concert of the Royal Philharmonic Society
8 August	Considers writing the *Hindemith Variations* for the RPS
September	Completes the orchestration of the *Gloria* (C72)
16 October	
November	Work commences on the building of La Mortella
24 November	
12 December	Decides to use the first 36 bars of the Hindemith Cello Concerto as the theme for the Variations
22 December	Begins to compose the *Hindemith Variations* (C76)
27 December	The proposed Suite Concertante loses 'its priority'

Works	*First performances*
What Cheer? (C73): Christmas Carol	
	The Quest – orchestral suite (C49a): BBC Concert Orchestra, conducted by Vilem Tausky, Royal Festival Hall, London
Concerto for Viola and Orchestra – revised version (C22)	
	Gloria (C72): Soloists with the Huddersfield Choral Society and the RLPO, conducted by M Sargent, Town Hall, Huddersfield

Date	Life
1962	
1 January	Commissioned for a song cycle by the City of London Festival for Elisabeth Schwarzkopf
18 January	
February	Begins to write *A Song for the Lord Mayor's Table* (C74)
4 February	Appointed accademico onorario di Santa Cecilia in Rome
March	Completes three of the songs of the song cycle (C74)
6 March	Signs a contract with Granada TV for the Prelude, Call Signs and End Music (C75)
Spring	Asked by Erich Leinsdorf to write a piece for the Boston Symphony Orchestra
May	Visits Canada for the first time
June	Visits the USA
7 June	
18 July	

Works	First performance
	Concerto for Viola and Orchestra – revised version (C22): John Coulling and the London Philharmonic Orchestra, conducted by M Sargent, Royal Festival Hall, London
	Gloria (C72): Soloists with the London Philharmonic Choir and Orchestra, conducted by M Sargent, Royal Festival Hall, London
A Song for the Lord Mayor's Table (C74): Six songs for soprano and piano	
	A Song for the Lord Mayor's Table (C74): E Schwarzkopf and G Moore, Worshipful Company of Goldsmiths Hall, City of London

Date	Life
1962	
August	Takes possession of La Mortella
9 August	
16 August	Decides to dedicate A *Song for the Lord Mayor's Table* (C74) to Edith Sitwell
23 August	Considers writing an opera based on Oscar Wilde's play The Importance of being Earnest
1963	
6 February	
8 March	
23 April	
21–25 July	Visits Israel
August	Visits the USA
October	Visits New York
November	*Second Symphony* (C68) receives the Nomination from the National Academy of Recording Arts and Sciences
1964	
February–April	Visits New Zealand and Australia

Works	First performances

Granada TV Prelude, Call Signs
and End Music (C75)

*Variations on a theme by
Hindemith* (C76) for orchestra

*Variations on a theme by
Hindemith* (C76): Royal
Philharmonic Orchestra,
conducted by Walton, Royal
Festival Hall, London

Troilus and Cressida – revised
version (C62): André Turp,
Marie Collier and soloists,
Covent Garden Opera Chorus
and Orchestra, conducted by M
Sargent, Royal Opera House,
Covent Garden, London

Date	Life
1965	
February	Begins to set Auden's poem *The Twelve* (C77)
March	Begins to set a *Missa Brevis* (C78)
25 March	Informs Benjamin Britten that he is '. . . seriously thinking of embarking on *The Bear*'
Spring	The libretto for *The Bear* (C79) is begun
10 May	
16 May	
6 June	Commissioned to write *Capriccio Burlesco* (C80) for the New York Philharmonic Orchestra
13 June	
1966	
2 January	
10 January	Has operation at the London Clinic for cancer
21 February	Returns to Ischia and resumes work on *The Bear* (C79)
4 March	Promises Piatigorsky that '. . . it won't be too long before I start on the Double Concerto'

Works	*First performances*

The Twelve (C77): Anthem for mixed chorus and organ

Missa Brevis (C78) for double mixed chorus and organ

The Twelve (C77): Christ Church Cathedral Choir with R Bottone (organ), conducted by Sidney Watson, Cathedral Church of Christ the King, Oxford

The Twelve (C77a) Arrangement of organ part for orchestra

The Twelve (C77a) with orchestral accompaniment: soloists with the London Philharmonic Choir and Orchestra, conducted by Walton, Westminster Abbey, London

Date	Life
1967 30 April	
3 June	
28 June	Receives a commission from the San Francisco Symphony Association for an orchestral work
12 July	
Summer	Considers writing the music for Tony Richardson's film The Charge of the Light Brigade
21 November	Receives the Order of Merit
11 December	Letter of agreement between Walton and the San Francisco Symphony Association
1968 26 April	Receives an honorary DLetts from the University of Sussex
May	Begins the final version of Capriccio Burlesco (C80)
June	Accepts a commission to write the music for the film The Battle of Britain (C81)
5 September	
8 September	Agrees the terms for The Battle of Britain (C81)

Works	First performances

The Bear (C79): An extravaganza
in one act

> The Bear (C79): Soloists with the
> English Chamber Orchestra,
> conducted by James Lockhart,
> Jubilee Hall, Aldeburgh

> The Bear (C79): Soloists with the
> English Chamber Orchestra,
> conducted by James Lockhart,
> Sadler's Wells Theatre, London

Capriccio Burlesco (C80) for
orchestra

Date	Life

1968

14 November   Alan Frank informs Walton that Gary Kerr, the American double bass player, wants to commission a double bass concerto from him

7 December

1969

January   Visits Houston in Texas (USA)

5 February

21 February   Music for The Battle of Britain (C81) recorded at Denham (1st session)

April   Second recording session for The Battle of Britain (C81)

August   Begins to compose *Improvisations on an Impromptu of Benjamin Britten* (C82)

15 September

November   Begins to compose music for the film Three Sisters (C83)

6 November   Mention of Elegiac Variations on a Theme of Benjamin Britten

11 November   Title changed to Improvisations

Works	First performances

Capriccio Burlesco (C80): New York Philharmonic Orchestra, conducted by A Kostelantz, Philharmonic Hall (Lincoln Center), New York

The Battle of Britain (C81): Music for the film

Capriccio Burlesco (C80): The BBC Symphony Orchestra, conducted by Colin Davis, Royal Festival Hall, London

The Battle of Britain (C81): Unnamed orchestra, conducted by M Arnold, Dominion Theatre, London

Improvisations on an Impromptu of Benjamin Britten (C82) for orchestra

Date	Life

1969

29 December   Attends recording session for Three Sisters (C83) at Shepperton Studios

1970

January   Considers writing music for the film 'Upon This Rock'

14 January

February   Decides not to compose the music for 'Upon This Rock'

3 March   Asked by OUP to contribute to *Carols for Choirs II* (*All this Time* (C84))

31 March   Asked by the Performing Right Society to contribute to *Music for a Prince*

25 April

Spring   Transcribes the piano part of A Song for the Lord Mayor's Table (C74a) for orchestra

27 June

7 July

Works	First performances

Three Sisters (C83) Music for the film

Improvisations on an Impromptu of Benjamin Britten (C82): San Francisco Symphony Orchestra, conducted by J Krips, War Memorial Opera House, San Francisco

All this Time (C84): Christmas carol

Theme (for Variations) (C85) for solo cello

Improvisations on an Impromptu of Benjamin Britten (C82): Royal Liverpool Philharmonic Orchestra, conducted by C Groves, The Maltings, Snape

A Song for the Lord Mayor's Table – transcribed for orchestra (C74a): J Baker and the English Chamber Orchestra, conducted by G Malcolm, The Mansion House, City of London

Date	Life
1970 26 August	
Autumn	Considers a setting of a C Day Lewis poem for the Brighton Festival
20 October	
2 November	
1971 Spring	Transcribes the guitar part of Anon in Love (C71a) for orchestra
April	Visits the USSR with the London Symphony Orchestra
May	Begins to compose *Five Bagatelles for Guitar* (C86)
21 June	
30 August	
September	Begins work on the *Sonata for String Orchestra* (C53a)
November	
December	Begins to compose a setting of the *Jubilate* (C87)

Works	First performances
	Three Sisters (C83): Session musicians, conducted by M Wilkinson, Sala Volpi, Venice
	Improvisations on an Impromptu of Benjamin Britten (C82): The London Philharmonic Orchestra, conducted by J Krips, Royal Festival Hall, London
	Three Sisters (C83): Session musicians, conducted by M Wilkinson, Cameo-Poly Cinema, London
	Anon in Love – transcribed for orchestra (C71a): R Tear and the London Mozart Players, conducted by H Blech, The Mansion House, City of London
Five Bagatelles for Guitar (C86)	
Sonata for String Orchestra (C53a)	

Date	Life

1972

17 January — Awarded the Benjamin Franklin Medal

February

March — Considers writing a third symphony for André Previn and the London Symphony Orchestra

2 March

15 March — Honorary membership of the Royal Northern College of Music conferred on Walton

28 March — Attends a 70th birthday concert in the Royal Festival Hall, London

29 March — Attends a birthday dinner, at 10 Downing Street, given by Edward Heath

22 April — Visits Oxford to hear the first performance of *Jubilate* (C87)

27 May

Works	First performances

Jubilate (C87) for double mixed
chorus and organ

Sonata for String Orchestra (C53a):
Academy of St Martin in the
Fields, conducted by N
Marriner, Octagon Theatre,
Perth (W Australia)

Jubilate (C87): Christ Church
Cathedral Choir and S
Darlington (organ), conducted by
S Preston, Cathedral Church of
Christ the King, Oxford

Sonata for String Orchestra (C53a):
Academy of St Martin in the
Fields, conducted by N
Marriner, Assembly Rooms,
Bath
Five Bagatelles for Guitar (C86): J
Bream, Assembly Rooms, Bath

Date	Life
1972 11 July	
28 July	Attends birthday celebrations at Aldeburgh
14 September	Attends a Promenade Concert at the Royal Albert Hall which includes the revised Act II of *Troilus and Cressida* (C62)
22 September	
October	Symphony No 3 'underway'
22 December	Agrees to write an *Anniversary Fanfare* (C89) for EMI
1973 21 January	
24 May	Invited to write a work for the 1974 Cork Festival
15 July	Considers a Te Deum for Chichester Cathedral
29 August	Agrees to the commission offered by the Cork Festival
September	Begins to compose *Cantico del Sole* (C90)

Works	First performances
	Sonata for String Orchestra (C53a): Academy of St Martin in the Fields, conducted by N Marriner, The Mansion House, City of London
	Façade – ballet in One Act, based on the Entertainment (C12a): The Maltings, Snape
	Siesta – a new pas de deux (C19d): V Lorrayne and B McGrath, The Maltings, Snape
Birthday Greetings to Herbert Howells (C88)	
	Five Bagatelles for Guitar (C86): J Bream, Queen Elizabeth Hall, London
Anniversary Fanfare (C89)	

Date	Life
1973 29 November	
December **1974** January	Revises the *Piano Quartet* (C7)
	Begins to compose a *Magnificat and Nunc Dimittis* (C91) for Chichester Cathedral
3 March	Considers writing a piece for the Bach Choir, including an elaborate version of *Cantico del Sole*
25 April	
Spring	Interviewed and filmed for *William and our Gracie* (LWT)
24 July	Mention of a piece for Piatigorsky in the nature of Chanson Poème
14 September	
October November	
23 November	
17 December	Sends a sketch of the new ending of the *Cello Concerto* to Piatigorsky

Works	First performances
	Anniversary Fanfare (C89): Kneller Hall Trumpeters, conducted by R Bashford, Royal Festival Hall, London
Cantico del Sole (C90): Motet for unaccompanied mixed chorus	
	Cantico del Sole (C90): BBC Northern Singers, conducted by S Wilkinson, University College, Cork
	Cantico del Sole (C90): BBC Northern Singers, conducted by S Wilkinson, BBC Studios, Manchester
Fanfare for the National (C92) *Magnificat and Nunc Dimittis* (C91) for mixed chorus and organ	
	Cantico del Sole (C90): L Halsey Singers, conducted by L Halsey, Queen Elizabeth Hall, London

Date	Life
1975	
27 January	Invited to write a short orchestral work by the GLC in celebration of the 25th Anniversary of the Royal Festival Hall
February	Re-writes the last two pages of the *Cello Concerto* (C65)
6 February	Accepts the commission from the GLC for a 'Ceremonial for Orchestra', for the Royal Festival Hall anniversary
25 February	Piatigorsky 'delighted' with the new ending of the *Cello Concerto* (C65)
12 March	Walton 'rather keen on the idea' of using *Anon in Love* (C71) and the *Bagatelles for Guitar* (C86) as a ballet
14 June	
24 June	Concert cancelled at which the Cello Concerto's new ending was to have been played
September	Offered a commission to write a choral work for the 250th Three Choirs Festival (1977)
October	Begins to transcribe *Five Bagatelles* (C86) for orchestra
1976	
January	Continues revising *Troilus and Cressida* (C62)
4 January	Informs Malcolm Arnold that he has abandoned the third symphony

Works	First performances

Magnificat and Nunc Dimittis
(C91): Choir of Chichester
Cathedral and Ian Fox (organ),
conducted by John Birch,
Cathedral Church of the Holy
Trinity, Chichester

Date	Life
1976	
16 April	
May	
4 May	
June	
3 June	
July	Considers setting 'Peace', a poem by Paul Dehn, for the Queen's Silver Jubilee, 1977
20 July	
25 July	Considers a bassoon concerto for Milan Turkovic
September	Commissioned to write an orchestral piece, entitled The Prospect, by Max Aitkin
4 September	Refuses to write a ceremonial piece for Nottingham County Council
16 September	Asked by OUP to contribute to *Carols for Choirs III* (*King Herod and the Cock* (C95))
12 November	

Works	First performances

Varii Capricci (C86a): free
transcriptions for orchestra

Roaring Fanfare (C93)

                                                   Varii Capricci (C86a): London
Symphony Orchestra, conducted
by A Previn, Royal Festival Hall,
London

Antiphon (C94) for mixed chorus
and organ

                                                   Roaring Fanfare (C93): Kneller
Hall Trumpeters, conducted by T
Platts, Zoological Gardens,
London

                                                   Fanfare for the National (C92):
Freelance players, conducted by H
Rabinowitz, LWT South Bank
Studios, London

                                                   Troilus and Cressida (C62) –
revised version: R Cassilly, J Baker
and soloists, Royal Opera Chorus
and Orchestra, conducted by L
Foster, Royal Opera House,
Covent Garden, London

Date	Life
1976	
30 November	Collapses during a celebratory dinner at the Garrick Club, London
1977	
January	Considers a work for double choir of St Alban's Abbey
22 March	Presented with the Incorporated Society of Musicians' 'Musician of the Year' award
25 March	
29 March	Attends a 75th birthday concert in the Royal Festival Hall, London
14 April	Prepares a setting of Psalm 130 for St Alban's Abbey
21 April	Prepares an unaccompanied setting for St Alban's Abbey
May	Approached by the National Brass Band Championships of Great Britain with a commission to write to work for brass band
10 May	Receives a commission from the USA for a work for concert band
24 June	
29 June	Agrees in principle to write a work for brass band
Summer	Re-writes the last movement of *Varii Capricci* (C86a)
24 August	Proposes to write Five Bagatelles for Brass Band
7 October	

Works	First performances

Façade Revived: R Baker (reciter) and the English Bach Festival Ensemble, Plaisterers Hall, London

King Herod and the Cock (C95): Christmas carol

Title music for the BBC-TV Shakespeare Series (C96)

Date	Life

1977

November · Lunches (as a member of the Order of Merit) with the Queen at Buckingham Palace

20 November

30 December · Decides that he is unable to write the concert band work

1978

12 January · Asked to write a work for Sir Lennox Berkeley's 75th birthday

22 January · Refuses to write the Berkeley 75th birthday piece, and a Mass for a San Francisco choir

26 January

Summer · Works on *Façade* 2

1979

26 February · Approached to write a setting of Horace's Odes for the Llandaff Festival

5 March · Confirmation that Walton would write an 'a cappella' work for the Llandaff Festival

13 March

5 June

Works	First performances
	Antiphon (C94): St Paul's Church Choir with D Craighead (organ), conducted by D Fetler, St Paul's Church, Rochester, New York
	Shakespeare Title Music (C96): English National Opera Orchestra, conducted by David Lloyd-Jones, BBC TV Studios, Lime Grove, London
Salute to Sir Robert Mayer (C97) for 12 trumpets	
	Salute to Sir Robert Mayer (C97): 12 ILEA trumpeters, Royal Festival Hall, London

Date	Life
1979 19 June	
12 October	Finishes the first movement of the Medley for Brass Band
19 November	Commissioned for an orchestral work by Rostropovitch for the Washington Symphony Orchestra
7 December	Accepts the commission for the Washington Symphony Orchestra work
1980 5 February	
15 April	Considers a companion piece for *The Bear*, libretto by Alan Bennett
19 December	
1981 28 January	
5 February	
19 April	Televising of Tony Palmer's film *At the Haunted End of the Day*
3 July	Completes the revision (first 10 pages) of *Prologo e Fantasia* (C100)
Summer	

Works	First performances
	Façade 2: P Pears (reciter) and ensemble, The Maltings, Snape
Medley for Brass Band	
The First Shoot (C29b) – arranged for brass band	
	The First Shoot (C29b) – arranged for brass band: Grimethorpe Colliery Band, conducted by Elgar Howarth, Goldsmith's College, London
	Varii Capricci (C86a) with revised ending: BBC Welsh Symphony Orchestra conducted by O A Hughes, BBC Studios, Cardiff
Passacaglia for Solo Cello (C98)	
A Birthday Fanfare (C99)	

Date	Life
1981 7 September	
10 October	
1982 3 January	
20 February	
16 March	
29 March	Attends an 80th birthday concert at the Royal Festival Hall, London
22 July	Filmed with Susana as the King and Queen of Bavaria in Tony Palmer's film *Wagner*
2 October	
1983 15 January	Attempts to write a motet in the style of Palestrina
15 February	

Works	First performances
	The First Shoot (C29b) – arranged for brass band: Grimethorpe Colliery Band, conducted by Elgar Howarth, Royal Albert Hall, London
	A Birthday Fanfare (C99): Members of the Westphalia Symphony Orchestra, conducted by K Rickenbacher, Recklinghausen, Germany
Prologo e Fantasia (C100) for orchestra	
	Prologo e Fantasia (C100): National Symphony Orchestra of Washington, conducted by M Rostropovitch, Royal Festival Hall, London
	Passacaglia for Solo Cello (C98): M Rostropovitch, Royal Festival Hall, London
Duettino for oboe and violin (C101)	
	Façade: a ballet choreographed and directed by Lindsay Kemp (C12b), Teatro Nuovo, Milan

Date	Life
1983	
March	Agrees to set the Stabat Mater for the 150th Anniversary of the Huddersfield Choral Society
7 March	
8 March	Dies at the age of 80
18 March	Frederick Ashton completes plans for a new ballet
19 April	
20 July	Memorial stone unveiled at memorial service by Lady Walton in Westminster Abbey, London

Works	First performances

Varii Capricci (C86b) – Coda for
the ballet

Varii Capricci (C86b): Royal
Ballet and unnamed orchestra,
conducted by A Lawrence,
Metropolitan Opera House, New
York

Varii Capricci (C86b): Royal
Ballet and orchestra of the Royal
Opera House, conducted by A
Lawrence, Royal Opera House,
Covent Garden, London

.

Manuscripts and First Editions

The majority of Walton's manuscripts are now to be found in New York, on permanent loan at the Pierpont Morgan Library (PML) as part of the Koch Collection. Between 1974 and 1978, I was able to examine and catalogue these while they resided at OUP in Conduit Street.

The results of these examinations appear in this section, arranged alphabetically by title of composition. The description of each falls into two sections: one giving details of the physical layout, the other the textual contents. Included are such details as the manuscript's size, its binding, a transcription of the title page, the number of pages, and whether it is signed and dated by the composer.

Particulars of orchestrations by Walton of works by other composers are not included in this volume.

Details of printed first editions of Walton's published scores follow with transcriptions of each title page, the number of pages, size, details of the cover, full date of publication, and print run (wherever possible) given.

Glossary

Holograph: manuscript written in Walton's hand
MS, MSS   Manuscript, manuscripts
[   ]:   Indicated editorial omissions; un-numbered pages

ALL THIS TIME (C84)

Carol for unaccompanied mixed chorus

Holograph in pencil.

The unbound score is written on both sides of one single sheet of 12-stave music paper, measuring 33.7 x 23.3 cms.

The manuscript paper printer's mark is shown, in the left hand margin, as Stamp.music.f.11i de Marino-Napoli-Porticato S. Francesco di Paola.

2 pages – pp. 1-2 Music

No date, place, dedication or signature of the composer apparent.

Present location: William Walton Museum, Ischia

First edition (Vocal Score)
No title page. Published by Oxford University Press, London in the 'Oxford Choral Songs' series (no X 201 SATB unacc.)

4 pages. 254 x 177 mm
White stiff paper. Lettered in black. Trimmed edges.

Publication: Published 16 July 1970 in *Carols for Choirs 2* at 15/-. Also published 16 July 1970, separately at 1/-.

ANNIVERSARY FANFARE (C89)

Holograph in pencil.

The unbound score is written on both sides of four single sheets of 12-stave music paper, measuring 33.3 x 23.4 cms.

The manuscript paper printer's mark, at the foot of the page on the left hand side, is shown as 12.Stamp.music.f.11i de Marino Napoli – Piazza Plebiscito.

Fanfare for the 75th anniversary of E.M.I. | for | 9 Trumpets in B flat (3.2.2.2) | 4 Tenor Trombones | 3 Bass Trombones | Timpani & Percussion | to be *immediately* followed by Coronation March 'Orb and Sceptre' (1953)

8 pages –   p. [i]   Title and Instrumentation
            pp. 1-6   Music. Duration indicated as c.55″
            p. 7   Blank

No date, place, dedication or signature of the composer apparent.

Present location: PML Koch manuscript 615

First edition (Score)
No title page.

6 pages. 253 x 177mm.
Stiff red and white paper wrappers. Lettered in red and white.
Trimmed edges.
Publication: 750 copies published 5 June 1975 at 75p.
Parts also on sale.

A note says 'A reference to *Happy Birthday to you* is used by arrangement with Keith Prowse Music Publishing Co. Ltd.'

ANON IN LOVE (C71)

Six songs for tenor voice and guitar

The following information was supplied by Mrs Lillias Sheepshanks
who holds the score:

Holograph in pencil.

The score is written on three double sheets of music paper, measuring
33 x 22.9 cms. Unable to ascertain whether the score is bound.

Unable to ascertain layout of the title page.

12 pages – p. [i]   Title page
          pp. 1-11   Music [?]

No date or place apparent. Dedication and composer's signature on the
title page.

Present location: Mrs Lillias Sheepshanks

First edition (Vocal Score)
To L.S. | *FOR PETER PEARS AND JULIAN BREAM* | ANON. IN
LOVE | Six Anonymous Sixteenth- and Seventeenth-Century Lyrics
set for Tenor voice and Guitar by | *WILLIAM WALTON* |
1. Fain would I change that note | 2. O stay, sweet love | 3. Lady, when I
behold the roses | 4. My Love in her attire | 5. I gave her Cakes and I
gave her Ale | 6. To couple is a custom | *Duration 9.5 minutes* |
OXFORD UNIVERSITY PRESS | MUSIC DEPARTMENT 44
CONDUIT STREET, LONDON, W.1

13 pages. 310 x 243 mm
Stiff turquoise and white paper wrappers. Lettered in black. Trimmed
edges.

The black and white photograph of 'La Gamme d'Amour' by Watteau is reproduced by courtesy of The Trustees of the National Gallery, London.

Publication: 1000 copies published 23 June 1960 at 10/6

OTHER VERSIONS

Rescored for tenor and small orchestra, 1971 (C71a)

Holograph in pencil.

The unbound score is written on both sides of twelve single sheets of 24-stave music paper, measuring 43.6 x 30.3 cms.

The manuscript paper printer's mark is shown as G.B.T. MARCHIO DEPOSITATO

No title page.

24 pages – pp. 1-5   'Fain would I change'
pp. 6-10   'O stay, sweet love'
pp. 10-12 'Lady, when I behold'
pp. 13-15 'My love in her attire'
pp. 15-19 'I gave her Cakes'
pp. 19-23 'To couple is a custom'
p. [24]   Blank

No date, place, dedication or signature of the composer apparent.

Present location: PML Koch manuscript 633

Unpublished

ANTIPHON (C94)

Anthem for mixed chorus and organ

Holograph in pencil.

The unbound score is written on one double and on both sides of four single sheets of 14-stave music paper, measuring 32.4 x 23.5 cms. The manuscript paper printer's mark, at the foot of the page on the left hand side, is shown as a large 'M' intertwined with a treble clef and *1105* EXTRA

Antiphon | George Herbert

12 pages – p. [i]   Title page
pp. 1-8   Music : An indication of the time at the head of page one is erased.
pp. [9-11] Blank

No date, place, dedication or signature of the composer apparent.

Present location: PML Koch manuscript 618

First edition (Vocal score)
No title page. Published by Oxford University Press, London in the
'Oxford Anthem' Series (A 326)
8 pages. 253 x 176 mm
White stiff paper. Lettered in black. Trimmed edges.

Publication: Published 9 February 1978 at 30p

AS YOU LIKE IT (C31)

Music for the film

Holograph in pencil.

The existing parts of the unbound score are laid out thus and are held
by PML (Koch manuscript 608A):-

Title Music
The score is written on seven double sheets of 27-stave music paper,
measuring 42.5 x 28 cms.

As You Like It | Title Music
28 pages – p.[i]   Title page
         pp.1-21   Music
         pp.[22-27] Blank

Fountain Music
The score is written on nine double sheets of 22-stave music paper,
measuring 35.5 x 26.3 cms.

The manuscript paper printer's mark is shown as a ship, within a circle,
with the following beneath: A.L. No. 16 | Printed in England

36 pages – p. [i]   Half Title page : As You Like It.
                      In the top right corner is written 'Efrem Kurtz
                      Covent Garden Opera (Stage door)'
       p. [ii]   Blank
       p. [iii]   Title page: Reel II | [Fountain Scene]
       pp.1-29   Music
       p. 30   Music: For 'March' | Fanfares
       pp.[31-33] Blank

First Rosalind theme (after Duke Frederick's exit)
The score is written on two double sheets of 22-stave music paper,
measuring 35.5 x 26.4 cms.

The manuscript paper printer's mark is shown as a ship,

within a circle, with the following beneath:
A.L. No. 16 | Printed in England

Reel III No.5 (after Duke's exit) at the head of page one
8 pages –   pp. 1-6   Music
            pp.[7-8]   Blank

Sunrise Music
The score is written on two double sheets of 22-stave music paper,
measuring 35.5 x 26.4 cms.

The manuscript paper printer's mark is shown as a ship, within a circle,
with the following beneath:
A.L. No. 16 | Printed in England

As You Like It | Reel 4 No.3 | Sunrise (28 secs) | *to be ready by 2 o'clock*

8 pages –   p. [i]   Title page
            pp. 1-6   Music
            p. [7]   Blank

Dinner Music
The score is written on one double sheet of 22-stave music paper,
measuring 35.5 x 26.4 cms.

No.1 Reel IV Dinner Scene at head of page one
4 pages –   pp. 1-3   Music
            p. [4]   Blank

Snake Scene
The score is written on two double sheets of 27-stave music paper,
measuring 42.6 x 28 cms.

Smoke [sic] Scene | (on a theme by Dr Paul Czinner) | Note for copyist –
The double bass is OK!

8 pages –   p. [i]   Title page
            pp. 1-4   Music
            pp. [5-7]   Blank

Procession
The score is written on five double sheets of 27-stave music paper,
measuring 42.6 x 27.8 cms.

Reel X | Procession
20 pages – p. [i]   Title page
            pp. 1-16   Music
            pp. [17-19] Blank

Prelude leading to ballet
The score is written on five double sheets of 27-stave music paper,
measuring 42.6 x 27.8 cms.

[Prelude leading to ballet/Choral ballet (SATB)]

20 pages – p. [i]   Blank
         pp. 1-17   Music
         pp. [18-19] Blank

Hymn
The score is written on three double sheets of 27-stave music paper, measuring 42.6 x 28 cms.

As You Like It | Reel X | Hymn [SATB]

12 pages – p. [i]   Title page
         pp. 1-8   Music
         pp. [9-11] Blank

Closing titles
The score is written on one double sheet of 22-stave music paper, measuring 35.6 x 26.3 cms.

The manuscript paper printer's mark is shown as a ship, within a circle, with the following beneath:
A.L. No.16 | Printed in England

As You Like It | Final Pass-out
4 pages – p. [i]   Title page
        pp.1-2   Music
        p. [3]   Blank

No dedication, date or signature of the composer apparent.

Present location: PML Koch manuscript 608A

Also at PML (Koch manuscript 636) is a setting by Walton of *Under the Greenwood Tree* (C31c) which was not used in the film:

Holograph in pencil, with amendments in blue pencil. The unbound score is written on one double sheet of 16-stave music paper, measuring 35.3 x 26.4 cms.

The manuscript paper printer's mark is shown as a ship within a circle, with the following beneath: A.L. No.10
Printed in England

Under the Greenwood Tree | from the film | 'As You Like It' | by | William Shakespeare | music by | William Walton

4 pages – p. [1]   Title page. A large '268R' is written in the top
              left hand corner in red pencil.
        pp. 1-2   Music [for solo voice]
        p. [3]   Blank – except the following which is written in

> Walton's hand: Hubert J Foss Esq | Oxford
> University Press | Amen House | Warwick
> Square | London EC2

Signed on the title page. No date or dedication apparent.

First edition (Version for solo voice and piano)
No title page.

4 pages. 308 x 242 mm
Stiff red (high key) or blue (low key) and white wrappers.
Lettered in black. Trimmed edges.

Publication: 500 copies published 29 July 1937 at 3/-

(Version for unison voices)

No title page. Published by Oxford University Press, London in the
'Oxford Choral Songs' series (no U 105)

4 pages. 253 x 177 mm
White stiff paper. Lettered in black. Trimmed edges.

Publication: © 1937 at 9d.

THE BATTLE OF BRITAIN (C81)

Music for the film

Holograph in pencil and ink (as indicated). Some parts in Walton's
hand, others in the hand of Malcolm Arnold.

The existing parts of the score (with the exception of 13.M.1: *Battle in
the Air* which is still held by United Artists) are laid out thus and are
held by PML (Koch manuscript 585). These scores were received at
OUP in London on 7 April 1972 after the successful attempt by the
then Prime Minister, Mr Edward Heath, of trying to persuade United
Artists to release them.

2.M.2
Walton holograph in pencil.

The unbound score is written on one double sheet of 14-stave music
paper, measuring 33.6 x 23.1 cms.

4 pages – p. [i]   Title page : 2.M.2
         pp.1-2   Music 2.M.2 and 3.M.1 (Bagpipe music)
         p. [3]   Blank
4.M.1
Walton holograph in pencil.

The unbound score is written on three double and on both sides of one single sheet of 14-stave music paper, measuring 33.6 x 23.3 cms.

14 pages – p. [i]	Title page : 4.M.1. Typewritten script attached. 'Young Siegfrieds' added but not in Walton's hand
	pp. 1-12	Music
	p. [13]	Blank, except script attached

6.M.1
Walton holograph in pencil.

The unbound score is written on two double and on both sides of one single sheet of 14-stave music paper, measuring 33.6 x 23.1 cms.

10 pages – p. [i]	Title page : 6.M.1. Typewritten script attached.
	pp.1-8	Music
	p. [9]	Blank, except script attached

6.M.2
Walton holograph in pencil.

The unbound score is written on one double sheet of 14-stave music paper, measuring 33.6 x 23.1 cms.

4 pages –	p. [i]	Title page : 6.M.2. Typewritten script attached.
	pp.1-2	Music
	p. [3]	Blank

6.M.3
Walton holograph in pencil.

The unbound score is written on one double sheet of 14-stave music paper, measuring 33.6 x 23.1 cms.

4 pages –	p. [i]	Title page : 6.M.3. Typewritten script attached.
	pp.1-3	Music

7.M.1
Walton holograph in pencil.

The unbound score is written on one double and on both sides of one single sheet of 14-stave music paper, measuring 33.6 x 23.1 cms.

6 pages –	p. [i]	Title page : 7.M.1. Typewritten script attached.
	pp.1-4	Music
	p. [5]	Blank

9.M.2
Walton holograph in pencil.

The unbound score is written on two double and on both sides of one single sheet of 20-stave music paper, measuring 33.6 x 23.3 cms.

No title page.
10 pages –	p. [i]	Typewritten script with 9.M.2 *Gay Berlin* written by Walton at the head of the page.
	pp.1-8	Music. Duration 1'15"
	p. [9]	Blank

10.M.1
Walton holograph in pencil.

The unbound score is written on two double sheets of 14-stave music paper, measuring 33.6 x 23.1 cms.

8 pages –	p. [i]	Title page : 10.M.1 with typewritten script attached.
	pp. 1-6	Music. Starts as old man walking into church hall. Duration 1'2"
	p. [7]	Blank : typewritten script attached.

13.M.1
Walton holograph in pencil [pp.1 - 15]
Arnold manuscript in ink [pp.16 - 24] Both unbound

Pages 1 to 15 are written on four double sheets of 28-stave music paper, measuring 46 x 30 cms.

No title page

6 pages –	pp. 1-15	Music : 13.M.1 [Battle in the Air]
	p. [16]	Blank

Unable to trace number of sheets. Pages 16 to 24 are written on 28-stave music paper, measuring 44 x 30.9 cms.

No title page. There is a note at the top of page 16 : (From here on all parts are transposed and the horns II and III are on different staves.)
13.M.1 (continued)

9 pages –	pp. 16-24	Music. The timing of the whole is given at the end, before the double bar line, as 5'08"

Introduction to the March
Walton holograph in pencil.

The unbound score is written on one double and on both sides of one single sheet of 28-stave music paper, measuring 46 x 32.5 cms.

6 pages –	p. [i]	Title page
	pp. 1-4	Music: another introduction to the March (14.M.3)
	p. [5]	Blank

No date, place, dedication or signature of the composer apparent.

Present location: PML Koch manuscript 585 (with the exception of *Battle in the Air* which is still held by United Artists).

THE BEAR (C79)

An extravaganza in one act for three soloists and orchestra

Holograph in pencil.

The unbound score is written on 20-stave music paper, measuring 40 x 30 cms.

The manuscript paper printer's mark is shown as G.RICORDI & C

The Bear | An extravaganza in one Act | Libretto adapted from A.Tchekov | by Paul Dehn | music by William Walton

239 pages –p. [i]   Title page
p. [ii]   Orchestration
p. [iii]   Characters/Action
pp.1-236   Music

The date and place indicated as: '30.4.67, Forio d'Ischia'.
Dedication on the title page.
Signed by the composer on the title page.

Present location: Koussevitsky Musical Foundation, Library of Congress, Washington DC, USA, which also holds the unbound revisions. The library received the manuscript on 5 June 1967.

The revisions were sent from Oxford University Press in New York City on 22 September 1967, and were received in the Music Division on 25 September.

These revisions consist of 11 double sheets of full orchestral score (in pencil: 26-stave music paper) which are kept in a separate envelope, laid in the manuscript. The following pages are marked 'new' in the full score: pp. 36; 39; 173; 174; 187; 188; 189; 190; 223; 224; 235 and 236.

First edition [Full Score]
Commissioned by the Serge Koussevitsky Music Foundation in the | Library of Congress and dedicated to the memory of Serge and | Natalie Koussevitsky | The Bear | An Extravaganza in One Act | Music by | William Walton | Libretto adapted from Anton Chekhov by | Paul Dehn and William Walton | Lyrics by | Paul Dehn | German translation by | Ernst Roth | Oxford University Press | Music Department, 44 Conduit Street, London W1R 0DE

212 pages. 278 x 216 mm

Stiff white paper wrappers. Lettered in grey and purple.
Trimmed edges.

Publication: Published 1 December 1977 at 12.00

[Vocal Score]
Commissioned by the Serge Koussevitsky Music | Foundation in the
Library of Congress and dedicated to | the memory of Serge and
Natalie Koussevitsky. | The BEAR | An Extravaganza in One Act |
Music by | WILLIAM WALTON | Libretto adapted from Anton
Chekhov by | PAUL DEHN | and | WILLIAM WALTON | Lyrics by |
PAUL DEHN | German translation by | ERNST ROTH | Pianoforte
arrangement by | ROY DOUGLAS | Oxford University Press | Music
Department. 44 Conduit Street. London. W.1

95 pages. 278 x 190 mm
Stiff orange paper wrappers with pictures of Smirnov and Popova
(cover design taken from photographs by Reg Wilson). Lettered in
black and white. Trimmed edges.

Publication: Published 8 June 1967 at 5/-

[Libretto]
THE BEAR | AN EXTRAVAGANZA IN ONE ACT | *Music by* WIL-
LIAM WALTON | *Libretto adapted from* | *ANTON TCHEKOV*
| By PAUL DEHN and WILLIAM WALTON | *Lyrics by* PAUL DEHN
| OXFORD UNIVERSITY PRESS | MUSIC DEPARTMENT 44
CONDUIT STREET LONDON W.1

7 pages. 254 x 177 mm
Stiff green paper wrappers. Lettered in black. Trimmed edges.

Publication: Published 8 June 1967 at 5/-

BELSHAZZAR'S FEAST (C23)

Cantata for baritone solo,double mixed chorus and orchestra

Whereabouts of holograph unknown

First edition [Full Score]
WILLIAM WALTON | BELSHAZZAR'S | FEAST for mixed chorus |
baritone solo | and orchestra | Text arranged from Biblical sources by |
OSBERT SITWELL | FULL SCORE | OXFORD UNIVERSITY
PRESS | MUSIC DEPARTMENT | 44 CONDUIT STREET LON-
DON W1

165 pages. 267 x 186 mm
Stiff purple paper wrappers. Lettered in orange, purple and white.
Trimmed edges.

Publication: Published 31 May 1957 at 25/-

[De Luxe Full Score]
BELSHAZZAR'S | FEAST | for baritone solo, mixed choir, and
orchestra | the text selected and arranged from the Bible by Osbert
Sitwell | the music by William Walton

165 pages. 315 x 235 mm
Hard blue, buff,black and white wrappers, featuring the front exterior
of Nebuchadnezzar II's royal chamber, Babylon. Trimmed edges.

Publication: 350 copies (boxed and signed by Walton) published 1978
at 60.00. This volume also included an essay on the origins
of 'Belshazzar's Feast' by Michael Kennedy, and was published in the 500th anniversary of OUP.

[Vocal Score]
BELSHAZZAR'S FEAST | *for Mixed Choir, Baritone Solo and Orchestra*
| *by* WILLIAM WALTON | *Text selected and arranged from the Holy*
Bible by | OSBERT SITWELL | *German Translation by* | Beryl de Zoete |
and | Baronin Imma Doernberg | *Price 3/-* | OXFORD UNIVERSITY
PRESS | Amen House | Warwick Square | London,EC4

120 pages. 252 x 175 mm
Stiff paper wrappers with cover designed by Severini in green and
white. Lettered in black. Trimmed edges.

Publication: Published 17 September 1931 at 3/-

Revised edition [Vocal Score]
WILLIAM WALTON | BELSHAZZAR'S | FEAST | FOR MIXED
CHOIR | BARITONE SOLO | AND ORCHESTRA | REVISED EDI-
TION 1955 | VOCAL SCORE | OXFORD UNIVERSITY PRESS |
(MUSIC DEPARTMENT) | 44 CONDUIT STREET, LONDON W1

120 pages. 251 x 175 mm
Stiff orange paper wrappers. Lettered in purple and white. Trimmed
edges.

Publication: Published 24 April 1959 at 12/-

First edition [Sol-Fa] No title page. Front cover:
BELSHAZZAR'S FEAST | *for Mixed Choir, Baritone Solo and Orchestra*
| *by* WILLIAM WALTON | *Text selected and arranged from the Holy*
Bible by | OSBERT SITWELL | Sol-Fa Edition | *Price 2/-* | OXFORD
UNIVERSITY PRESS | 36 Soho Square, Oxford Street, London W1

88 pages. 255 x 170 mm
Stiff off-white paper wrappers. Lettered in black. Trimmed edges.

Publication: © 1933 at 2/-

[Two separate choruses]
Two choruses | from | BELSHAZZAR'S FEAST | WILLIAM WAL-
TON | (Printed for the Blackpool Music Festival, 1934) | OXFORD
UNIVERSITY PRESS

50 pages [pp. 70-120 : taken from the 1931 vocal score]
Stiff white paper wrappers. Lettered in black. Trimmed edges.

Publication: © 1935

A BIRTHDAY FANFARE (C99)

For seven trumpets in Bb and percussion

Details taken from a copy:
Holograph in black felt-tipped pen(?)

The unbound manuscript is written on one side of a single sheet of 21-
stave music paper.

2 pages –   p. [1]   Music. *Fanfare* for Karl on his 70th birthday.
                       Greetings from Susana and William' is written
                       at the top of the score.
           p. [2]   Blank

No date or place apparent.

Present location: Dr Karl Still, Germany

First edition [Score]
No title page

4 pages. 253 x 177 mm
Stiff white paper. Lettered in black. Trimmed edges.

Publication: Published 19 May 1983 at 60p

BIRTHDAY GREETINGS TO HERBERT HOWELLS (C88)

Written for the occasion of Herbert Howells's 80th birthday

Holograph in black biro.

The unbound score is written on half of one single sheet of 16- stave
music paper, measuring 27 x 18.5 cms.

2 pages – p. [1]   Music
           p. [2]   Blank

Signed by the composer and dated 22.9.72

Present location: Royal College of Music, London. MS 5274/6

Unpublished

THE BOY DAVID (C30)

Incidental music for J M Barrie's play in three acts
Whereabouts of holograph unknown

BUCOLIC COMEDIES (C15)

Five songs to words by Edith Sitwell
Whereabouts of holograph unknown

CANTICO DEL SOLE (C90)

Motet for unaccompanied mixed chorus

Holograph in pencil.

The unbound score is written on one double and on both sides of five single sheets of 14-stave music paper, measuring 32.4 x 23.4 cms.

The manuscript paper printers's mark, at the foot of the page on the left hand side, is shown as Casa Musicale G.RICORDI & C. S.p.A.-ROMA

To| Sir Robert & Lady Mayer | Cantico del Sole | S.Francesco d'Assisi | Motet for mixed voices a capella | William Walton

14 pages – p. [i]   Title page
           pp. 1-10   Music
           pp. [11-13] Blank

No date or place apparent.
Dedication on the title page.
Signed by the composer on the title page.

Present location: PML Koch manuscript 616

First edition [Vocal Score]
No title page

15 pages. 254 x 177mm

Stiff orange paper wrappers. Lettered in white. Trimmed edges.

Publication: 4000 copies published 31 October 1974 at 50p.

CAPRICCIO BURLESCO (C80)

For orchestra

Holograph in pencil.

The unbound score is written on both sides of 25 single sheets of 28-stave music paper, measuring 46.4 x 32.4 cms.

The manuscript paper printer's mark is shown as G.B.T.
MARCHIO DEPOSITATO.

Philharmonic Overture N.Y.'68 [crossed out] | Capriccio burlesco | William Walton

50 pages –	p. [i]	Title page
	p. [ii]	Commissioned by the New York Philharmonic
	p. [iii]	To	André	Kostelanetz - Orchestra [tion] (on 17 lines) – Duration 7'0" circa
	p. [iv]	Blank
	p. 1	Music
	p. [2]	Orchestra - crossed out
	pp.2-4	Music
	p. [5]	Blank
	pp.4[sic]-42	Music: 6'50"c. indicated as the timing – at the end of the music
	p. [43]	Music – erased with sketch and other scribblings

Date and place indicated as 'Forio 5.9.68'
Dedication on page [iii] of the preliminaries.
Signed by the composer on the title page and initialled after the double bar line on p.42.

Present location: PML Koch manuscript 598

Also at PML are old pages (i.e. originals now replaced in the above by amendments) – these are written on four separate pieces of 28-stave music paper.

First edition: [Score]
WILLIAM WALTON | Capriccio Burlesco | Oxford University Press | Music Department 44 Conduit Street London W1R 0DE

68 pages. 253 x 178 mm

Stiff chocolate brown, light brown (two shades), mauve and white paper wrappers. Lettered in light brown (2 shades), mauve and white. Trimmed edges.

Publication: 1000 copies published 27 November 1969 at 2.00

CHORAL PRELUDE ON WHEATLEY (C3)

For organ

Holograph in ink.

The unbound score is written on both sides of a single sheet of 12-stave music paper, measuring 30.5 x 24 cms.

No title page
2 pages – pp. [1-2] Music. It is 39 bars in length.

No dedication. Dated 'August 16th 1916' at the end of the music, under the double bar line.
Signed by the composer at the head of page [1].

Present location: Manuscript Collections, the British Library, Add.
MS 52384

Unpublished

CHORAL PRELUDE 'Herzlich Thut Mich Verlangen' (C25)

By J S Bach, freely arranged for solo piano

Holograph in ink.

The score is written on one side of a single sheet of 16-stave music paper, measuring 28 x 24 cms.
The wrapper is inscribed by Harriet Cohen with the title, and 'Gift to the Library of the Hebrew University in Jerusalem, Palestine from Harriet Cohen CBE'.

No title page apparent.
1 page – p.[1] Music. It is 18 bars in length.

Dedication 'For Harriet Cohen' at the head of the score.
Also the word 'BACH' and 'arr. by William Walton'
'4 Mus' appears in the bottom right hand corner.

Present location: The Music Department, the Jewish National and University Library, Jerusalem, Israel

First edition [Piano Score]
A | BACH | BOOK | *for Harriet Cohen* | Transcriptions for pianoforte
from the | works of J.S.Bach made by Granville | Bantock, Arnold Bax,
Lord Berners, | Arthur Bliss, Frank Bridge, Eugene | Goossens,
Herbert Howells, John | Ireland, Constant Lambert, R.Vaughan | Wil-
liams, William Walton, and W. | Gillies Whittaker | OXFORD
UNIVERSITY PRESS | PRICE 5/-

32 pages (Walton's contribution appears on p. 30). 310 x 240 mm
Stiff yellow wrappers. Lettered in green. Trimmed edges.

Publication: © 1932 at 5/-

CHRISTOPHER COLUMBUS (C46)

Incidental music for Louis MacNeice's play

Holograph in pencil.

The existing parts of the score (originally bound by the BBC in stiff
grey paper boards with a blue leather re-inforced spine) are laid out
thus:

Act One
Introduction and Chorus
The score is written on five double sheets of 27-stave music paper,
measuring 44.3 x 29 cms.

20 pages –	p. [i]	Title page: 'Introduction' written in Walton's hand but erased.
	p. [ii]	Blank
	p. [iii]	Introduction and chorus	all 2 bar repeats to be copied in full. Cue 1 is written in red pencil on p.[i] and p. [iii]
	pp.1-16	Music
	p. [17]	Blank

Background to Columbus and Prior
The score is written on one double sheet of 24-stave music paper,
measuring 36.2 x 27 cms.

| 4 pages – | p. [i] | Title page : CC – Pt. 1 | Background to Col. & Pr. p. 10 – written in Walton's hand but erased. Cue 5A is written in red pencil |
| | pp. [1-3] | Music |

Recitative and Chorus
The score is written on two double sheets of 27-stave music paper, measuring 44.3 x 29 cms.

8 pages – p. [i] Title page: CC – Pt. 1 | Recitative & Chorus p.13 & 14 – written in Walton's hand but erased.
Cue 6 is written in red pencil

  pp. [1-6] Music
  p. [7] Blank

Fanfares for Talavera, Medina-Sidonia, Medina Celi and Mendoza
The score is written on one double sheet of 24-stave music paper, measuring 36.7 x 27 cms.

4 pages – p. [i] Title page: CC Pt. 1 | Fanfares p.14-15,15 | & | C. music p.16-17 – written in Walton's hand but page references erased.
Cues 7,8,9,10,11 are written in red pencil.

  pp. 1-2 Music
  p. [3] Blank

Note: C. music refers to 'Court Music' (a Sarabande) which was not used in the original broadcast.

Down in the Kingdom of Granada: song for voice and guitar

Holograph held by the estate of the late Hedli Anderson.
Unable to see and examine the material.

No-no-never again!
The score is written on two double sheets of 24-stave music paper, measuring 36.7 x 27 cms.

8 pages – p. [i] Title page: CC Part 1 | Male Chorus p.31 | No-no-never again! – written in Walton's hand but page references erased.
Cue 15 is written in red pencil.

  pp. [1-5] Music
  pp. [6-7] Blank

Beatriz's Song
The score is written on one double sheet of 16-stave music paper, measuring 36.7 x 27 cms.

4 pages – p. [i] Title page: CC (Part 1) | Beatriz's Song (p.31 of script) – written in Walton's hand but page references erased.
Cue 17 is written in red pencil.

  pp. [1-3] Music

Kyrie
The score is written on one double sheet of 16-stave music paper, measuring 36.7 x 27 cms.

4 pages – p. [i] Title page: CC (Pt 1) | Melody of Beatriz's Song c/f into Kyrie p.34 – written in Walton's hand but page references erased.
Cue 18 is written in red pencil.

p. 1 Music
pp. [2-3] Blank

Granada has fallen
The score is written on six double sheets of 32-stave music paper, measuring 48 x 31.4 cms.

24 pages – p. [i] Title page: CC (Pt. 1) | Chorus 'Granada' p.34 | Background music pp.36-36 – written in Walton's hand but page references erased. Cue 19 is written in red pencil. There is also a note: 'Copyist note that all 2 bar repeats to be copied in full'. The cues are attached to the page.

pp. 1-19 Music
pp. [20-23] Blank

Fanfares
The score is written on one double sheet of 24-stave music paper, measuring 36.5 x 27 cms.

4 pages – p. [i] Title page: CC (Pt. 1) | Fanfares p.40- | Fanfare and background written in Walton's hand but page references erased.
Cue 20,21,23,23A,23B are written in red pencil. The cues are attached to the page.

pp. [1-2] Music
p. [3] Blank

Note: The Fanfare for Queen Isabella was not used in the original 1942 broadcast

Act Two
Port Music
The score is written on three double sheets of 24-stave music paper, measuring 44.2 x 29.6 cms.

12 pages – p. [i] Title page: CC (Pt. II) Introduction: Port music | and background p.46.
Cue 24 is written in red pencil.

pp. 1-8 Music
pp. [9-11] Blank

There be three ships, etc.
The score is written on one double sheet of 16-stave music paper, measuring 36.5 x 27 cms.

4 pages –   p. [i]   Title page: CC (Pt II) | Women's Song p.48-49 | Background music on Beatriz's song p.50-51 | Drumming p. 54 – written in Walton's hand but page references erased.
Cues 25,26 and 27 are written in red pencil.

           pp. 1-3   Music

Per Dominum, etc
The score is written on one double sheet of 16-stave music paper, measuring 36.5 x 27 cms.

4 pages –   p. [i]   Title page: CC - | Per Dominum | Litany of the Saints | Capstan Shanty – written in Walton's hand but page references erased.
Cues 27A and 28 are written in red pencil.

           pp. [1-2] Music
           p. [3]   Blank

We're gone away/Sea Music
The score is written on two double sheets of 24-stave music paper, measuring 36.5 x 27 cms.

8 pages –   p. [i]   Title page: Shanty 'We're gone away' p. 55 | & | Sea Music pp. – written in Walton's hand but page references erased.
Cue 29 is written in red pencil.

           pp. [1-5] Music
           pp. [6-7] Blank

Night Music
The score is written on one double sheet of 24-stave music paper, measuring 36.5 x 27 cms.

4 pages –   p. [i]   Title page: 'CC (Pt II)' | Night Music p. – written in Walton's hand but page references erased.
Cue 31 is written in red pencil.

           pp. [1-3] Music

Gold Gold Gold
The score is written on two double sheets of 24-stave music paper, measuring 36.5 x 27 cms.

8 pages –   p. [i]   Title page: 'CC (Pt II)' | Gold Gold Gold p. – written in Walton's hand but page references erased.
Cue 33 is written in red pencil.

pp. 1-6   Music
p. [7]   Blank

Look Look Look/Te Deum
The score is written on two double sheets of 24-stave music paper, measuring 36.5 x 27 cms.

8 pages –   p. [i]   Title page: 'CC (Pt II)' Speaking Chorus p. – |
                      Look Look Look | & | Te Deum – written in
                      Walton's hand but page references erased.
                      Cue 34 is written in red pencil.
       pp. [1-7]   Music

Indian Chorus
The score is written on two double sheets of 24-stave music paper, measuring 36.5 x 27 cms.

8 pages –   p. [i]   Title page: Indian Chorus | Fanfare | Reprise
                      Indian Chorus – written in Walton's hand but
                      page references erased.
                      Cues 34A and 35 written in red pencil.
       pp. 1-7   Music

Background and speaking chorus
The score is written on six double sheets of 28-stave music paper, measuring 44.9 x 31.2 cms.

24 pages – p. [i]   Title page: Background and speaking chorus –
                      written in Walton's hand but page references
                      erased.
       p. [ii]   Blank
       pp. 1-21   Music
       p. [22]   Blank

Glory to God
The score is written on four double sheets of 32-stave music paper, measuring 48 x 31.7 cms.

16 pages – p. [i]   Title page: Final Chorus – written in Walton's
                      hand but page references erased.
                      Cue 37 written in red pencil.
       pp. 1-15   Music

No dedication, date or signature of the composer apparent.

Present location: PML Koch manuscript 623

First edition [Vocal Score] *Beatriz's Song* (C46b)
No title page

4 pages. 311 x 231 mm

Stiff black, grey and white paper wrappers. Lettered in black and white. Trimmed edges.

Publication: 1000 copies published 11 July 1974 (in the Oxford Solo Song Series) at 35p.

CONCERTO FOR VIOLA AND ORCHESTRA (C22)

Original version

Holograph in ink.

The score is written on sixteen double and one single sheet of 28-stave music paper, measuring 38.75 x 28.5 cms.

The manuscript is in a crude cloth binding – it was already in this form before it became a possession of the Royal College of Music. There has been a good deal of repair and re-inforcement at the joints involving adhesive strips.

CONCERTO for VIOLA | and | ORCHESTRA | WILLIAM WAL-TON
In the top right hand corner is the number '4234', i.e. the number of this manuscript in the RCM's collection.

66 pages – p. [i]   Title page
        p. [ii]   Details of the instrumentation required and a note from Walton for the engraver
        pp. 1-16 First movement
        pp. 17-35 Second movement
        pp. 36-61 Third movement
        pp.[62-64] Blank

Dedication at the head of the score of the first movement, p.1. Signed by the composer on the title page.

Present location: The Royal College of Music, London (MS 4234)

First edition [Full score – original version]

No title page

71 pages. 343 x 257 mm
Stiff paper wrapper with cover designed by Severini in green and white. Lettered in black. Trimmed edges.

Publication: © 1930 by OUP at 21/-

[Miniature Score]

No title page

71 pages. 216 x 141 mm
Stiff papers wrappers with cover designed by Severini in green and white. Lettered in black. Trimmed edges.

Publication: © 1930 by OUP at 4/-

[arranged for viola and piano]

CONCERTO FOR VIOLA | AND ORCHESTRA | WILLIAM WALTON | Piano Score | OXFORD UNIVERSITY PRESS

43 pages. 309 x 235 mm
Stiff paper wrappers with cover designed by Severini in green and white. Lettered in black. Trimmed edges.

Publication: Published 3 July 1930 at 7/6

[Solo viola part, ed. by Lionel Tertis]

CONCERTO FOR VIOLA | AND ORCHESTRA | WILLIAM WALTON | VIOLA SOLO

12 pages. 307 x 243 mm
Stiff white paper wrappers. Lettered in black. Trimmed edges.

Publication: Published and included with the above.
Available separately at 1/6

Revised version 1936
Unable to examine the manuscript
Present location: PML Koch manuscript 586A

Revised version 1961
Holograph in pencil.

The score (loose in a folder) is written on 61 sheets of 28-stave music paper, measuring 37 x 26.5 cms.

Concerto for Viola and Orchestra | [rule] | [Reduced] (written in blue pencil) | William Walton

122 pages – p. [i]   Title page
              pp. [ii-iii]   Blank
              p. [iv]   Instrumentation
              pp. 1-30   First movement
              pp. 31-66   Second movement
              pp. 67-118   Third movement

Dedication at the head of the score of the first movement, p.1. Signed by the composer on the title page.

Present location: PML Koch manuscript 586B

First edition [Score – revised version]
William Walton | CONCERTO | FOR VIOLA | AND ORCHESTRA | I-Andante Comodo | II-Vivo, con molto preciso | III-Allegro moderato | OXFORD UNIVERSITY PRESS | Music Department, 44 Conduit Street, London, W1

136 pages. 254 x 178 mm
Stiff green paper wrappers. Lettered in yellow. Trimmed edges.

Publication: Published 19 March 1964 at 30/-

CONCERTO FOR VIOLIN AND ORCHESTRA (C37)

Original version

Holograph in pencil(?)

The score, bound in blue cloth covers, is written on 24-stave music paper, measuring 38 x 25.6 cms.

No title page apparent.

144 pages – p. [i]   Half title page (not in Walton's hand)
      pp. 1-40   First movement
      p. [ii]   Half title page (not in Walton's hand – for movements II and III)
      pp.41-82   Second movement
      pp.83-142 Third movement

Dedication ('for Jascha Heifetz') at the top of page 1.
No signature apparent. Dated '2/6/39: New York' at the end of the score.

Present location: whereabouts unknown. The above details are taken from a copy at Oxford University Press.

[Arrangement for violin and piano]

Holograph in ink. The first movement uses a combination of black and red inks; the second and third movements use black only.

The work is laid out thus:

First movement on 12-stave music paper, measuring 36 x 27 cms.
Second and third movements on 16-stave music paper, measuring 37 x 27 cms.

The manuscript is not bound, (12) Durand & Cie.4, Place de la Madeleine, Paris only appearing as the manuscript paper printer's mark on the 12-stave music paper (1st movement).

Violin and Pianoforte (top right hand corner) | Violin Concerto | I (in black ink) Walton's name (handwriting undetermined but in large blue lettering) appears above the words 'Violin Concerto' in a crudely drawn parallelogram.
Above Walton's name, also in blue pencil, is 'about 27 1/2 minutes'. In the top left hand corner of the title page, the word 'Revised' is underscored twice and written directly below the encircled 'orch.' and the initials 'J.H.' At the very top of the title page (above the initials 'J.H.') is the number '35a'.

68 pages – p. [i]   Title page
        pp. 1-15)
        p. [16])   First movement
        pp. [ii-iv] Blank
        p. [v]   Half title page
        pp. 17-32 Second movement
        pp. [vi-viii]Blank
        p. [ix]   Half title page
        pp. 33-56 Third movement
        pp. [x-xii] Blank

No dedication apparent, nor signature of the composer.
The only date indicated is at the end of the first movement: 'New York: 15/5/39'

[Solo violin part]

Holograph in ink. All three movements use a combination of black and red inks.

Unable to ascertain the number of sheets. The work is laid out thus:

> First movement on 12-stave music paper, measuring 36 x 27 cms. Second and third movements on 16-stave music paper, measuring 37 x 27 cms.

The manuscript is not bound, (12) Durand & Cie.4, Place de la Madeleine, Paris only appearing as the manuscript paper printer's mark on the 12-stave music paper (1st movement).

Solo (in pencil, and the only word in Walton's hand).
The word 'violin' is written (in pencil) after 'solo' in a square as is 'Walton' above the Roman numeral 'I' in the centre of the page. Handwriting undetermined. There is evidence that some notes and other musical notation was originally written on this sheet but later

erased. In the top left hand corner of the title page, the word 'Revised' is underscored twice directly below the encircled 'orch.' and the initials 'J.H.'

44 pages –	p. [i]	Title page
	pp. 1-11	Music
	pp. [ii-iv]	Blank
	p. [i]	Half title page
	pp. [1-8]	Music
	pp. [ii-iv]	Blank
	p. [i]	Half title page
	pp. [1-14]	Music
	p. [ii]	Blank

No dedication, date or signature of the composer apparent.

Present location of the violin/piano arrangement and the solo violin part: Music Division, Library of Congress, Washington DC, USA. Also at the Library of Congress is a sheet of instructions and emendations for Heifetz, written on a piece of 16-stave music paper.

Revised version (1943)
Holograph in pencil.

The score, bound in blue cloth covers, is writen on 24-stave music paper, measuring 43.8 x 31.6 cms.

No title page.

158 pages –	p. [i]	Half title page (Walton's initials appear in the top right hand of this page)
	pp. [ii-iii]	Blank
	pp. 1-40	First movement
	pp. [iv-viii]	Blank
	p. [ix]	Half title page
	p. 41-82	Second movement ('6 mins' is written after the double bar line')
	p. [x]	Blank
	p. [xi]	Half title page
	pp. 83-142	Third movement
	pp. [xii-xvi]	Blank

Dedication (for 'J.H.') at the top of page 1.
No signature apparent – only the initials as indicated above.
Dated 'New York: 2/6/39; revised 30/11/43' at the end of the score.

Present location: PML Koch manuscript 597

First edition [Full Score]
No title page

172 pages. 264 x 188 mm
Stiff paper wrappers with cover designed by Severini in green and white. Lettered in black. Trimmed edges.

Publication: 1000 copies published 29 November 1945 by OUP at 12/6

[Arrangement for violin and piano by Franz Reizenstein]
No title page

60 pages. 310 x 230 mm
Stiff paper wrappers with cover designed by Severini in green and white. Lettered in black. Trimmed edges.

Publication: Published 18 September 1941 by OUP at 15/-

[Solo violin part]

CONCERTO FOR VIOLIN AND ORCHESTRA | Violin Solo part edited by | JASCHA HEIFETZ | VIOLIN SOLO | WILLIAM WAL-TON

25 pages. 306 x 240 mm
Stiff white paper wrappers. Lettered in black. Trimmed edges.

Published and included with the arrangement for violin and piano

CONCERTO FOR VIOLONCELLO AND ORCHESTRA (C65)

The following information was supplied by the late Gregor Piatogorsky:

Holograph in pencil.

Unable to ascertain the number of sheets or details of the music paper, which measures 44.4 x 31.5 cms.

Unable to ascertain details of the title page, although it is signed by the composer and the dedication is written on it.

Also unable to ascertain the pagination, although the first movement occupies 20 pages, the second movement 38 pages and the third 30 pages. There is a blank between each movement.

'Forio d'Ischia, Feb-Oct 1956' appears at the end of the third movement.

Present location: Mrs Daniel B Drachman, Piatigorsky's daughter

New ending for the Concerto   Starting 5 before 19 in the printed score
on page 112 (total length – 23 bars)

Holograph in pencil

The unbound score is written on one side of two separate single sheets of 24-stave music paper, measuring 43.1 x 30 cms.

These are marked Ⓐ and Ⓑ

The manuscript paper printer's mark is shown as G.B.T. MARCHIO DEPOSITATO.

Present location: Mrs Drachman (USA)

Piano Score (movements 2 and 3 only)

Holograph in pencil

The unbound score is written on six double (with four single sheets stuck on either side of two separate pieces of blank card as indicated) sheets of 16-stave music paper, measuring 33.7 x 23.2 cms.

The music paper has been used upside down, the manuscript paper printer's mark is shown (in the top right hand corner) as 16. Stamp music.f1le de Marino-Napoli-Porticato S.Francesco di Paola.

II (with: William Walton | Cello Concerto | Piano Score, added in another hand)

28 pages – p. [i]	Title page: 'II' written only in Walton's hand. A large 619R is written in the top right hand corner – in blue pencil. A large 619R is written in the bottom right hand corner – in red pencil.
pp. 1-9	Music
p. 10A	One line of music (3 staves) stuck to plain cardboard with sellotape
p. [ii]	Blank
pp. 10B-11A	Music
p. 11B	Two lines of music (9 staves) stuck to plain cardboard with sellotape
p. [iii]	Blank
pp. 12-21	Music: alterations on pages 16 and 17 (not used) are stuck together with sellotape
pp. [22-23]	Blank

Holograph in pencil.

The unbound score is written on six double and one single sheet of 12-stave music paper, measuring 33.7 x 23.2 cms.

The music paper has been used upside down, the manuscript paper printer's mark is shown (in the top right hand corner) as 12. Stamp music. f.11e de Marino-Napoli-Porticato S. Francesco di Paola.

III (with: Walton | Cello Concerto | [Piano Score], added in another hand)

26 pages – p. [i]   Title page: 'III' written only in Walton's hand
           pp. 1-23   Music
           pp. [24-25] Blank

No date, place, signature of the composer or dedication apparent

Present location: PML Koch manuscript 627

First edition [Full Score]
WILLIAM WALTON | CONCERTO | for | Violoncello and Orchestra | Full Score | OXFORD UNIVERSITY PRESS | MUSIC DEPARTMENT | 44 Conduit Street, London W.1

114 pages. 255 x 178 mm
Stiff light green, russet and white papers wrappers. Lettered in russet. Trimmed edges.

Publication: Published 12 December 1957 at 21/-

[Arrangement for violoncello and piano]

WILLIAM WALTON | CONCERTO | FOR | VIOLONCELLO | AND ORCHESTRA | OXFORD UNIVERSITY PRESS | Music Department 44 Conduit Street London W.1

42 pages. 309 x 231 mm
Stiff grey paper wrappers. Lettered in purple. Trimmed edges.

Publication: Published 19 December 1957 at 18/-

[Solo cello]

WILLIAM WALTON | CONCERTO | FOR | VIOLONCELLO | AND ORCHESTRA | VIOLONCELLO SOLO | OXFORD UNIVERSITY PRESS

18 pages. 311 x 229 mm
Stiff white paper wrappers. Lettered in black. Trimmed edges.

Publication: Published and included with the above.

CORONATION TE DEUM

for two mixed choruses,two semi-choruses,boys' voices,organ orchestra and military brass (C58)

Holograph in pencil.

The full score is written on 32-stave music paper, measuring 48 x 32 cms.

This manuscript was presented to the British Library by Sir William Walton on 16 May 1953 in an unbound condition. It was later bound (in November/December 1974) in red leather, with gold tooling.

Te Deum Laudamus | by | William Walton | set to music for | The Coronation of Her Majesty Queen Elizabeth II | in | Westminster Abbey June 2nd 1953

55 pages – p. [i]   Title page
        pp. 1-46   Music. '7'40"' appears at the end of the music, after the double bar line
        pp. [47-55] Blank. Some sketch (now erased) appears on p. [48]

'47898' is written at the foot of the title page, on the left hand side. This refers to the British Library's Manuscript Collections's manuscript number.

Walton's pagination (1-46) at the top of each page has been crossed out and a number added to each even-numbered page.

No date, place or dedication apparent
Signed by the composer on the title page.

Present location: The British Library, London. Manuscript Collections Add.MS 47898

Vocal Score

Holograph in pencil.

The unbound score is written on nine double sheets of 16-stave music paper, measuring 33.5 x 23.3 cms.

The manuscript paper has been used upside down, the manuscript paper printer's mark is shown (in the top right hand corner) as Stamp. music. f.11e de Marino-Napoli-Porticato S.Francesca di Paola.

Coronation Te Deum | William Walton

36 pages – p. [i]   Title page
        pp. 1-34   Music
        p. [35]   Blank

No date, place or dedication apparent. Signed by the composer on the title page.

Present location: PML Koch manuscript 629

First edition [Vocal Score]
WILLIAM WALTON | CORONATION TE DEUM | COMPOSED
FOR THE CORONATION OF | H.M. QUEEN ELIZABETH II | IN
WESTMINSTER ABBEY | ON TUESDAY, 2 JUNE 1953 | [rule]
INSTRUMENTATION | Full orchestra and organ. The triple wood-
wind may | be reduced to double if necessary. Additional | parts for 4
trumpets, 3 trombones, and side-drums are | optional. Full score and
orchestral parts on hire. | *Duration, 7 minutes 45 seconds* | [rule]
OXFORD UNIVERSITY PRESS | LONDON NEW YORK TOR-
ONTO | *Price 3s. net*
36 pages. 246 x 180 mm
Stiff blue paper wrappers. Lettered in pale blue and black. Also
featured are five bars of the manuscript vocal score on a pale blue
background. Trimmed edges.

Publication: Published 20 April 1953 by Novello & Co. Ltd in the
Coronation Service Book
Published separately 30 April 1953 by OUP at 3/-

Arrangement for choir and organ [Vocal Score]
First edition
No title page

39 pages. 254 x 177 mm
Stiff white paper wrappers. Lettered in black. Trimmed edges.

Publication: © 1988 by OUP at 4.50

CROWN IMPERIAL (C32)

Coronation March for full orchestra

Holograph in pencil.

The score, bound in a buff coloured paper binder, is written on 24-
stave music paper, measuring 44.4 x 30.3 cms. Pages 2 to 17 are
photocopies, in Walton's hand, and are reduced to 34.6 x 24 cms.

No title page apparent

54 pages – p. [i]   Title page [this may be attached to the binding]
         pp. 1-45   Music: *8 mins 10 secs* appears after the double
                     bar line at the end of the music
         pp. [46-53] Blank

No date, place, dedication or signature of the composer apparent.

Present location: PML Koch manuscript 595B

[Short/Piano Score]

Details taken from a copy:
Holograph in pencil (?)

The unbound score is written on three double sheets of 16-stave music paper, measuring 35.5 x 26.5 cms.

The manuscript paper printer's mark is shown as a ship within a circle with A.L. No 10 and Printed in England underneath.

12 pages – p. [i]   Title page: in the top right hand corner is William Walton original short score of 'Crown Imperial' Coronation March, April 1937. The remainder is blank, except for some scribblings.
pp.[1-11]   Music

No place, dedication or signature of the composer apparent.

Present location: PML Koch manuscript 595A

First edition: [Full Score]

Unable to trace a copy of the printed 1937 full score

– – – – – [Full Score incorporating authorised cuts made by Walton in 1963]

WILLIAM WALTON | CROWN IMPERIAL | Coronation March (1937) | OXFORD UNIVERSITY PRESS | Music Department, 44 Conduit Street London W.1

41 pages. 254 x 175 mm
White stiff paper wrappers. Lettered in orange and white on red background. Trimmed edges.

Publication: Published 28 September 1967 at 21/-

– – – – – [Arranged for small orchestra with piano by Hyam Greenbaum]

No title page

17 pages (piano conductor). 311 x 243 mm
Buff stiff paper wrappers. Lettered in red. Trimmed edges.

Publication: Published 2 September 1937 by OUP at 10/- per set.

– – – – – [Arrangement for amateur orchestra]

WILIAM WALTON | CROWN IMPERIAL | *Coronation March (1937)* | Arranged by | DAVID STONE | Oxford University Press | Music Department, 44 Conduit Street, London W.1

50 pages (piano conductor). 305 x 228 mm

Brown, purple and white stiff paper wrappers. Lettered in purple and white. Trimmed edges.

Publication: Published 11 September 1969 at 25/- per set.

– – – – – [Arrangement for military band]

No title page

23 pages (piano conductor). 310 x 238 mm
Buff stiff paper wrappers. Lettered in blue. Trimmed edges.

Publication: Published (by Boosey & Hawkes Ltd as QMB 76)
8 June 1937 at 20/- per set

– – – – – [Arrangement for piano]

No title page

15 pages. 309 x 239 mm
Buff stiff paper wrappers. Lettered in orange. Trimmed edges.

Publication: Published 10 May 1937 by OUP at 2/6

– – – – – [Arrangement for piano duet]

No title page

24 pages. 308 x 244 mm
Yellow stiff paper wrappers. Lettered in green. Trimmed edges.

Publication: Published 4 August 1949 by OUP at 5/-

– – – – – [Arrangement for organ]

No title page

18 pages. 309 x 240 mm
White paper covers. Lettered in black. Trimmed edges.

Publication: Published (in the Oxford Organ Music Series)
10 May 1937 at 2/6

DR SYNTAX (C10)

A Pedagogic Overture

What appears to be a page of the original score was formerly at Oxford University Press in London. It was written in Walton's early hand:

Holograph [fragment] in ink

This fragment is written on one double and on both sides of a single sheet of music paper, measuring 36 x 26.7 cms.

6 pages – p. [1]   Blank
        pp. [2-3] Music
        pp. [4-6] Blank

Also at Oxford University Press was another fragment, the title page (in ink), on music paper, of a projected ballet, measuring 30.9 x 23.6 cms:

Dr Syntax | a ballet in one act | by | Sacheverell Sitwell and Percy Wyndham Lewis | Music by | W.T.Walton | Scenery by Percy Wyndham Lewis

Unpublished

DREAMING LIPS (C34)

Whereabouts of holograph unknown

DUETS FOR CHILDREN (C39)

Original versions

A. Holograph in pencil

The unbound score is written on three double sheets of 16-stave music paper, measuring 34.2 x 27.3 cms.

The manuscript paper printer's mark is shown as G.Schirmer Imperial Bond No.4-16 Staves Printed in U.S.A.

Tunes for my niece

12 pages –p. [i]	Title page
p. [1]	I – Allegretto
pp.[1-2]	II – Vivo
p. [2]	III – Andante
p. [3]	IV – Slow and deliberate
p. [4]	V – Quick
pp.[4-5]	VI – Slow
pp.[5-6]	VII –
pp.[6-7]	VIII –
pp.[8-9]	IX –
pp.[10-11]	Blank

Dedication ('for Elizabeth') at the top of page 1.
No signature apparent, nor date or place.

I	Allegretto	became 1. The Music Lesson
II	Vivo	became 2. The Three Legged Race
III	Andante	became 3. The Silent Lake
IV	Slow and deliberate	became 7. Swing-Boats
V	Quick	became 6. Hop-Scotch
VI	Slow	became 8. Song at Dusk
VII	–	became 4. Pony Trap
VIII	–	became 5. Ghosts
IX	–	became 9. Puppet's Dance

This, for solo piano, is apparently the original version. Later Walton brought in his nephew, Michael, and the pieces became duets. The solo manuscript consists of nine not ten pieces, *Trumpet Tune* not being included. It is possible that this was added later, probably at the suggestion of OUP, as a finale for the duet publication.

Present location: PML Koch manuscript 624A

B. Holograph in black pencil, with some red pencil alterations and annotations.

The unbound score is written on five double sheets of 14-stave music paper, measuring 34 x 27.2 cms.

The manuscript paper printer's mark is shown as G.Schirmer Imperial Bond No. 3-14 Staves Printed in U.S.A.

Duets for Children [written by Walton in pencil] | by William Walton [written by Alan Frank in pencil]

20 pages – p. [i] Title page: also on the title page is written, in blue ink:

for | Alfred Chenhalls (Cheneg) | in celebration (surtax!) | from | William | May 15th 1940

p. 1 - I
pp. 2-3 - II-III
p. 3 - III
pp. 4-5 - IV
pp. 5-6 - V
pp. 6-7 - VI
pp. 7-9 - VII
pp. 10-11 - VIII
pp. 12-14 - IX
pp. 14-18 - X
p. [19] - Blank

Dedication ('for Elizabeth and Michael') at the top of page 1.
No signature apparent or place. It is dated May 15th 1940 (see above).

Present location: PML Koch manuscript 624B

C. Holograph in pencil

The unbound score is written on two double sheets of 12-stave music paper, measuring 28.9 x 22 cms.

Galop Final. Also written (below the title) in blue biro, by Alan Frank is:

(written as an extra finale | for Boris Kochno's ballet | Music for Children 1949-50 (?) | William Walton thinks Kochno | has a score.)

8 pages – p. [i]   Title page
          pp. [1-7]   Music (3'0" is written at the end of the music, after the double bar line)

Galop Final (C39b) was written for piano but not used as the finale for the ballet 'Devoirs de Vacances', danced to an orchestrated version of *Music for Children*.

Present location: PML Koch manuscript 624D

First edition [Piano Score]
No title page
Book One: 19 pages. 310 x 241 mm
              White stiff paper wrappers. Lettered in yellow and red. Trimmed edges.
Book Two: 16 pages. 311 x 241 mm
              White stiff paper wrappers. Lettered in blue and green. Trimmed edges.
Publication: Published 6 June 1940 by OUP at 3/6

– – – – – [Three Duets: Piano Score]

No title page

8 pages. 311 x 243 mm
White stiff paper wrappers. Lettered in blue and white.
Trimmed edges.

Publication: Published 21 November 1940 by OUP at 2/6

– – – – – [Arranged for piano solo]
No title page
Book One: 11 pages. 311 x 242 mm
              Green stiff paper wrappers. Lettered in orange and blue. Trimmed edges.
Book Two: 11 pages. 311 x 244 mm
              Green stiff paper wrappers. Lettered in green and purple. Trimmed edges.

Publication: Published 1 December 1949 by OUP at 4/-

Orchestral version
Holograph in pencil

The score (bound in a brown paper cover, reinforced at the spine) is written on ten double sheets of 24-stave music paper, measuring 36.7 x 27.1 cms.

Music for Children | William Walton

40 pages – p. [i]   Title page
          pp. 1-2   I
          pp. 2-5   II
          p. 6   III
          pp. 7-8   IV
          pp. 9-11 V
          pp. 12-13 VI
          pp. 14-21 VII
          pp. 22-27 VIII
          pp. 28-30 IX
          pp. 31-37 X pp. [38-39] Blank

No dedication, date or place indicated
Signed on the title page

Present location: PML Koch manuscript 624C

First edition [Full Score]
No title page

48 pages. 265 x 192 mm
Stiff paper wrappers with cover designed by Severini in green and white. Lettered in black. Trimmed edges.

Publication: 500 copies published 11 December 1941 by OUP at 10/6

DUETTINO FOR OBOE AND VIOLIN (C101)

Holograph in blue biro

The score is written on one double sheet of 3-stave music paper, measuring 10 x 17.3 cms.

2 pages – p. [1]   Music
          p. [2]   Blank

Dedication at the head of the music: To Barnaby and Cordelia Craggs. Signed by the composer and dated 2.10.82

Present location: Stewart R Craggs

Unpublished

ESCAPE ME NEVER (C28)

Music for the film

Holograph in pencil.

The existing parts of the unbound score are laid out thus and are held by PML (Koch manuscript 609):-

Title Music
The score is written on three double sheets of 24-stave music paper, measuring 36.6 x 27.1 cms.

No.1 | Title Music

12 pages –	p. [i]	Title page
	pp. 1-10	Music
	p. [11]	Blank

Venetian Scene
The score is written on three double sheets of 24-stave music paper, measuring 36.6 x 27.1 cms.

No.2 | Venetian Scene

12 pages –	p. [i]	Title page
	pp. 11-20	Music
	p. [21]	Blank

Baker's Shop
The score is written on two double sheets of 24-stave music paper, measuring 36.6 x 27.1 cms.

Car [sic] and Baker's Shop

8 pages –	p. [i]	Title page
	pp. 1-6	Music
	p. [7]	Blank

Well Head I | Car | Well Head II
The score is written on five double and twelve single sheets of 24-stave music paper, measuring 36.6 x 27.1 cms.

Well Head No.1

44 pages –	p. [i-ii]	Blank
	p. [iii]	Title page
	pp. 1-11	Music: on page 11 at F, a *car* sequence begins
	pp. 12-13	Car sequence continues (11 secs): on page 13 at G, the *Well Head No.2* sequence begins

pp. 14-40 Well Head No.2 continues (2'7").
           After the double bar line on p.40, *Seque: Dolomites* is written
p. [41]   Blank

Dolomites
The score is written on five sheets of 24-stave music paper, measuring 36.6 x 27.1 cms.

Dolomites

20 pages – p. [i]   Title page
            pp. 41-56 Music
            pp. [57-59] Blank

No dedication, date or signature of the composer apparent.

First edition [Ballet Music: arranged for piano]
No title page

5 pages. 310 x 240 mm
Stiff buff and cream paper wrappers with cover showing scenes from the film in black and white. Lettered in black. Trimmed edges.

Publication: 1000 copies published © 1935 by OUP at 2/-

FAÇADE (C12)

An entertainment for reciter and chamber ensemble

Manuscripts held by the Humanities Research Center, University of Texas at Austin, USA:

Black Mrs Behemoth
Holograph in black and red ink, with pencil notes in another hand

The unbound score is written on both sides of one single sheet of 14-stave music paper, measuring 25.8 x 35.3 cms.

The manuscript paper printer's mark is shown as a ship, within a circle, the letters 'A L' beneath, with 'No 41' beneath that.

2 pages – pp. [1-2]   Music

By the Lake
Holograph in black ink, with some pencil notes in another hand

The unbound score is written on one double sheet of 14-stave music paper, measuring 25.8 x 35.5 cms.

The manuscript paper printer's mark is shown as a ship within a circle, the letters 'A L' beneath, with 'No.41' beneath that.

4 pages – pp. [1-3]   Music
          p. [4]   Blank

Country Dance
Holograph in black ink, with some pencil notes in another hand

The unbound score is written on one double sheet of 14-stave music paper, measuring 25.8 x 35.4 cms.

The manuscript paper is upside down, the paper printer's mark appearing in the top right hand corner, and shown as a ship within a circle, the letters 'A L' beneath, with 'No 41' beneath that.

4 pages – pp. [1-3]   Music
          p. [4]   Blank, except for a number (telephone?) written in the top right hand corner '9158' followed by the word 'Kensington'.

Fox-trot : 'Old Sir Faulk'
Holograph in pencil

The unbound score is written on three double sheets of 16-stave music paper, measuring 33 x 23.7 cms.

The manuscript paper printer's mark is shown as 16 Stamp mark. f.11i de Marino Napoli-Piazza Plebiscita

12 pages – pp. 1-7   Music
           pp. [8-11]   Music
           p. [12]   Blank

Another version now in the British Library (Add. MS 64120):

Holograph in pencil

The unbound score is written on two double sheets of music paper, measuring 32.4 x 24.8 cms.

8 pages – p. [i]   Title page (?)
         pp.[1-7]   Music

Four in the Morning
Holograph in black ink

The unbound score is written on one double sheets of 14-stave music paper, measuring 25.9 x 35.5 cms.

The manuscript paper printer's mark is shown as a ship within a circle, the letters 'A L' beneath, with 'No 41' beneath that.

4 pages – pp. [1-4]   Music

Hornpipe
Holograph in blue ink

The unbound score is written on one double sheet of 10-stave music paper, measuring 29 x 22.1 cms.

4 pages –   pp. 1-4   Music

The Last Gallop
Holograph in black ink

The unbound score is written on one double and on both sides of one single sheet of 15-stave music paper, measuring 23.4 x 30.3 cms. [The original manuscript may have been 28 or 30-stave, but halved and used for this music]

6 pages –   pp. [1-5]   Music
            p. [6]   Blank (?)

Long Steel Grass
Holograph in black and red ink, with pencil notes in another hand

The unbound score is written on both sides of three separate single sheets of 14-stave music paper, measuring 25.7 x 35.5 cms.

The manuscript paper printer's mark is shown as a ship within a circle, the letters 'A L' beneath, with 'No 41' beneath that.

6 pages –   pp. [1-5]   Music
            p. [6]   Blank [?]

Lullaby for Jumbo
Holograph in black and red ink with pencil notes in another hand.

The unbound score is written on one double sheets of 14-stave music paper, measuring 25.7 x 35.5 cms.

The manuscript paper printer's mark is shown as a ship within a circle, the letters 'A L' beneath, with 'No 41' beneath that.

4 pages –   p. [i]   Title page: LULLABY FOR JUMBO (20)
                     'Façade' is also written in the top right hand corner – in an unknown hand.
                     Several numbers have been written on the title page with circles round them but crossed out.
                     A figure '7' within a circle (but not erased) appears in the top left hand corner.
           pp.[1-3]   Music

March
Holograph in black ink

The unbound score is written on both sides of one single sheet of 14-stave music paper, measuring 25.9 x 35 cms.

The manuscript paper printer's mark is shown as a ship within a circle, the letters 'A L' beneath, with 'No 41' beneath that.

2 pages – pp. [1-2]   Music

Polka
First version: Holograph in black ink with pencil notes in another hand and some holograph notes.

The unbound score is written on one double sheet of 14-stave music paper, measuring 25.7 x 35.3 cms.

The manuscript paper printer's mark is shown as a ship within a circle, the letters 'A L' beneath, with 'No 41' beneath that.

4 pages – pp. [1-4]   Music

Second version: Holograph in ink

The unbound score is written on one double sheet of 12-stave music paper, measuring 29 x 24 cms.

4 pages – pp. [1-3]   Music
      p. [4]   Blank

Present location: Thomas Balstan Papers in the Washington State University Library, Pullman, Washington, USA

Draft version (1922): Holograph in pencil

The unbound score is written on one double and on both sides of one single sheet of 16-stave music paper, measuring 33 x 24 cms.

6 pages – pp. [1-5]   Music
      p. [6]   Blank

Present location: Manuscript Collections, The British Library. Egerton MS 3771

Popular Song
Holograph in black and red ink

The unbound score is written on one double and on both sides of one single sheet of 14-stave music paper, measuring 25.8 x 35.3 cms.
The title page is written on one side of a separate, single sheet of 14-stave music paper.

The manuscript paper printer's mark is shown as a ship within a circle, the letters 'A L' beneath, with 'No 41' beneath that.

7 pages – p. [i]   Title page: Popular Song (written in Constant Lambert's hand). 'Façade' is also written in the

top right hand corner in an unknown hand. Several numbers have been written on the tile page with circles round them but crossed out. A figure '19' within a circle (but not erased) also appears in the top right hand corner.

pp.[1-6]   Music. At the end of the music on p.[6] Constant Lambert has written 'Don't engrave this bar but leave a space for the composer's altered version'.

Scotch Rhapsody
Holograph in black ink

The unbound score is written on one double sheet of 14-stave music paper, measuring 25.8 x 35.4 cms.

The manuscript paper printer's mark is shown as a ship within a circle, the letters 'A L' beneath, with 'No 41' beneath that.

4 pages –   pp. [1-4]   Music

Sir Beelzebub
Holograph in pencil

The unbound score is written on two double sheets of 16-stave music paper, measuring 33 x 23.7 cms.

The manuscript paper printer's mark is shown as 16 Stamp mark. f.11i de Marino Napoli-Piazza Plebiscita

8 pages –   p. [i]   Title page: Sir Beelzebub (not in Walton's hand), with a large figure '21' written above it.
            p. [ii]   Blank
            pp. 1-4   Music
            p. [5]   Music
            p. [6]   Blank

Manuscripts held by PML (New York) Koch manuscript 638:

Aubade / The Owl

Manuscript (not Walton's) in blue ink

The unbound score is written on three double sheets of 12-stave music paper, measuring 35 x 27 cms.

12 pages – p. [i]   Title page. No 22 (written in red pencil but crossed out) Aubade 14 (written in red pencil) | No 23 The Owl (crossed out) | Foxtrot 15 (written by Constant Lambert in red pencil)
            pp. [1-4] Music: Aubade

pp. [5-10]   Music: The Owl
p. [11]   Blank

En famille
Two versions with different scorings:

A - Holograph in pencil

The unbound score is written on one double and on both sides of one single sheet of 16-stave music paper, measuring 33 x 24 cms.

6 pages –   pp. [1-5]   Music
p. [6]   Blank

B - Holograph in pencil

The score, bound in a buff coloured cover, is written on two double sheets of 16-stave music paper, measuring 35.3 x 27.8 cms.

The manuscript paper printer's mark is shown as J & W Chester, within a circle, LONDON, No 16

8 pages –   p. [i]   Title page: En famille (group 1) with a large figure 2, written in blue pencil and underlined.

pp. [1-7]   Music

Fanfare
Holograph in pencil

The unbound score is written on both sides of one single sheet of 16-stave music paper, measuring 32.4 x 24 cms.

2 pages –   pp. [1-2]   Music

Hornpipe
Holograph in pencil

The unbound score is written on two double sheets of 16-stave music paper, measuring 32.5 x 24 cms.

8 pages –   p. [i]   Title page: 1 Hornpipe | 2 En famille | 3 Mariner Man The numbers are written in red pencil, the titles in ordinary lead pencil.
There are also 12 other titles written on this title page, together with their timings and an indication of the total time involved.

pp. [1-6]   Music: Hornpipe
p. [7]   Mariner Man [second version]

Mariner Man / Hornpipe
First version: Holograph in pencil

The score, bound in a green cover, is written on one double sheet of 12-stave music paper, measuring 30.4 x 23.7 cms.

4 pages –   p. [i]   Title page: Mariner Man (group 1) with a large
                          figure 3, written in blue pencil and underlined.
                          There is also another large figure 3, within a
                          circle, written in red pencil.
            pp.[1-3]   Music

Small talk | By the Lake | Said King Pompey
Holograph in blue ink

The unbound score is written on four double sheets of 12-stave music paper, measuring 35 x 27 cms.

16 pages – p. [i]   Title page. Nos 7,8,9 are crossed out and 4,5,6
                          are substituted above, written in red pencil.
                          Small talk (crossed out) | By the Lake | Said King
                          Pompey – written in lead pencil
           pp. [1-5]   Music: Small Talk
           pp. [6-8]   Music: By the Lake
           p.[9-12]   Music: Said King Pompey
           pp.[13-15]   Blank

Something lies beyond
First version: Holograph in pencil

The score, bound in a buff coloured cover, is written on one double sheet of 16-stave music paper, measuring 35.6 x 26.2 cms.

The manuscript paper printer's mark is shown as J & W Chester Ltd, within a circle, LONDON, No.16.

4 pages –   p. [i]   Title page: Something lies beyond (group 7) with
                          a large figure '20', within a circle, written in blue
                          pencil.
            pp. [1-3]   Music

Second version: Manuscript (may be Constant Lambert's hand) in ink

The unbound score is written on one double sheet of 14-stave music paper, measuring 35.3 x 26 cms.

The manuscript paper has been used upside down, the manuscript paper printer's mark is shown (in the top right hand corner) as a ship within a circle, the letters 'A L' beneath, with 'No 41' beneath that.

4 pages –   pp. [1-4]   Music
            p. [4]   Blank

Tarantella | Mazurka
Holograph in pencil

The unbound score is written on three double and on both sides of three single sheets of 14-stave music paper, measuring 37 x 27.5 cms.

18 pages – pp. [1-6]   Music: Tarantella
           p. [7]   Music erased: Mazurka
           pp. [8-10] Sketches erased
           pp. [11-17] Music: Mazurka
           p. [18]   Blank

Title page for the definitive printed version (1951)
It is written by Walton in blue ink and pencil on one double sheet of 12-stave music paper, measuring 29 x 22 cms.

4 pages – p. 1   Title page: To Constant Lambert | Façade | An entertainment | with poems by | Edith Sitwell | and music by | William Walton
          p. 2   Instrumentation: additions and amendments written in pencil, with 'No.134' also written at the top of the page in blue pencil.
          p. 3   Contents 1-21 (1951): The word 'CONTENTS' is written at the top of the page in pencil.
                            Each number is written in blue ink with blue pencil ticks against each number. There are page numbers, written in biro and blue ink, by each number.
          p. 4   Blank

Through Gilded Trellises | The Octogenarian | Herodiade's Flea
Manuscript (not Walton) in black ink

The unbound score is written on three double sheets of 12-stave music paper, measuring 35.2 x 27 cms.

12 pages – pp. [1-5]   Music: Through Gilded Trellises
           p. [6]   Blank, except for a sketch in pencil
           pp. [7-9]   Music: The Octogenarian
           pp. [10-12] Music: Herodiade's Flea. There is also a duplicate sketch of the opening of 'Through Gilded Trellises' on the last page, p.[12] of this number.

Manuscript held in private hands

Valse
Holograph in pencil

The unbound score is written on two double and on both sides of two single sheets of 16-stave music paper, measuring 32.4 x 23.8 cms.

Valse [not in Walton's hand] written across the top half of the page, and a large figure '20' in the top right hand corner, with a sketch (?) in pencil (10 bars) written in the bottom half.

12 pages – p. [i]   Title page
         pp. [2-12] Music: Valse is written at the top of p.[2], in pencil, in Constant Lambert's hand. 'Don't do Fl & Cl' written in the top left hand corner also by Lambert.

Signed on p. [12], at the end of the music, after the double bar line, by the composer. The duration is given as 2 mins 22 secs.

Present location: Mr Francis Sitwell

First edition [Score]
To Constant Lambert | FAÇADE | AN ENTERTAINMENT | *with Poems by* | EDITH SITWELL | *and Music by* | WILLIAM WALTON | OXFORD UNIVERSITY PRESS | Music Department | 44 CONDUIT STREET, LONDON W.1 New York: Toronto: | 114 Fifth Avenue 480 University Avenue

112 pages. 252 x 178 mm
Buff stiff paper wrappers. Lettered in black on pink and buff panels on upper, and in black on lower cover. Trimmed edges.
John Piper's design for the curtain used at the 1942 performance in the Aeolian Hall is featured on the lower cover.

Publication: 2,000 copies published 26 July 1951 at 16/-
– – – – – [De-luxe score]

To mark the occasion of the composer's 70th birthday, and the 50th anniversary of the first performance, Oxford University Press published, on 2 March 1972 (the actual birthday was 29 March), a limited, finely-bound edition of *Façade Entertainment* in two forms:

(1) 250 copies, signed by the composer and numbered, at 30.00

(2) 750 copies, numbered, at 12.00

Both editions were printed on heavy cartridge paper, the signed edition quarter-bound in leather, the other edition in buckram. Both editions were boxed. Besides the re-engraved score of the music itself they both included a newly commissioned cover and colour illustrations by John Piper, colour reproductions of the John Piper curtain and of John Armstrong's ballet designs, new essays by Sacheverell Sitwell and Frederick Ashton, a Note – mainly about the poems – by Edith Sitwell (the poems themselves are printed separately as well as in the music score), a hitherto unpublished, rejected setting, reproduced in facsimile of Walton's manuscript, and – perhaps most valuable of all – a new pressing specially manufactured by Decca for this edition of the original recording of the *Entertainment* made in 1929 with Constant Lambert and Edith Sitwell as speakers.

FAÇADE *an entertainment* | *the poems by Edith Sitwell. the music by William Walton* | London Oxford University Press 1972

111 pages. 315 x 240 mm

FAÇADE 2

Details taken from a copy:
Holograph in pencil (?)

The score is written on seven double sheets of 15-stave music paper.

FAÇADE 2 | Poems by Edith Sitwell | Music by William Walton
28 pages – p. [i]   Title page
           p. [11]   Dedication : 'To Cathy Berberian'
           p. [iii]   Instrumentation required
           pp.1-23   Music
           pp.[24-25] Blank

Signed by the composer on the title page.
No date or place apparent.

Present location: unable to trace

First edition [Facsimile score]
FAÇADE 2 | Poems by Edith Sitwell | Music by William Walton
3 un-numbered pages (preliminaries), followed by 23 numbered pages (music), followed by 5 un-numbered pages (notes and texts of the poems)

White stiff paper wrappers. Lettered in black, green and red. Trimmed edges. The cover also features an illustration by John Piper.

Publication: Published 28 June 1979 at 4.75

Façade: Version for Male (1) and Female (2) Voices
Arranged by Walton for the 1964 Adelaide Festival (Australia)

Details taken from a copy:
Holograph in pencil (?)

The unbound score is written on one double sheet of 16-stave music paper, measuring 30.5 x 20.3 cms.

4 pages – pp. 1-4   Music

No date, place or signature of the composer apparent.

Present location: Kevin McBeath (Australia)

Unpublished

OTHER VERSIONS
Façade: First Suite for Orchestra (C12c)
Holograph in pencil with several passages gone over in heavier pencil and one passage in black ink. This superimposing was done by Walton himself since the score was used by him for conducting and became rather faint for easy reading. There are one or two additions to the manuscript (mostly names of instruments) which are in the hand of Constant Lambert who also conducted from this score.

The unbound score is written on 24, 28 and 30-stave music paper (as indicated), measuring 43.7 x 29 cms.

62 pages – p. [i]		Title page (28-stave): not in Walton's hand 'FAÇADE' SUITE I | *WILLIAM WALTON* | In this score the numbers [are] II,III,I,IV,V. Further down the page is Oxford University Press' stamp.
	p. [ii]	Correct order (30-stave): not in Walton's hand: Polka Valse Jodelling Song Tango Tarantella
	pp. [1-16]	II Valse (24-stave). '2.5 mins' indicated after the double bar line.
	pp. [17-21]	III Swiss Jodelling Song (or the Waiter's Lament) (24-stave).
	pp. [22-28]	I Polka (24-stave). This number was originally No. III – but this is crossed out and No. I substituted.
	pp. [29-36]	IV Tango Pasodoble: I do like to be beside the seaside (14-stave). '1.5 mins.' indicated after the double bar line.
	pp. [37-59]	V Tarantella Sevillana (24-stave: pp.[37-53]; 30-stave: pp.[54-59], i.e. from the second bar after [J] to the end).
	p. [60]	Blank (28-stave)

No date, place, dedication or signature of the composer apparent.

Present location: Humanities Research Center, University of Texas at Austin, U.S.A.

First edition [Score]
No title page

72 pages. 265 x 187 mm
Stiff paper wrappers with cover designed by Severini in green and white. Lettered in black. Trimmed edges.

Publication: Published 8 October 1936 by OUP at 7/6

(The score was re-engraved, corrected and re-published in 1968)

FAÇADE: Second Suite for Orchestra (C12e)
Details taken from a copy:
Part holograph in pencil (?): Country Dance and Noche Espagnole are in Walton's hand

The score is written on 20-stave music paper, measuring 30.4 x 26.7 cms.

No date, place or signature of the composer apparent.

Present location: PML Koch manuscript 638

First edition [Score]
No title page

43 pages. 267 x 187 mm

Stiff paper wrappers with cover designed by Severini in green and white. Lettered in black. Trimmed edges.

Publication: Published 28 April 1938 by OUP at 6/-

(The score was re-engraved, corrected and re-published in 1968)

FAÇADE: Arrangements for Concert Band by Robert O'Brien (C12f)

First edition: [Full Score]
FULL SCORE | WILLIAM WALTON | Fanfare and Scotch Rhapsody | FROM | FAÇADE | ARRANGED FOR BAND BY | ROBERT O'BRIEN | Full Score and Parts for Complete Band (97.815-70) ...$15.00 | Full Score, separately (97.815)... $5.00 | Separate parts... Each .25 | New York | Oxford University Press

16 pages. 304 x 228 mm Stiff green paper wrappers. Lettered in white. Trimmed edges.

Publication: Published 26 June 1969 at $15 by OUP (New York)

Title page as above, except 'Jodelling Song' to be substituted on the 3rd line

10 pages. 304 x 228 mm

Stiff green paper wrappers. Lettered in white. Trimmed edges.

Publication: Published 26 June 1969 at $15 by OUP (New York)

Title page as above, except 'Polka' to be substituted on the 3rd line

10 pages. 304 x 228 mm
Stiff green paper wrappers. Lettered in white. Trimmed edges.

Publication: Published 26 June 1969 at $15 by OUP (New York)

Title page as above, except 'Popular Song' to be substituted on the third line

17 pages. 304 x 228 mm
Stiff green paper wrappers. Lettered in white. Trimmed edges.

Publication: Published 26 June 1969 at $15 by OUP (New York)

Title page as above, except 'Old Sir Faulk' to be substituted on the third line

14 pages. 304 x 228 mm
Stiff dark green paper wrappers. Lettered in white. Trimmed edges.

Publication: Published 26 June 1969 at $15 by OUP (New York)

FOUR DANCES FROM FAÇADE: Arranged for small orchestra (C12g)
First edition [Piano Conductor]
No title page

18 pages. 311 x 243 mm
Stiff buff paper wrappers. Lettered in blue. Trimmed edges.

Publication: Published 23 November 1939 at OUP at 3/6

THREE PIECES FROM FAÇADE: Arranged for harmonica and piano (C12j)
First edition [Score]
WILLIAM WALTON | THREE PIECES FROM | 'FAÇADE' | ARRANGED FOR | HARMONICA AND PIANO | BY | ROY DOUGLAS | price 8s.6d. net | OXFORD UNIVERSITY PRESS | MUSIC DEPARTMENT 44 CONDUIT STREET LONDON W1

14 pages. 310 x 230 mm
Stiff buff paper wrappers. Lettered in red. Trimmed edges.

Publication: 750 copies published 17 December 1959 at 8/6d.

– – – – – [Harmonica part]

WILLIAM WALTON | THREE PIECES FROM | 'FAÇADE' | HAR-
MONICA SOLO | OXFORD UNIVERSITY PRESS

8 pages. 310 x 230 mm
Stiff white paper wrappers. Lettered in black. Trimmed edges.

Publication: Published and included with the above.

FAÇADE: Concert Version of the Valse (C12k)
First edition [Score]
No title page

9 pages. 343 x 258 mm
Stiff paper wrappers with cover designed by Severini in green and
white. Lettered in black. Trimmed edges.

Publication: Published 24 October 1928 by OUP at 3/6d.

FAÇADE: Piano Solo Arrangements (C12l)

First edition: Popular Song (Suite No 2)
No title page

6 pages. 311 x 239 mm
Stiff paper wrappers with cover designed by Severini in green and
white. Lettered in black. Trimmed edges.

Publication: Published 24 September 1942 by OUP at 2/6

– – – – – Old Sir Faulk (Suite No 2)

No title page

5 pages. 302 x 238 mm
Stiff paper wrappers with cover designed by Severini in green and
white. Lettered in black. Trimmed edges.

Publication: Published 30 December 1943 by OUP at 2/6

– – – – – Polka (Suite No 1)

No title page
3 pages. 303 x 238 mm
Stiff paper wrappers with cover designed by Severini in green and
white. Lettered in black. Trimmed edges.

Publication: Published 30 December 1943 by OUP at 2/-

– – – – – Scotch Rhapsody (Suite No 2)

SCOTCH RHAPSODY | from Façade | Arrangement for Pianoforte Solo by | ROY DOUGLAS | WILLIAM WALTON

5 pages. 303 x 238 mm
Stiff paper wrappers with cover designed by Severini in green and white. Lettered in black. Trimmed edges.

Publication: Published 30 December 1943 by OUP at 2/6

– – – – – Swiss Jodelling Song (Suite No 1)

No title page

4 pages. 309 x 244 mm
Stiff paper wrappers with cover designed by Severini in green and white. Lettered in black. Trimmed edges.

Publication: Published 5 February 1948 by OUP at 3/-

FAÇADE: Piano Duet Arrangements (C12m)

Suite No 1

First edition
No title page

35 pages. 343 x 257 mm
Stiff paper wrappers with cover designed by Severini in green and white. Lettered in black. Trimmed edges.

Publication: Published 6 October 1927 by OUP at 6/6d.

Suite No 2

First edition
No title page

36 pages. 351 x 255 mm
Stiff paper wrappers with cover designed by Severini in green and white. Lettered in black. Trimmed edges.

Publication: Published 8 September 1938 by OUP at 6/-

FAÇADE: Two Piano Arrangements (C12n)

Valse (Suite No 1)

First edition
No title page

12 pages. 306 x 239 mm
Stiff orange and white paper wrappers. Lettered in black. Trimmed edges.

Publication: Published 22 March 1934 by OUP at 3/6d.

Swiss Jodelling Song (Suite No 1)
First edition
SWISS JODELLING SONG | from 'FAÇADE' | Arranged for Two Pianos by | HERBERT MURRILL | WILLIAM WALTON

5 pages. 309 x 242 mm
Stiff paper wrappers with cover designed by Severini in green and white. Lettered in black. Trimmed edges.

Publication: Published 21 April 1949 by OUP at 4/-

Popular Song (Suite No 2)
First edition
No title page

9 pages. 309 x 238 mm
Stiff orange and cream paper wrappers. Lettered in black. Trimmed edges.

Publication: Published 29 June 1939 by OUP at 3/6d.

Polka (Suite No 1)
First edition
No title page

4 pages. 309 x 238 mm
Stiff paper wrappers with cover designed by Severini in green and white. Lettered in black. Trimmed edges.

Publication: Published 8 December 1949 by OUP at 3/6d.

Old Sir Faulk (Suite No 2)
First edition
No title page

7 pages. 309 x 239 mm
Stiff paper wrappers with cover designed by Severini in green and white. Lettered in black. Trimmed edges.

Publication: Published 6 January 1949 by OUP at 4/6d.

Tarantella Sevillana (Suite No 1)
First edition
No title page

12 pages. 309 x 242 mm
Stiff paper wrappers with cover designed by Severini in green and white. Lettered in black. Trimmed edges.

Publication: Published 29 June 1950 by OUP at 6/-

FANFARE FOR THE NATIONAL (C92)

Holograph in pencil

The unbound score is written on three double sheets of 14-stave music paper, measuring 32.3 x 23.5 cms.
The manuscript paper printer's mark, at the foot of the page, is shown
as a large 'M' intertwined with a treble clef and $\dfrac{1105}{\text{EXTRA}}$

Fanfare for the National | W.W.

12 pages – p. [i]   Title page
        pp. 1-8   Music
        pp. [9-11]   Blank

No date, place or dedication apparent.
Initialled by the composer on the title page.

Present location: PML Koch manuscript 617

Unpublished

FANFARES FOR THE RED ARMY (C48)
Whereabouts of holograph unknown

OTHER VERSIONS
Memorial Fanfare for Henry Wood (C48a)
for full orchestra

Holograph in pencil

The unbound score is written on two double sheets of 32-stave music paper, measuring 45 x 31.6 cms.

Memorial Fanfare | for | Henry Wood | by | William Walton

8 pages – p. [i]   Title page
        pp. 1-7   Music

No dedication apparent.

Signed on the title page, and after the double bar line at the end of the music on p.7. The date 'Feb 5th 1945' is also written after the double bar line as is '2-25'.

Present location: Mr O W Neighbour, London

Unpublished

FANTASIA CONCERTANTE (C14)

for two pianos, jazz band and orchestra

Whereabouts of holograph unknown

THE FIRST OF THE FEW (C45)

Music for the film

Whereabouts of holograph unknown

OTHER VERSIONS
Prelude and Fugue ('The Spitfire') (C45a)
Arranged by the composer for full orchestra

Holograph in ink

The score (bound in blue leather covers) is written on 24-stave music paper, measuring 37.7 x 27 cms.

Prelude and Fugue (The 'Spitfire') | from | Leslie Howard's film 'The First of the Few'

38 pages – p. [i]   Title page
          pp.1-13   Music : Prelude
          – – – – – – – – – – – – – –
          p. [ii]   Title page - 'Spitfire' fugue
          pp.1-19a Music: Fugue
          pp.[20-23a]Blank

No date, place, dedication or signature of the composer apparent.

Present location: PML Koch manuscript 607

First edition [Full score]
WILLIAM WALTON | PRELUDE AND FUGUE | (The 'Spitfire') | OXFORD UNIVERSITY PRESS | MUSIC DEPARTMENT 44 CONDUIT STREET LONDON W.1

39 pages. 254 x 179 mm
Stiff turquoise paper wrappers. Lettered in white. Trimmed edges.

Publication: Published 25 May 1961 at 10/6

Prelude ('The Spitfire') arranged for organ by Dennis Morrell (shortened version)
First edition
No title page

4 pages. 311 x 232 mm
White paper covers. Lettered in black. Trimmed edges.

Publication: Published 5 May 1966 (in the Oxford Organ Music series) at 3/6

Spitfire Prelude, arranged for military band by Rodney Bashford
First edition
No title page

14 pages (piano conductor). 310 x 236 mm
Stiff grey paper wrappers. Lettered in blue. Trimmed edges.

Publication: Published [by Boosey & Hawkes Ltd.] as QMB 273, 30 December 1966 at 35/- per set

Spitfire Fugue arranged for military band by J L Wallace
First edition
No title page

24 pages (piano conductor). 309 x 235 mm
Stiff grey paper wrappers. Lettered in blue. Trimmed edges.

Publication: Published [by Boosey & Hawkes Ltd.] as QMB 288, 31 December 1970 at 50/- per set

THE FIRST SHOOT (C29)

Ballet with choreography by Frederick Ashton

Whereabouts of holograph unknown

A photocopy of a piano reduction of the ballet music (not in Walton's hand) exists.

The score is written on 11 single sheets of 12-stave music paper, measuring 29.8 x 21.2 cms

Ballet – Piano | Francis Collinson | The First Shoot | Ballet by | William Walton | Follow the Sun, Adelphi Theatre, 1936.

11 pages – p. [i]   Title page
          pp. 1-10   Music

Unpublished

OTHER VERSIONS
The First Shoot (C29b)
Arranged for Brass Band

Details taken from a copy:
Holograph in pencil (?)

The score is written on 13 double sheets of 16-stave music paper, measuring 31 x 23.5 cms.

In Mem. | C B Cochran and his Young Ladies | 'The First Shoot' | ballet | devised by Frederick Ashton and Cecil Beaton | Music revised and arranged for Brass Band by | William Walton | 'Follow the Sun' Adelphi Theatre 1936

52 pages – p. [i]   Title Page
          pp. 1-50   Music
          p. [51]   Blank

No date or place of arrangement apparent.
Signed by the composer on the title page.

Present location: PML Koch manuscript 594

First edition [Score]
No title page

52 pages. 296 x 210 mm
Stiff white paper wrappers. Lettered in black. Trimmed edges.

Publication: © 1986 by Studio Music Ltd

FIVE BAGATELLES FOR GUITAR (C86)

Holograph in pencil

The score is written on two double and on both sides of one single sheet of 18-stave music paper, measuring 32 x 24 cms.

Unable to ascertain the manuscript paper printer's mark, although there is a lyre at the foot of the page, on the left hand side and $\frac{1107}{\text{EXTRA}}$ at the foot of the page, on the right hand side.

Sir William arranged for the score to be bound in morocco leather, and on the front cover is the title 'Five Bagatelles for Guitar | William

Walton', under which is the dedication 'To Malcolm Arnold with admiration and affection for his 50th birthday.'

Five Bagatelles | for | Guitar | William Walton (edited by Julian Bream) [The above dedication was added later to the title page, on presentation to Malcolm Arnold]

10 pages – p. [i]   Title page
       pp. 1-9   Music: I Allegro 1-3
                        II Lento 3-4
                        III Alla Cubana 5-6
                        IV - - 6
                        V Con Slancio 7-9

No date, place, dedication apparent.
Signed by the composer on the title page.

Present location: William Walton Museum, Ischia

First edition [Score]
To Malcolm Arnold | Five Bagatelles for Guitar | WILLIAM WALTON | Edited by Julian Bream | *Five Bagatelles* were written for Julian Bream and | dedicated to Malcolm Arnold 'with admiration and | affection for his 50th birthday'. | They were given their first performance by Julian Bream | on 27 May 1972 at Bath and have been recorded by him | on RCA SB 6876 | Duration 12.5 minutes. | Oxford University Press

16 pages. 301 x 223 mm
Stiff mustard paper wrappers. Lettered in black and white.
Trimmed edges.

The black and white photograph of 'Sketches of Guitar Players' by Watteau is reproduced by permission of the British Museum, London.

Publication: Published 26 September 1974 at 1.50

OTHER VERSIONS
VARII CAPRICCI (C86a)
Free transcriptions of the 5 Bagatelles - for orchestra

Holograph in pencil
The unbound score is written on twelve double sheets of 28 and 30-stave music paper, measuring 46 x 33 cms.

Varii Capricci (free transcriptions of Five Bagatelles for Guitar | I
48 pages – p. [i]   Title page
       pp. 2-15 I : Allegro Assai 92 bars
       pp. 16-22 II : Lento sognando 116 bars
       pp. 23-29 III : Alla Cubana 51 bars

pp. 30-33   IV : Lento 24 bars
p. 34   Blank
pp. 35-45   V : Con slancio 88 bars
pp. [46-48] Blank

No date, place, dedication or signature of the composer apparent.

In 1977, the composer completely re-wrote the last movement. This re-working is included in the printed score of *Varii Capricci*, published by OUP in 1978.

Manuscript of No 5, the revised finale
Holograph in pencil

The unbound score is written on both sides of nine single sheets of 28-stave music paper, measuring 47.2 x 32.5 cms.

The manuscript paper printer's mark, at the foot of the page on the left hand side, is shown as a harp with GBT Marchio Depositato printed under it and 28 | EXTRA

Varii Capricci No. 5 2nd version | WW

18 pages – p. [i]   Title page
pp. 1-17   Music. The speed of the piece is given as = 138 - 144 c. and the sub title changed to *Presto con slancio*.
An indication of the duration is given as 3'5'c. after the double bar line at the end of the music. Blue pencil markings appear on pp. 6; 10; 13; 14 and 15 of the score.

No date, place, dedication or signature of the composer apparent.

Present location : PML Koch manuscript 613

Ending used for the ballet: short score (C86b)
A nine bar coda, written on a piece of 4-stave music paper.

Present location: unable to trace

First edition [Score]
William Walton | Varii Capricci | I Allegro assai | II Lento sognando | III Alla Cubana | IV Lento | V Presto con slancio | Oxford University Press | Music Department | 44 Conduit Street, London | W1R 0DE

73 pages. 253 x 178 mm
Stiff olive green paper wrappers. Lettered in dark blue and white. Trimmed edges.

Publication: Published 7 September 1978 at 7.00

THE FOREMAN WENT TO FRANCE (C44)

Music for the film

Whereabouts of holograph unknown

THE FORSAKEN MERMAN (C4)

Cantata for soprano and tenor soli, double female chorus and orchestra

Details taken from a copy:
Holograph in pencil (?)

The score is written on five double sheets of 12-stave music paper, measuring 25.6 x 20 cms.

20 pages - pp. [1-20] Music

Signed by the composer at the head of the score on p. [1]. No place apparent and dated 'Summer 1916' at the end of the music.

Present location: unable to trace

GLORIA (C72)

For contralto, tenor and bass soloists, double mixed chorus and orchestra

Full orchestral score
Holograph in pencil

The score, loose, in a blue binder, is written on one side of 111 single sheets of 36-stave music paper, measuring 50.7 x 36.2 cms.

No title page : presumably missing
111 pages - pp. 1-111 Music (written on the recto of each sheet)

No date, place, dedication or signature of the composer apparent.

Vocal Score
Holograph in pencil

The unbound score is written on 12 double and on both sides of 18 single sheets of 16-stave music paper, measuring 33.5 x 23.5 cms.

The manuscript paper has been used upside down, the manuscript paper printer's mark is shown (in the top right corner) as 16.Stamp. music. f.11e de Marino Napoli-Porticato S.Francesca di Paola.

84 pages – p. [i] Title page : blank, except for GLORIA IN EXCELSIS DEO | WILLIAM WALTON written in the hand of Alan Frank (in pencil)

pp. 1-80 Music: there is an amendment stapled to the score on page 78. There are also one or two written amendments in blue ink. 17'30" appears after the double bar line on page 80.

pp. [81-83] Blank on the last page [83] there is a large '143' written in blue pencil at the bottom of the page and a large 'R' written in black biro.

No place, dedication or signature of the composer apparent. A date is written in the top left hand corner of the first page of music : 23.12.60

Present location: PML Koch manuscript 603 (full and vs) There are also some sketches and alterations on 16-stave music paper, written in pencil. Some are sellotaped to the above holograph.

First edition [Vocal score]
WILLIAM WALTON | GLORIA | For contralto, tenor and bass soloists, | chorus, and orchestra | Vocal score | OXFORD UNIVER-SITY PRESS | MUSIC DEPARTMENT, 44 CONDUIT STREET LONDON, W.1

85 pages. 253 x 177 mm
Stiff lilac paper wrappers. Lettered in purple. Trimmed edges.

Publication: Published 28 September 1961 at 10/6

GRANADA TELEVISION MUSIC (C75)

Holograph in pencil

The unbound score is written on thirteen double sheets of 32-stave music paper, measuring 48 x 33 cms.

The manuscript paper printer's mark, at the foot of the page on the left hand side, is shown as G.RICORDI & C.

'GRANADA' Prelude - End Music - Call Signs | William Walton

52 pages – pp. [i-ii] Blank
p. [iii] Title page
pp. 1-36 Prelude
pp. [37-39] Blank
pp. [40-43] Call Signs
pp. [44-46] End Music
pp. [47-49] Blank

Pages 1 to 34 of the Prelude are indicated and numbered.
Pages 25 and 26 are numbered twice by Walton, with the result that the remaining pagination is wrong.

No dedication apparent.

'© 1962' appears at the foot of page one [this is not in Walton's autograph; it may have been added by OUP]

Signed by the composer on the title page.

Present location: PML Koch manuscript 601

Unpublished

OTHER VERSIONS
Prelude arranged for Concert Band (C75b)

First edition [Full Score]
WILLIAM WALTON | MARCH FOR CONCERT BAND | Full Score and Parts for Complete Band (97.819-70) ... $25.00 | Full Score Separately (97.819) ... 4.00| Separate Parts ... Each .65 | NEW YORK | OXFORD UNIVERSITY PRESS

26 pages. 303 x 238 mm
Stiff blue paper wrappers. Lettered in white. Trimmed edges.

Publication: 1000 copies published 10 August 1972 at $25.00 by OUP, New York

HAMLET (C54)

Music for the film

Holograph in pencil.
The existing parts of the unbound score are laid out thus and are held by PML (Koch manuscript 583):-

Something is rotten in the state of Denmark (2.M.1)
The score is written on one double sheet of 32-stave music paper, measuring 47.8 x 33 cms.

Hamlet | 2.M.1 [also written in green felt tipped pen] Sc. 17-19

4 pages –	p. [i]	Title page. At the top of this page is a note in pencil that the music was recorded 18.XII.47
	pp. [1-2]	Music: 'Something is rotten in the state of Denmark'. The duration is given, after the double bar line, as 2'48"
	p. [3]	Blank

Oh that this too too solid flesh (3.M.4)

The score is written on one double sheet of 24-stave music paper, measuring 34.2 x 27.2 cms.

The manuscript paper printer's mark is shown as Paramount Brand No. 19 - 24 lines. Printed in USA. Belwin Inc. New York, USA.

Hamlet | 3.M.4 [also written in green felt tipped pen] | Sc.32

| 4 pages – | p. [i] | Title page. At the top of the page are the words 'Checked 24.XI.47' |
| | pp. [1-3] | Music: 'Oh that this too too solid flesh'. The duration is given, after the double bar line, as 3'26". |

O cursed spite (6.M.1)
The score is written on two double sheets of 24-stave music paper, measuring 34.2 x 27.3 cms.

Hamlet | 6.M.1 [also written in green felt tipped pen] | S.106

8 pages –	p. [i]	Title page. Recorded 28.11.47/8.1.48
	pp. [1-4]	Music: 'O cursed spite that ever I was born to set it right'.
	pp. [5-7]	Blank

Hamlet and Ophelia (7.M.1)
The score is written on one double sheet of 24-stave music paper, measuring 34.2 x 27.2 cms.

Hamlet | 7.M.1 [Also written in greenfelt tipped pen] | Sc.128

| 4 pages – | p. [i] | Title page. Recorded 28.11.47 |
| | pp. 1-3 | Music: 'Hamlet and Ophelia'. The duration is given, after the double bar line, as 2'32". |

3To be or not to be (8.M.1)
The score is written on two double and on both sides of one single sheet of 32-stave music paper, measuring 47.7 x 32.9 cms.

Hamlet | 8.M.1 [also written in green felt tipped pen]

| 10 pages – p. [i] | Title page. At the foot of the page is written: Miss Branson 142 Charing X Road | WC2 |
| | pp. [1-9] | Music: Prelude 'To be or not to be' |

Ophelia by the stream (13.M.1)
The score is written on three double sheets of 24-stave music paper, measuring 34.2 x 27.3 cms.

Hamlet | 13.M.1 [also written in green felt tipped pen] | Sc.242

| 12 pages –p. [i]   Title page. Recorded 4.XII.47
           pp. [1-10]   Music: 'Ophelia by the stream'
           p. [11]   Blank

The Death of Ophelia (14.M.3)
The score is written on one double and on both sides of one single sheet of 24-stave music paper, measuring 34.2 x 27.2 cms.

Hamlet | 14.M.3 [also written in green felt tipped pen] | Sc. 283 - 285

6 pages –   p. [i]   Title page, with a pencil sketch written on it
           pp. [1-3]   Music: 'The Death of Ophelia'
           pp. [4-5]   Blank

Other parts of the score (see the catalogue) have since been re-discovered but I have been unable to examine these.

No dedication, date or signature of the composer apparent.

OTHER VERSIONS

Funeral March (C54a)
Holograph in pencil, with amendments, timings etc., in red, green and blue biro and pencil.

The unbound score is written on five double sheets of 32-stave music paper, measuring 47.6 x 32.8 cms.

Sellotape has been used to repair several pages.

Hamlet | 1.M.1 (erased) | William Walton
Underneath is written in another hand, in blue pencil:
'Hamlet' | Funeral March | Walton

20 pages – p. [i]   Title page
           pp. [1-17]   Music
           pp. [18-19] Blank, except for ORIGINAL | Hamlet | 1.M.1
                        on page [18]. Also, at the foot of this page, is
                        written Miss Branson | 142 Charing Cross Road
                        | WC2

First edition [Full Score]
William Walton | FUNERAL MARCH | FROM 'HAMLET' | FULL SCORE | OXFORD UNIVERSITY PRESS | MUSIC DEPARTMENT 44 CONDUIT STREET LONDON W.1

15 pages. 253 x 179 mm
Stiff purple paper wrappers. Lettered in white. Trimmed edges.

Publication: Published 26 September 1963 at 8/6

Hamlet and Ophelia (C54b)
It is made up of *2.M.1* (74 bars); *6.M.1* (29 bars); *8.M.1* (56 bars); *14.M.3* (10 bars) and *7.M.1* (42 bars)

First edition [Full Score]
WILLIAM WALTON | HAMLET AND OPHELIA | a poem for orchestra | 'I hoped thou shouldst have been my Hamlet's wife; | I thought thy bride-bed to have decked, sweet maid, | And not have strewed thy grave.' | Oxford University Press | Music Department 44 Conduit Street London W.1

33 pages. 354 x 176 mm
Stiff blue paper wrappers. Lettered in white. Trimmed edges.

Publication: 1000 copies published 25 January 1968 at 18/-

Fanfare for a great occasion (C54d)
Whereabouts of holograph unknown

First edition [Full Score]
No title page

5 pages. 258 x 177 mm
Stiff red and white paper wrappers. Lettered in red and white. Trimmed edges.

Publication: 500 copies published 6 May 1965 by OUP at 6/6

HAPPY BIRTHDAY TO YOU (C57)

Whereabouts of holograph unknown

A copy reveals that the setting is written on two single sheets (9 bars) of music paper with text. Signed and dated 6.8.51

HENRY V (C50)

Music for the film

The following parts of the score are laid out thus and are held by PML (Koch manuscript 582):-

Titles
Holograph in pencil, with some blue pencil expression marks.

The unbound score is written on one double sheet of 24-stave music paper, measuring 38.1 x 25.4 cms.

4 pages – p. [1]   *Titles IIB* is written in the top right hand corner
                       – in blue pencil.
                       No chorus is written in the middle of the page,
                       also in blue pencil. Neither in Walton's hand.
            p. [2-4]   Music

Holograph in pencil, with some blue pencil expression marks.

The unbound score is written on one double and on both sides of one single sheet of 24-stave music paper, measuring 38.1 x 25.4 cms.

6 pages – p. [i]   *Titles IIC* is written in blue pencil. Henry V –
                       with Sop. and Alto – is written in the middle of
                       the page, also in blue pencil.
            pp. [1-5] Music

The French prepare for battle
Holograph in pencil, with some blue pencil expression marks.

The unbound score is written on three double sheets of 24-stave music paper, measuring 38 x 25.2 cms.

Reel 11 | Henry V | Bourbon: 'The Sun doth gild' 178 ft. | Side 5?

12 pages – p. [i]   Title page
            pp. [1-9]   Music
            pp. [10-11]   Blank

Miscellaneous fanfares
Holograph in pencil with some red pencil expression marks.

The unbound score is written on one double sheet of 24-stave music paper, measuring 38 x 27.3 cms.

Fanfares | Reels 16 and 17

4 pages – p. [i]   Title page
            p. [1]   7 Fanfares (for trumpet in C)
            pp. [2-3]   Blank

Threre are also three pages of *unidentified music* with references to French foot soldiers. It may be part of the Battle music.

Holograph in pencil, with some blue, green and red pencil expression marks.

The unbound score is written on one double sheet of 24-stave music paper, measuring 38.1 x 25.4 cms.

4 pages – pp. [1-3]   Music
            p. [4]   Blank

Charge and Battle
Holograph in pencil, with some expression marks in blue ink. Muir Mathieson's amendments for the printed score are sellotaped to the manuscript.

The unbound score is written on one double sheet of 24-stave music paper, measuring 38.1 x 25.4 cms.

Reel 12 (Shot 147 p.98) | Henry: '… gentle herald' (115 ft.)

4 pages –   p. [i]   Title page
            pp. [1-3]   Music

No dedication, date or signature of the composer apparent.

Unpublished

Charge and Battle
Holograph in pencil – in a cloth case.

It is described as having 36 pages, with a few corrections, unbound (the recto of leaves 4 and 5 badly stained but still legible), n.d. (not later than 1944).

Present location: H B Vander Poel, USA

First edition [Full Score]
William Walton | SUITE FROM | 'HENRY V' | PAGE | I Overture ‑ The Globe Playhouse 1 | II Passacaglia – Death of Falstaff (*strings only*) 14 | III Charge and Battle 16 | IV Touch her soft lips, and part (*strings only*) 50 | V Agincourt Song 52 | OXFORD UNIVERSITY PRESS | MUSIC DEPARTMENT | 44 CONDUIT STREET LONDON W.1

68 pages. 258 x 177 mm
Stiff turquoise paper wrappers. Lettered in white. Trimmed edges.

Publication: Published 19 March 1964 at 21/-

OTHER VERSIONS

Two pieces for strings
First edition [Full Score]
No title page

4 pages. 308 x 240 mm
Stiff grey paper wrappers. Lettered in black. Trimmed edges.

Publication: Published 10 April 1947 by OUP at 2/6

Passacaglia 'The death of Falstaff'
Arranged for organ

First edition [Score]
PASSACAGLIA | 'Death of Falstaff' | FROM THE FILM MUSIC
HENRY V | WILLIAM WALTON | ARRANGED FOR ORGAN BY
| HENRY G. LEY

4 pages. 307 x 241 mm
Stiff white paper wrappers. Lettered in black. Trimmed edges.

Publication: Published 17 February 1949 by OUP at 2/-

Two pieces from Henry V
Arranged for piano duet

First edition [Score]
No title page

5 pages. 278 x 214 mm
Stiff reddish-brown and white wrappers. Lettered in white.
Trimmed edges.

Publication: 1500 copies published (in the Oxford Piano Duets series) 2
March 1972 at 25p

A HISTORY OF THE ENGLISH SPEAKING PEOPLES: MARCH (C70)

Holograph in pencil

The unbound score is written on one double and on both sides of ten
single sheets of 30-stave music paper, measuring 43.8 x 32 cms.

The manuscript paper printer's mark, at the foot of the first page, on
the top left hand side, is shown as f.11i de Marino-portic. S.Franc. di
Paola - Napoli.

No title page apparent

24 pages – p. [i]   Blank
        pp. 1-22   Music
        p. [23]   Blank

No date, place or composer's signature apparent. 4'20" approx.
appears after the double bar line.

Present location: PML Koch manuscript 632

Unpublished

IMPROVISATIONS ON AN IMPROMPTU OF BENJAMIN BRITTEN (C82)

For orchestra

Holograph in pencil

The unbound score is written on both side of 30 separate sheets of 28-stave music paper, measuring 46.2 x 32.6 cms.

The manuscript paper printer's mark is shown as G.B.T. MARCHIO DEPOSITATO

To the San Francisco Symphony Orchestra | Josef Krips Conductor and Music Director | in memory of Adeline Smith Dorfman | Improvisations on an Impromptu of Benjamin Britten | William Walton

60 pages – p.[i]   Title page
          p.[ii]   Instrumentation
          pp.1-58   Music: Theme p. 1
                           1   pp. 1-8
                           2   pp. 8-18
                           3   pp. 18-29
                           4   pp. 30-38
                           5   pp. 39-58

No date or place apparent.

Dedication on the title page.

Signed by the composer on the title page and initialled at the end of the music, after the double bar line.

Present location: PML Koch manuscript 622

First edition [Full Score]
WILLIAM WALTON | IMPROVISATIONS | ON AN IMPROMPTU OF BENJAMIN BRITTEN | Oxford University Press | Music Department 44 Conduit Street London W1R 0DE

73 pages. 254 x 177 mm
Sea green, light blue (two shades) and white paper wrappers. Lettered in sea green, one shade of blue and white. Trimmed edges.

Publication: 1500 copies published 5 November 1970 at 45/-

IN HONOUR OF THE CITY OF LONDON (C33)

Cantata for mixed chorus and orchestra

Full Score
Details taken from a copy:
Holograph in pencil (?)

The score is written on twenty-one double sheets of 32-stave music paper.

84 pages – p. [i]   Title page (?)
        pp. 1-83   Music

No place or signature of the composer apparent.
Initialled and dated 'Sept 5th 1937' at the end of the score.

Present location: unable to trace. Walton presented this score as a raffle prize to LCMC in 1952

Vocal Score (Part only)
Holograph in pencil (black, with some red pencil annotations and alterations in the piano part)

The unbound score is written on one double and twelve single sheets of 14-stave music paper, measuring 32.9 x 24.3 cms.

In Honour of the City of London | a poem by | William Dunbar | set to music for chorus and orchestra by | William Walton

28 pages – p. [i]   Title page. A large 267 R appears on the title page in the top left hand corner, written in red pencil.
        pp. 1-25 Music: up to and including the penultimate line of the third verse
        pp. [26-27] Blank

Signed by the composer on the title page.
No dedication or date apparent.

Present location: PML Koch manuscript 596

First edition [Vocal Score]
IN HONOUR OF | THE CITY OF LONDON | *for Mixed Choir and Orchestra* | *by* WILLIAM WALTON | *The poem by* | WILLIAM DUNBAR (1465-1520) | OXFORD UNIVERSITY PRESS | 36 Soho Square, Oxford Street, London, W.1

51 pages. 251 x 177 mm

Stiff paper wrappers with cover designed by Severini in green and white. Lettered in black. Trimmed edges.

Publication: 2000 copies published 16 September 1937 at 2/6

JOHANNESBURG FESTIVAL OVERTURE (C66)

For Orchestra

Holograph in pencil

The score (bound in blue cloth covers) is written on 30-stave music paper, measuring 43.5 x 32 cms.

The manuscript paper printer's mark is shown as 30 F.11i de Marino-Porticato S.Francesco di Paola - Napoli

Johannesburg Festival Overture (1956) | William Walton

72 pages – p. [i] Title page
        pp. 1-71 Music: pages 41 and 2 are indicated as (revised) [sic] and are stuck down together. The following five pages [42-46] are unnumbered.

The manuscript is dated '31.5.56' and the place indicated as 'Forio d'Ischia'
No dedication apparent.
Signed by the composer on the title page.

First edition [Full Score]
WILLIAM WALTON | JOHANNESBURG | FESTIVAL | OVER-TURE | FULL SCORE | OXFORD UNIVERSITY PRESS | MUSIC DEPARTMENT | 44 CONDUIT STREET LONDON W.1

84 pages. 254 x 177 mm
Stiff green, light blue and white paper wrappers. Lettered in green and white. Trimmed edges.

Publication: Published 6 February 1958 at 10/6

JUBILATE DEO (C87)

For double mixed chorus and organ

Holograph in pencil

The unbound score is written on one double (12-stave) and on both sides of five single sheets of 14-stave music paper, measuring 32.3 x 23.3 cms.

The manuscript paper printer's mark is shown as G.B.T. MARCHIO DEPOSITATO

14 pages – p. [i] Title page: William Walton written by Alan Frank in pencil.
Jubilate Deo written by Walton in pencil.

p. [ii] Blank

pp. 1-10 Music: 3'15" indicated after the double bar line at the end of the music

pp. [11-12] Blank

No date, place, dedication or signature of the composer apparent.

Present location: PML Koch manuscript 614

First edition [Vocal Score]
S601 | *Oxford Church Services* | *General Editor* David Willcocks | WILLIAM WALTON | Jubilate Deo [within a double rule] S.S.A.A.T.T.B.B. | and Organ | OXFORD UNIVERSITY PRESS

11 pages. 258 x 177 mm
White stiff paper. Lettered in black. Trimmed edges.

Publication: 3000 copies published 1 March 1973 at 13p

KING HEROD AND THE COCK (C95)

Christmas carol for unaccompanied mixed chorus

Holograph in pencil

The unbound score is written on one side of a single sheet of 12-stave music paper, measuring 33.8 x 22.8 cms.

The manuscript paper printer's mark is shown in the left hand margin, as 12 Stamp. Music. f11i de marino-Napoli-Porticato S.Francesco di Paola

2 pages – p. [1] Music

p. [2] Blank, except for a large figure one within a circle

No date, place, dedication or signature of the composer apparent.

Present location: PML Koch manuscript 621

First edition [Vocal Score]
Included in *Carols for Choirs 3* (© OUP 1978) as no 46, p. 186

LAI (C51)

For solo piano

Whereabouts of holograph unknown

A LITANY (C1)

Motet for unaccompanied mixed chorus

Holograph in ink

The unbound score is written on one double sheet of 12-stave music paper, measuring 31 x 24.4 cms.

4 pages – pp. [1-4]   Music

No dedication apparent.
It is dated 'Easter 1916' at the bottom of p.[4].
Also 'Chris' [i.e. Christmas] erased
Signed by the composer at the top of p.[1]

Present location: PML Koch manuscript 591

First edition [Vocal Score]
No title page.

6 pages. 254 x 177 mm
White stiff paper. Lettered in black. Trimmed edges.

Publication: © 1930 by OUP at 4d.

MACBETH (C43)

Incidental music for Shakespeare's play

Holograph in pencil. Black, blue and red pencil instructions (some in red ink in places) appear on several pages of the score. The existing parts of the unbound score are laid out thus and are held by PML (Koch manuscript 581):-

Act One
Scene 1 (Allegro Furioso)

The score is written on three double sheets of 24-stave music paper, measuring 36.6 x 27.1 cms.

Macbeth | Act 1 Sc. 1 | between opening & ⬛3⬛ about 38 to 40 secs
Underneath, in red ink but not in Walton's hand, are some timings

In the top right-hand corner is (in red and blue pencil) a large figure 1, the word 'and' underneath, with a large figure 2 underneath that. Both figures are circled. In the top left hand corner is the word 'copied' written in red pencil.

12 pages –	p. [i]	Title page
	pp. 1-10	Music - at figure $\boxed{5}$ [last two bars of p.9 and the 4 bars on p. 10]: *Slow march - Transition between Scs.I and II*, about 15 secs.
	p. 11	*Act I Transition between Scs.II and III* [4 bars of music]

Transitions between scenes

The score is written on one double sheet of 24-stave music paper, measuring 36.6 x 27.1 cms.

Macbeth Act I | Transition between Scs III & IV 20 secs | IV & V 20 secs

In the top left hand corner is (in red pencil) a large figure three underlined with ' + 4' (in blue pencil) in brackets next to it. In the top left hand corner is the word 'copied' written in red pencil.

4 pages –	p. [ii]	Title page
	p. 12	*Transition between Sc. III and IV*
	p. 13	*Transition between Sc IV & V*
	p. 14	Blank

Transitions between scenes
The score is written on two double sheets of 24-stave music paper, measuring 36.6 x 27.1 cms.

Macbeth Act 1 between Scs V & VI | Festal entrance music 35-40 secs (fading out)

In the top right hand corner is a large figure five, underlined, written in blue pencil.

8 pages –	p. [i]	Title page
	pp. 1-4	Music
	pp. [5-7]	Blank

Transition between scenes and Banquet music

The score is written on two double sheets of 24-stave music paper, measuring 36.6 x 27.1 cms.

Macbeth Act 1 between Scs VI & VII | Festal & Banquet music 1-5 | from about $\boxed{1}$ onwards there's chatter & noise going on | The music is supposed to stop on the words 'success success' | in M's opening speech in Sc 7 | Banquet music cont. 50-55 secs | Start from 'thy love' Lady M's speech line 39. Stop after unmake line 54 | Use this piece cutting bars 5 & 6 | VI I II | Violas Cut 4 & 6 | after ③ use repeat bars cut 5 & 8.

There is a large letter A within a circle and a large figure 6 in a circle (written in blue pencil) in the top right hand corner and the words 'Banquet music ①' appear in the top left hand corner, within a circle (written in red pencil). The words 'Banquet music ③,' again within a circle, appear at the left hand side further down the page, opposite the words 'Act I for Sc 7', together with a large figure 8, again within a circle (written in blue pencil).

8 pages –   p. [i]   Title page
            pp. 1-6   Music
            p. [7]   Blank

Banquet Music 2

The score is written on two double sheets of 24-stave music paper, measuring 36.6 x 27.1 cms.

Macbeth Act I Sc 7 [underlined] 'B' written in red pencil (in a square) | Banquet music cont. 30 secs [underlined] | start after 'words own lips' (line 12) & finish on 'taking off' (line 20) | Take from piece marked Ⓐ . After opening bar (see overleaf) continue from beginning of 2nd bar after ① page 3 (repeat included) until end of 3rd bar after ② page 4 - | for finish see overleaf.

Underneath (in bottom right hand corner) some timings are written in red ink (not in Walton's hand).
In the top left hand corner are the words 'Banquet music 2' within a circle, and in the top right hand corner a large 7 in a circle (written in blue pencil).

8 pages –   p. [i]   Title page
            pp. [1-4]   Music: not in Walton's hand
            p. [5]   Blank
            p. [6]   Music: not in Walton's hand
            p. [7]   Blank

Banquet 3

The score is written (none in Walton's hand) on two double sheets of 24-stave music paper, measuring 36.6 x 27.1 cms.

Act 1 Banquet Music 3 | Banquet music cont 50-55 sec | Start from 'My love' Lady M speech line 39 | Stop after unmake line 54.

There is a large figure eight in the top left hand corner (written in blue pencil)

8 pages –   p. 1   Title page
           pp. 2-6   Music
           pp. [7-8]   Blank

Banquet 4 and transition between scenes

The score is written on two double sheets of 24-stave music paper, measuring 36.6 x 27.1 cms.

Macbeth Act 1 Sc 7 ['D' - written in red pencil] Banquet music cont. 1 min 35 secs & *transition to Sc.* 8 15-20 secs | Start after 'And will not fail' line 61 to the end of Sc.

There is a large figure nine, in a red pencil circle, in the top right hand corner (written in blue pencil); in the top left hand corner are the words, in a circle 'Banquet music 4'

8 pages –   p. [i]   Title page
           pp. 1-7   Music [last 7 bars on p. 7]:
                        Transition to Sc.8 (15-20 secs)

Act Two
Prelude to Act II

The score is written on one double sheet of 18-stave music paper, measuring 36.6 x 27.1 cms.

Macbeth Act II before Sc.I 40 secs.
(Underneath are some timings written in red ink, not in Walton's hand)

In the top right hand corner is (written in red pencil) a large figure 10 within a circle written in blue pencil. The words 'Act II' are also written across the page at the top. In the top left hand corner is the word 'copied', written in red pencil.

4 pages –   p. [i]   Title page
           pp. 1-2   Music
           p. [3]   Blank

Fanfare, murder music and transition between scenes

The score is written on one double sheet of 18-stave music paper, measuring 36.6 x 27.1 cms.

Macbeth Act II Sc.2 (Sc.I Act III in original) | After the words 'in hope'. Fanfare 20 secs. [bar] 12- not in Walton's hand (written in blue pencil) : Between Scs. 2A & 3 murder music 20 secs [bar] 13- not in Walton's hand (written in blue pencil) : Between Scs. 3 & 4 murder music & fanfare 20 secs.

In the top right hand corner are the figures 11 | 12 | 13 underneath each other (written in blue pencil), the 11 within a circle. In the top left hand corner is the word 'copied' written in red pencil.

4 pages –   p. [i]   Title page
            p. [1]   Music
            p. [2]   Music: Act II between Scs. 2A & 3 murder
                      music
            p. [4]   Music: Act II between Scs. 3 & 4

Banquo's Ghost

The score is written on one double sheet of 18-stave music paper, measuring 36.6 x 27.1 cms.

Act II Sc 4 (III 4) Banquo's ghost 22 secs.

In the top right hand corner are the figures 14 14a 14b underneath each other (written in blue pencil). In the top left hand corner is the word 'copied' written in red pencil.

4 pages –   p. [i]   Title page
            p. [1]   Music
            p. [ii]   Half title page :
                      14a 14b (written in blue pencil) | for two further
                      appearances of this jolly figure | we will repeat
                      the 1st 4 bars 10 secs each time [most likely
                      written in Ernest Irving's hand]
            p. [2]   Blank

Act Three
Act III : before Scene I

The score is written (in ink but not in Walton's hand) on one single side of a single sheet of 20-stave music paper, measuring 35.7 x 26.7 cms.

2 pages –   p. [1]   Fanfare. At the head of the music is *Macbeth Act
                      III before scene I.* A large figure 15 is written (in
                      blue pencil) in the top left hand corner.
            p. [2]   Blank

Witches music

The score is written on four double sheets of 24-stave music paper, measuring 36.6 x 27.1 cms.

Macbeth Act III Sc.II (Act IV Sc.I in original version) | Witches Music

(Underneath are some timings, written in red ink, but not in Walton's hand)

In the top right hand corner is the figure 16 (written in blue pencil) within a circle. In the top left hand corner is the word 'copied' written in red pencil.

16 pages – p. [i]   Title page
        pp. 1-14   Music: *Allegro Furioso*
        p. [15]   Blank

Apparitions
The score is written on two double sheets of 24-stave music paper, measuring 36.6 x 27.1 cms.

Macbeth Act III Sc.II 1st, 2nd & 3rd apparitions

In the top right hand corner are the figures 17a | 17b | 17c underneath each other (written in blue pencil).

8 pages – p. [i]   Title page
       pp. 1-2   Music: 1st apparition
       pp. 3-4   Music: 2nd apparition
       pp. 5-6   Music: 3rd apparition
       p. [7]   Blank

March of the Eight Kings
The score is written on two double sheets of 18-stave music paper, measuring 36.6 x 27.1 cms.

Macbeth Act III Sc.II March of the eight kings

In the top right hand corner is the figure 18 (written in blue pencil). In the top left hand corner is the word 'copied' written in red pencil.

8 pages – p. [i]   Title page
       pp. 1-4   Music
       pp. [5-7]   Blank

Transition between scenes
The score is written on both sides of one single sheet of 20-stave music paper, measuring 36.6 x 27.1 cms.

2 pages – p. 1   Macbeth Act III before Sc.I (Act III Sc.VI original): Fanfare
                Act III between Scs 3 & 4 (original Act IV Sc III)

In between the above is written, not in Walton's hand, in blue pencil, Witches music here 16,17. In the top left hand corner is a figure 15, written in blue pencil and in the middle a large figure 19, also in blue pencil, and at the foot of the page is written: over for 20,21,22 – in blue pencil.

p. 2   Act III between Scs 5 & 6 (original Act V Sc.II):
         Fanfare

Below is written, not in Walton's hand:

21 (written in blue pencil) for Act III between 6 & 7 repeat with addition of Tmpts.
22 (written in blue pencil) for Act III between 7 & 8 repeat version for 5 & 6.

In the top left hand corner is a large figure 20, written in blue pencil.

Transition between scenes

The score is written on both sides of one single sheet of 16-stave music paper, measuring 36.6 x 27.1 cms.

2 pages –   p. 3 [sic]   Macbeth Act III between Scs 8 & 9: Fanfare

Below is written, not in Walton's hand:

24 (written in blue pencil) the same for between Scs 9 & 10 Act III
25 (written in blue pencil) between 10 & 11 the same as Act III Sc. 1

At the top left hand corner is a large figure 23, written in blue pencil

p. 4 [sic]   During Sc.II Act III: Fanfare [to be repeated] ad
              lib no timing given

Below is written, not in Walton's hand:

27 (written in blue pencil) During Sc.II Act III Fanfare 10 secs.

In the top left hand corner is a large figure 26, written in blue pencil.

Final Lines

The score is written on one double sheet of 24-stave music paper, measuring 36.6 x 27.1 cms.

Macbeth | Act III | Final Lines [not in Walton's hand]

In the top right hand corner is the figure 28 in black lead pencil
4 pages –   p. [i]   Title page
            pp. 1-3   Music

No dedication, date or signature of the composer apparent.

Unpublished

MAGNIFICAT AND NUNC DIMITTIS (C91)

For mixed chorus and organ

Holograph in pencil

The score is written on both sides of eight single sheets of 14-stave music paper, measuring 30 x 22.5 cms.

The manuscript was bound (for presentation to the Dean of Chichester) in dark blue cloth with the inscription MAGNIFICAT | AND | NUNC DIMITTIS WILLIAM WALTON, in gold, on the front cover.

The manuscript paper printer's mark, at the foot of the page, is shown as a large 'M' intertwined with a treble clef and *1105* EXTRA

for | Walter Hussey | Dean of Chichester Cathedral | Magnificat and Nunc Dimittis | William Walton

16 pages – p. [i]   Dedication and title page
           pp. 1-10   Magnificat
           p. [11]   Blank
           – – – – – – – – – – – – –
           p. [i]   Half title page
           pp. 1-3   Nunc Dimittis

No date or place apparent.
Dedication on the title page.
Signed by the composer on the title page.

Present location: West Sussex Record Office Add. MS. 19,979

First edition [Vocal Score]
Oxford Church Services | *General Editor* David Willcocks | OXFORD UNIVERSITY PRESS. MUSIC DEPARTMENT. 44 CONDUIT STREET LONDON W1R 0DE WILLIAM WALTON | Magnificat and Nunc Dimittis | S 609 | S.A.T.B. | OXFORD UNIVERSITY PRESS

15 pages. 254 x 177 mm
Stiff white paper wrappers. Lettered in black. Trimmed edges.

Publication: Published 12 February 1976 at 60p

MAKE WE JOY NOW IN THIS FEST (C24)

Old English carol for unaccompanied mixed chorus

Whereabouts of holograph unknown

First edition [Vocal Score]
No title page. Published by Oxford University Press, London in the 'Oxford Choral Songs' series (no.750 - mixed voices)

3 pages. 254 x 178 mm
Stiff white paper. Lettered in black. Trimmed edges.

Publication: Published 6 October 1932 at 3d.

MEDLEY FOR BRASS BAND

Details taken from a copy:
Holograph in pencil (?)

The score is written on twelve double sheets of 18-stave music paper,
measuring 32.5 x 23.5 cms.

Medley for Brass Band | W.W.

48 pages – p. [i]   Title page
     pp. 1-17   Music : movement I
     p. [ii]   Half title page: 'Medley for Bra Ba', pp.18 to 34
     pp. 18-21   Music: movement II
     pp. 22-25   Music: movements III and IV
     p. [iii]   Half title page (same as above)
     pp. 26-34   Music
     pp. 31-41   Music : movement V

No date or place apparent.
Initialled by the composer on the title page.

Present location: PML Koch manuscript 612

Unpublished

MISSA BREVIS (C78)

For double mixed chorus and (in the Gloria) organ

Holograph in pencil

The unbound score is written on both sides of eight single sheets of 16-
stave music paper, measuring 33.6 x 23.4 cms.

The mansucript paper printer's mark is shown as 16.Stamp. music.
f.11i de Marino Napoli - Porticato S. Francesco di Paola.

No title page
16 pages – p. [i]   Title page: blank - except for Missa Brevis |
                     William Walton written in pencil by Alan
                     Frank
     pp. 1-15   Music - Kyrie: 1-2 (timing indicated as 1'35"c.)
                     Sanctus & Benedictus: 3 (1'8"c.)

(Hosanna): 3-4
Agnus Dei: 5-6 (1'15")
Gloria: 7-15 (3'5")

Pages 11 to 14 were originally numbered wrongly but subsequently altered to become 11 to 12; 12 to 13; 13 to 14; 14 to 15. There is an amendment, written in pencil, stapled to page 14.

No date, place, dedication or signature of the composer apparent.

Present location: PML Koch manuscript 635

First edition [Vocal Score]
No title page (English or Latin texts available)

19 pages. 254 x 176 mm
Stiff grey paper wrappers. Lettered in black and white. Trimmed edges.

Publication: 2500 copies published 21 July 1966 (in the Oxford Church Services Series as S 577) at 4/-

THE NATIONAL ANTHEM (C60)

Arranged for full orchestra (1953)

Holograph in pencil

The unbound score is written on one double sheet of 32-stave music paper, measuring 48 x 31.5 cms.

No title page apparent
4 pages –   p. [i]   Blank
           pp. 1-3   Music

No date, place or composer's signature apparent.

Present location: PML Koch manuscript 626

First edition [Full Score]
No title page

5 pages. 296 x 209 mm
Stiff white paper wrappers. Lettered in blue and black with a union flag featured in red, blue and white. Trimmed edges.

Publication: Published 3 March 1988 by OUP at 3.50

ORB AND SCEPTRE (C59)

Coronation March for full orchestra

Holograph in pencil

The unbound score is written on nine sheets of 32-stave music paper, measuring 48 x 31.5 cms.

Orb and Sceptre | Coronation March (1953) | by | William Walton

36 pages – p. [1] Title page
    pp. 2-22 Music
    p. [23] Blank, except for the following instructions:
        p. 3 becomes p. 23
        p. 4 becomes p. 24 - 1 becomes 9
        p. 5 becomes p. 25
        p. 6 becomes p. 26 - 2 becomes 10
        p. 7 becomes p. 27 p. 8 becomes p. 28 - 3 becomes 11
        p. 9 becomes p. 29 p.10 becomes p. 30
        p.11 becomes p. 31 - 4 becomes 12
        p.12 becomes p. 32
    p. [24] Blank
    pp.33-42 Music
    pp.[43-44] Blank

No date, place or dedication apparent. Signed by the composer on the title page.

Present location: PML Koch manuscript 628

Unpublished

– – – – – [Arranged for small orchestra]

No title page (Piano Conductor)

20 pages. 311 x 244 mm
Stiff grey paper wrappers. Lettered in red. Trimmed edges.

Publication: Published 22 October 1953 by OUP at 6/-

– – – – – [Arranged for military band]

First edition
William Walton | Orb and Sceptre | *Coronation March* | *Arranged for Military Band* by | *Norman Richardson* | *Conductor* | *This Coronation March was commissioned by The Arts Council of Great Britain and in its original* | *form, for full orchestra, it was first heard in Westminster Abbey at*

the Coronation of Her Majesty | Queen Elizabeth II on June 2nd 1953. The present arrangement is issued by agreement with the | publishers of the original version and owners of the copyright Oxford University Press. | Quarto Military Band No. 188 | Boosey & Hawkes

20 pages. 312 x 233 mm
Stiff green and light brown paper wrappers. Lettered in black. Trimmed edges.

Publication: Published 27 May 1953 (as QMB 188) by Boosey & Hawkes Ltd. at 30/- per set.

– – – – – [Arranged for brass band]

[double rule] | William Walton | [treble rule] | Orb & Sceptre | Arranged for brass band | by Eric Ball | [single rule] | Oxford University Press

41 pages. 279 x 215 mm
Stiff red paper wrappers. Lettered in black and white. Trimmed edges.

Publication: © 1979 at 5.25

– – – – – [Arranged for organ]

No title page
11 pages. 310 x 243 mm
Stiff white paper wrappers. Lettered in black. Trimmed edges.

Publication: 3000 copies published 4 June 1953 (in the Oxford Organ Music Series) at 3/6

– – – – – [Arranged for piano]

ORB AND | SCEPTRE | CORONATION MARCH (1953) | [bar] | William Walton | ARRANGED FOR PIANO SOLO BY | ROY DOUGLAS | [Royal Coat of Arms] | *Price 3s. net* | OXFORD UNIVERSITY PRESS

8 pages. 309 x 242 mm
Stiff light blue paper wrappers with black crest. Lettered in royal blue. Trimmed edges.

Publication: Published 4 June 1953 at 3/-

PARTITA FOR ORCHESTRA (C67)

Holograph in pencil

The score, bound in blue cloth covers, is written on 30-stave music paper, measuring 43.5 x 32 cms.

The manuscript paper printer's mark is shown as 30 f.11i de Marino-porticato S. Francesco di Paola-Napoli

To | George Szell and the Cleveland Orchestra | Partita | for | Orchestra | William Walton

124 pages – pp. [i-ii]   Blank
          p. [iii]   Title page
          p. [iv]   Commissioned by the Cleveland Orchestra for its 40th Anniversary season
          p. [v]   Partita | for | Orchestra | I Toccata
          pp. 1-46   Music ('4'30"c.' at the end of the music)
          p. [vi]   Blank
          p. [vii]   Half title page: II | Pastorale Siciliana
          pp. 47-66   Music ('5'10"c.' at the end of the music)
          p. [viii]   Blank
          p. [ix]   Half title page: III | Giga Burlesco
          pp. 67-113   Music ('4'45"c.' at the end of the music)
          pp. 114-115   Blank

No date or place apparent. Dedication and signature of the composer on the title page.

Present location: PML Koch manuscript 631

First edition [Full score]
WILLIAM WALTON | PARTITA FOR ORCHESTRA | MOVE-MENTS | 1. TOCCATA *p.*1 | 2. PASTORALE SICILIANA *p.*57 | 3. GIGA BURLESCA *p.*81 | OXFORD UNIVERSITY PRESS | *MUSIC DEPARTMENT* | 44 CONDUIT STREET, LONDON W. 1

130 pages. 253 x 178 mm
Stiff buff, blue and white paper wrappers. Lettered in blue and white. Trimmed edges.

Publication: Published 21 August 1958 at 18/-

PASSACAGLIA FOR SOLO CELLO (C98)

Details taken from a copy:
Holograph in pencil (?)

The manuscript is written on two double sheets of 18-stave music paper, measuring 32 x 23.5 cms.

Passacaglia | for | 'Cello Solo
8 pages –   p. [i]   Title page
            pp. 1-4   Music
            p. [5]   New page 4
            pp. [6-7] Blank

No date, place or signature of the composer apparent.

Present location: PML Koch manuscript 611

First edition [Score]
No title page

4 pages. 310 x 230 mm
Stiff turquoise paper wrappers. Lettered in black and white. Trimmed edges.

Publication: Published 16 December 1982 by OUP at 1.40

PORTSMOUTH POINT (C17)

Overture for orchestra

Holograph in pencil

The unbound score is written on 30-stave music paper, measuring 44 x 29.1 cms.

PORTSMOUTH POINT | AN | OVERTURE (after a print by Thomas Rowlandson | for | ORCHESTRA | by | W.T.WALTON | Time of performance is 5.5 to 6 minutes
64 pages –   p. [i]   Title page
             p. [ii]   Blank
             pp. 1-39   Music
             pp. [40-50] Blank
             pp. [51-52] Music(?) - a sketch (in pencil)
             pp. [53-62] Blank

No dedication apparent. The dedication to Siegfried Sassoon was added later in the printed copy.
Signed by the composer on the title page.

Present location: PML Koch manuscript 588

First edition [Full Score]
No title page

40 pages. 343 x 260 mm
Stiff paper wrappers with cover designed by Severini in green and white. Lettered in black. Trimmed edges.

Publication: Published 6 June 1928 by OUP at 15/-

— — — — — [Miniature Score]
No title page

40 pages. 196 x 145 mm
Stiff white and pale green paper wrappers. Lettered in black. Trimmed edges.

Publication: Published 17 May 1928 by OUP at 3/6

— — — — — [arranged for piano duet by the composer]

PORTSMOUTH POINT | [Copy of the Rowlandson print, 114 x 117 mm] | An Overture | *by* William Walton | *Pianoforte Duet Arrangement* | *by the Composer* | *Cover designed by Gino Severini* | OXFORD UNIVERSITY PRESS

20 pages. 344 x 254 mm
Stiff paper wrappers with cover designed by Severini in green and white. Lettered in black. Trimmed edges.

Publication: © 1927 at 6/6
It is dated by the composer: London, November 1925

PROLOGO E FANTASIA (C100)

for orchestra

Details taken from a copy:
Holograph in pencil (?)

The unbound score is written on eight double sheets of 32-stave music paper, measuring 47 x 32.5 cms.

32 pages – p. [i]   Title page (?)
        p. [ii]   Orchestration (the score is written in C)
        pp. 1-28 Music
        pp. [29-30] Blank

No place, date or signature of the composer apparent.

Present location: PML Koch manuscript 610

First edition [Score]
No title page

24 pages. 253 x 178 mm
Stiff green, red and white wrappers. Lettered in green, red and white.
Trimmed edges.

Publication: Published 26 April 1984 by OUP at 3.95

QUARTET FOR PIANO AND STRINGS (C7)

Whereabouts of holograph unknown

First edition [Score]
No title page. Front cover:

[Within an ornamental rule]
CARNEGIE COLLECTION | of British Music | QUARTET | for
Violin, Viola, Violoncello & Pianoforte | by | W.T.WALTON |
Copyright Price 9/- net cash | STAINER & BELL LTD | 58 Berners
Street, London W1 | PUBLISHED UNDER THE SCHEME OF THE
CARNEGIE UNITED KINGDOM TRUST

74 pages. 309 x 245 mm
Buff stiff paper wrappers. Lettered in maroon. Trimmed edges.

Publication: © 1924 at 9/-

At the top of page 3 of the printed copy is the dedication 'To the Right
Rev. Thomas Banks Strong, Bishop of Ripon'. It is dated at the foot of
p. 74 'Oxford 1918 - 19'

Revised edition [Score]
William Walton | QUARTET | for Violin, Viola, Cello and Piano |
Oxford University Press | Music Department, 44 Conduit Street,
London W1R 0DE

74 pages. 309 x 229 mm
Blue, white, pink and purple stiff paper wrappers. Lettered in blue,
white, pink and purple. Trimmed edges.

Publication: Published 26 February 1976 at 5.00

QUARTET [NO.1] FOR STRINGS (C11)

Holograph in ink

The unbound score of the first movement is written on six double
sheets of 4-stave music paper, measuring 9.8 x 31 cms.

QUARTET | (Chosen for the International Festival of Contemporary Chamber Music at Salzburg 1923) | I | (Moderato) Walton also added later on this title page, in ink:
'for Bumps [i.e.Hyam Greenbaum] from | William | September 28th 1936'

24 pages –	p. [i]	Title page
	pp. 1-22	Music: first movement (181 bars)
	p. [23]	Blank

_ _ _ _ _ _ _ _ _ _ _ _

The unbound score of the *second* movement is written on fifteen double and two single sheets of 4-stave music paper, measuring 9.8 x 31 cms.

64 pages –	p. [ii]	Half title page: II	Scherzo	(Allegro molto vivace, e ritmico)
	pp. 1-62	Music: second movement (402 bars)
	p. [63]	Blank

_ _ _ _ _ _ _ _ _ _ _ _

The unbound score of the *third* movement is written on thirteen double and one single sheet of 4-stave music paper, measuring 9.8 x 31 cms.

54 pages –	p. [iii]	Half title page: III	Fuga	(Lento, ma non troppo, e molto espressivo)
	pp. 1-47	Music: third movement (266 bars)
	pp. 48-51	Missing
	p. 52	Music
	p. [53]	Blank

No dedication.
Initialled and dated: (WTW- | Amalfi | 23.11.22) by the composer at the foot of p. 52 (3rd movement). The composer's initials and '1920-22' are also added at the foot of p. 22 (1st movement) and p. 62 (2nd movement).

Present location: PML Koch manuscript 590

Unpublished

QUARTET [No.2] FOR STRINGS (C53)

Holograph in ink

It is difficult to ascertain the number of sheets as the manuscript was mounted on larger manuscript paper for publication. The unbound score is written on 48 pages (I-20; II-8; III-8; IV-12) of 24-stave music paper, measuring 32 x 25 cms.

No date or place apparent.

Signed by the composer at the top of page one, together with the dedication: To | Ernest Irving | String Quartet in A minor | William Walton

Present location: PML Koch manuscript 606A

First edition [Score – a facsimile of the composer's manuscript]
No title page

48 pages. 252 x 178 mm
Stiff paper wrappers with cover designed by Severini in green and white. Lettered in black. Trimmed edges.

Publication: Published 14 August 1947 by OUP at 5/-

OTHER VERSIONS

Sonata for String Orchestra (C53a)
Holograph (first three movements) in pencil. Unbound.
Manuscript (last movement) in black biro, in the hand of Malcolm Arnold, with a few pencil annotations. Unbound.

The manuscript paperprinter's mark is shown as G.B.T. MARCHIO DEPOSITATO

The *first* movement is written on both sides of 11 single sheets of 18 and 20-stave music paper, measuring 32.5 x 23.5 cms.

pp. 1-21 Music: I Movement

The *second* movement is written on both sides of 5 single sheets of 20-stave music paper, measuring 32.5 x 23.5 cms.

pp. 22-33 Music: II Movement

The *third* movement is written on both sides of 9 single sheets of 20-stave music paper, measuring 32.5 x 23.5 cms, with 2 single sheets of 14-stave music paper interpolated where indicated.

pp. 33-36   Music: III Movement
p. [i]   Title page: Sonata for String Orchestra | (adapted from String Quartet 1947)
p. [ii]   Blank
pp. 36   [sic] - 49 Music: III Movement. Incorrectly numbered by the composer. Correct sequence should be 37-50.
pp. [iii-iv] Blank

The *fourth* movement is written on five double sheets of 20-stave music paper, measuring 32.5 x 23.5 cms.

pp. 50-56 Music: IV Movement

pp. [67-69] Blank

No dedication, date or signature of the composer or arranger apparent.

Present location: PML Koch manuscript 606B

First edition [Full Score]
WILLIAM WALTON | SONATA | FOR STRING ORCHESTRA |
page | I Allegro 1 | II Presto 35 | III Lento 59 | IV Allegro molto 73 |
OXFORD UNIVERSITY PRESS | Music Department 44 Conduit
Street London W1R 0DE

94 pages. 267 x 190 mm
Stiff green, yellow, blue and white paper wrappers. Lettered in green,
yellow, blue and white. Trimmed edges.

Publication: Published 20 December 1973 at 3.90

A QUEEN'S FANFARE (C69)

Holograph in pencil

The unbound score is written on one double sheet of 12-stave music
paper, measuring 24.9 x 23.5 cms.

The manuscript paper printer's mark is shown, on page 4, as 16.
Stamp.music. f.11i de Marino-Napoli-Porticato S.Francesco di Paola.

No title page: 'Fanfare' written at the top of page one.

4 pages –   pp. 1-4   Music. '40″ approx' and 'N.B. This can be per-
                      formed without Tr.B flat 5,6,7 and Bass Trb 2'
                      appear at the end after the double bar line.

No date, place or dedication apparent. Signed by the composer on the
first page.

Present location: Manuscript Collections. The British Library (Refer-
                  ence Division) Add.MS 59813 (Part of the *MacNagh-
                  ten Concerts Collection*)

First edition [Score]
No title page

5 pages. 254 x 178 mm
Stiff dark blue, light blue and white paper wrappers. Lettered in blue
and white. Trimmed edges.

Publication: 750 copies published 28 April 1972 by OUP at 40p

THE QUEST (C49)

Ballet in five scenes

The majority is holograph in pencil; the rest is manuscript in ink (unable to trace).
The existing parts of the score are laid out thus and are held by PML (Koch manuscript 605B):-

SCENE ONE

The score (loose in a blue folder, several leaves bound together with adhesive tape) is written on 32-stave music paper, measuring 44.5 x 30.5 cms.

Dedicated to the | Sadler's Wells Ballet Company | and in particular to | Ninette, Margot, Constant, Bobbie and Freddie | THE QUEST | A BALLET IN FIVE SCENES FROM SPENSER'S 'FAERIE QUEENE' | Choreography by Frederick Ashton | Scenery by John Piper | Music by William Walton | Scene I

51 pages – p. [i]   Title page
            pp. [1-46] Music: Scene I
            pp. [47-50] Blank

Many notes, re-timings and expression notes (in black and blue pencil) appear in the score. These are in Constant Lambert's hand.

SCENE TWO

The score is written on 32-stave music paper, measuring 44.5 x 30.5 cms.

THE QUEST | W.Walton | Scene II. *Quest* | *Sc II* is also written (in pencil) at the top of the page in Constant Lambert's hand.

44 pages – p. [51]   Title page
            pp. [52-70] Music: Scene II
            pp. [71-72] Blank
            p. [73]   Half title page: Scene II cont.
            p. [74]   Blank
            pp. [75-93] Music
            p. [94]   Blank

SCENE THREE

The score is written on 32-stave music paper, measuring 44.5 x 30.5 cms.

The Quest | Sc.3 | Hermaphrodite's dance. *Scene III – beginning* is also written (in pencil) in the top right hand corner, in Constant Lambert's hand.

76 pages – p. [95]   Title page
           pp. [96-105] Music
           pp. [106-108] Blank
           p. [109]   Half title page: The Quest | 7 Deadly Sins Sc. III
           pp. [110-137] Music – In ink, not in Walton's hand
           p. [138]   Variation 7: Pride – pencilled out
           p. [139]   Half title page: 'Variation 7 Pride' written at the head of the page in ink
           pp. [140-145] Music
           p. [146]   Blank
           p. [147]   Half title page: Scene III continued.
                        Scene III – Section III is also written (in pencil) in the top right hand corner, in Constant Lambert's hand
           pp. [148-170] Music

SCENE FOUR

The score is written on 32-stave music paper, measuring 44.5 x 30.5 cms

THE QUEST | Scene IV. Scenes IV and V are also written (in pencil) in the top right hand corner, in Constant Lambert's hand.

28 pages – Spp. [171-176] Blank
           p. [177]   Title page
           pp. [178-189] Music
           p. [190]   (Pencilled out)
           p. [191]   Half title page: The Quest Scene IV continued WILLIAM WALTON (written at the head of the page – not in Walton's hand)
           pp. [192-198] Music

SCENE FIVE

The score is written on 32-stave music paper, measuring 44.5 x 30.5 cms

No title page

20 pages – pp. [199-217] Music: *The Quest – Scene V* is written at the top of p. [199]. Not in Walton's hand.
           p. [218]   Blank

Dedication on the title page.
Signed by the composer on the title page and also initialled at the foot of the last page p. [217], below the last two bars.
The date (March 29th 1943) is written beneath these initials.

Unpublished

First edition [Full Score]
WILLIAM WALTON | THE QUEST | *BALLET SUITE* | FULL
SCORE OXFORD UNIVERSITY PRESS | MUSIC DEPARTMENT
44 CONDUIT STREET LONDON W.1.

80 pages. 254 x 177 mm
Stiff blue paper wrappers. Lettered in white. Trimmed edges.

Publication: 1000 copies published 3 May 1962 at 21/-

– – – – – [Piano reduction]

Details taken from a copy:
Holograph in pencil (?)

The score is written on 14-stave music paper, measuring 36 x 20.7 cms
as follows:

SCENE ONE

p. [i]   Title page: Scene 1
pp. 1-13   Music
pp. [14-15] Blank

SCENE TWO

p. [i]   Title page: The Quest | Scene II
pp. [1-12] Music
pp. [14-15] Blank

SCENE THREE

p. [i]   Title page: Scene III – St George and Duessa's entry (The
             remainder is missing)
pp. 1-7   Music

SCENE FOUR

p. [i]   Title page: Scene IV
pp. 1-6   Music
p. [7]   Blank

SCENE FIVE
p. [i]   Title page: Scene V
pp. 1-6   Music
p. [7]   Blank

No date, place or signature of the composer apparent.

Present location: The Walton Museum, Ischia

Unpublished

RICHARD III (C63)

Music for the film

Holograph in pencil except where indicated.
The existing parts of the unbound score are laid out and are held by
PML (Koch manuscript 584):-

Prelude
The score is written on two double sheets of 28-stave music paper,
measuring 43.8 x 30.3 cms.

The manuscript paper printer's mark is shown as J & W CHESTER.
LONDON (within a circle).

Opening titles (2'-18.5) | Muir Mathieson | c/o Mrs. Buck (in ink) at the
foot of the page

8 pages –   p. [i] –   Title page
             pp. 1-7   Music. It contains red pencil/green biro mark-
                        ings with timings in black pencil. Recorded 29.3
                        55

Fanfare (King Edward IV's Coronation) 1.M.1
The score is written on both sides of one single sheet of 30-stave music
paper, measuring 44.1 x 31.7 cms.

No title page
(At the head of the page is written Richard III 1.M.1 0-to 38″ to be
taken wild)

2 pages –   p. [1]   Music. It contains dark green pencil markings
                       with regard to timings

                       Recorded 24.2.55
             p. 2   Blank except 1.M.1 which is written at the foot
                       of the page in blue pencil.

Fanfare; March; Fanfare 1.M.2 1.M.3 1.M.4
The score is written on one double sheet of 12-stave music paper,
measuring 31 x 24.4 cms.

1.M.2 (9″) | 1.M.3 (1'4″) | 1.M.4 (16″) recorded 22.2.55

4 pages –   p. 1   1.M.2) Each contain
             pp. 1-3   1.M.3) green pencil markings
             p. 4   1.M.4) with regard to timings

The King greets his Queen/King and escort leave Coronation 1.M.5B

The score is written on one double and on both sides of one single
sheet of 30-stave music paper, measuring 43.8 x 32 cms.

The manuscript paper printer's mark is shown as 30 f.11i de Marino-porticato S.Francesco di Paola-Napoli

1.M.5 B (1'5")

6 pages –   p. [i]   Title page
            pp. 1-5   Music: It contains red pencil markings with
                        regard to timings. Recorded 22.2.55

Procession pauses, leaving Richard alone 2.M.1 A
The score is written on 2 double sheets of 30-stave music paper,
measuring 43.8 x 32 cms.

The mansucript paper printer's mark is shown as 30 f.11i de Marino-
porticato S. Francesco di Paola-Napoli

2.M.1 A (53")

8 pages –   p. [i]   Title page
            pp. 1-5   Music
            p. 6   Music: crossed out Recorded 22.2.55
            p. [7]   Blank

Richard speaks: Now is the winter 2.M.1 B
The score is written on one double and on both sides of one single
sheet of 30-stave music paper, measuring 43.6 x 32 cms.

The manuscript paper printer's mark is shown as 30.f.11i de Marino-
porticato S. Francesco di Paola-Napoli

2.M.1 B (55")

6 pages –   p. [i]   Title page
            pp. 1-5   Music: It contains red and green pencil mark-
                        ings with regard to timings. Recorded 25.2.55

I'll drown more sailors 2.M.2
The score is written on one double and on both sides of one single
sheet of 30-stave music paper, measuring 43.6 x 32 cms.

The manuscript paper printer's mark is shown as 30f.11i de Marino-
porticato S. Francesco di Paola-Napoli

2.M.2 (44")

6 pages –   p. [i]   Title page
            pp. 1-4   Music: it contains red pencil markings with
                        regard to timings. Recorded 22.2.55
            p. [5]   Blank

Set down - set down 3.M.1
The score is written on both sides of half a single sheet (15 staves) of 30-
stave music paper, measuring 31.8 x 23 cms.

3.M.1 (32″)

2 pages – p. [1] Music
         p. [2] Blank. 3.M.1 is written in blue pencil.

Then I must count my gains – Clarence beware 3.M.2
The score is written on one double sheet of 30-stave music paper, measuring 43.6 x 31.9 cms.

The music paper has been used upside down, the manuscript paper printer's mark is shown (in the top right hand corner) as 30f.11i de Marino-porticato S. Francesco di Paola-Napoli

3.M.2 (45.5″) [The figure '2' is crossed out in pencil]

4 pages – p. [i] Title page
         pp. 1-3 Music: it contains green pencil markings with regard to timings. Recorded 24.2.55

Clarence to the Tower 4.M.1
The score is written on two double sheets of 30-stave music paper, measuring 43.6 x 31.9 cms.

The music paper has been used upside down, the manuscript paper printer's mark is shown (in the top right hand corner) as 30f.11i de Marino-porticato S. Francesco di Paola-Napoli

4.M.1 (2′3″)

8 pages – p. [i] Title page
         pp. 1-6 Music: it contains red pencil markings with regard to timimgs. Recorded 22.2.55
         p. 7 Blank

To wear this ring 4.M.2
The score is written on one double and on both sides of one single sheet of 30-stave music paper, measuring 43.6 x 31.9 cms.

The music paper has been used upside down, the manuscript paper printer's mark is shown (in the top right hand corner) as 30f.11i de Marino-porticato S.Francesco di Paola-Napoli

4.M.2 (1′31″)

6 pages – p. [i] Title page
         pp. 1-5 Music: it contains red pencil markings with regard to timings. Recorded 22.2.55

Shine out fair sun till I have bought a glass 4.M.3
The score is written on one double sheet of 30-stave music paper, measuring 43.6 x 31.9 cms.

The music paper has been used upside down, the manuscript paper printer's mark is shown (in the top right hand corner) as 30f.11i de Marino-porticato S.Francesco di Paola-Napoli

4.M.3 (23")

4 pages – p. [i] Title page
pp. 1-2 Music: it contains red pencil markings with regard to timings. Recorded 24.2.55
p. [3] Blank

Clarence's nightmare in the Tower 5.M.1
The score is written on one double sheet of 30-stave music paper, measuring 43.6 x 31.9 cms.

The music paper has been used upside down, the manuscript paper printer's mark is shown (in the top right hand corner) as 30f.11i de Marino-porticato S.Francesco di Paola-Napoli

5.M.1 (37")

4 pages – p. [i] Title page
pp. 1-3 Music: it contains red pencil markings with regard to timings. Recorded 22.2.55

See how he requites me 5.M.2
The score is written on one double sheet of 20-stave music paper, measuring 33.6 x 23.2 cms.

The music paper has been used upside down, the manuscript paper printer's mark is shown (in the top right hand corner) as 20 Stamp music f.11i de Marino-Napoli-Porticato S. Francesco di Paola

5.M.2 (58")

4 pages – p. [i] Title page
pp. 1-2 Music: it contains red pencil markings with regard to timings. Recorded 22.2.55
p. [3] Blank

Who comes here? 6.M.1
The score is written on one double sheet of 20-stave music paper, measuring 33.7 x 23 cms.

The music paper has been used upside down, the manuscript paper printer's mark is shown (in the top right hand corner) as 20 Stamp music f.11i de Marino-Napoli-Porticato S. Francesco di Paola

6.M.1 (22")

4 pages – p. [i] Title page
pp. 1-3 Music: it contains red pencil markings with regard to timings. Recorded 22.2.55

Clarence being dropped into a wine butt 6.M.2
The score is written on one double sheet of 30-stave music paper, measuring 43.6 x 31.9 cms.

The music paper has been used upside down, the manuscript paper printer's mark is shown (in the top right hand corner) as 30 f.11i de Marino-Porticato S.Francesco di Paola-Napoli

6.M.2 (32")

4 pages – p. [i]   Title page
           pp. 1-2   Music Recorded 22.2.55
           p. [3]   Blank

Madam, His Majesty doth call 7.M.1
The score is written on one double sheet of 30-stave music paper, measuring 43.6 x 31.9 cms.

The music paper has been used upside down, the manuscript paper printer's mark is shown (in the top right hand corner) as 30f.11i de Marino-Porticato S.Francesco di Paola-Napoli

7.M.1 (29")

4 pages – p. [i]   Title page
           p. 1   Music. They contain red pencil
           p. [2]   Music with markings with regard to timings. Recorded 22.2.55
           p. [3]   Blank

The King's Bedchamber 7.M.2
Holograph in blue ink

The score is written on one double sheet of 12-stave music paper, measuring 30.8 x 24.2 cms.

No. 57.M.2 (2'57") | organ – erased

4 pages – p. [i]   Blank – pencil markings erased
           pp. [1-2]   Music, with amendments in pencil
           p. [3]   Blank

The Princes in the Tower 7.M.3
The score is written on both sides of one single sheet of 30-stave music paper, measuring 43.8 x 31.6 cms.

The manuscript paper printer's mark is shown as 30.f11i de Marino-porticato S.Franceso di Paola-Napoli

7.M.3 (31")

2 pages – p. [i]   Music Recorded 25.2.55

> p. [2]   Blank, except for pencil sketch at the foot of the
> page

Straight shall post to Ludlow 8.M.1
The score is written on two double sheets of 30-stave music paper,
measuring 43.7 x 32 cms.

The manuscript paper printer's mark is shown as 30f.11i de Marino-
porticato S.Francesco di Paola-Napoli

8.M.1 (2'34")

8 pages –   p. [i]   Title page
            pp. 1-7   Music: it contains red and green pencil mark-
                      ings with regard to timings. Recorded 25.2.55

The tiger now hath seized the gentle hand 8.M.2
The score is written on one double and on both sides of one single
sheet of 30-stave music paper, measuring 43.8 x 32 cms.

8.M.2 (2'30")

6 pages –   p. [i]   Title page
            pp. 1-5   Music: it contains red pencil markings with
                      regard to timings. Recorded 22.2.55

Go with them 9.M.1
The score is written on one double sheet of 30-stave music paper,
measuring 43.8 x 32 cms.

The manuscript paper printer's mark is shown as 30f.11i de Marino-
porticato S.Francesco di Paola-Napoli

9.M.1 (49")

4 pages –   pp. 1-3)   Music: it contains green pencil
            p. [4])   markings with regard to timings. Recorded
                       25.2.55

Here comes the Duke of York 9.M.2
The score is written on one double sheet of 30-stave music paper,
measuring 43.8 x 32 cms.

The manuscript paper printer's mark is shown as 30f.11i de Marino-
porticato S.Francesco di Paola-Napoli

9.M.2 (43")

4 pages –   p. [i]   Title page
            pp. 1-3   Music: it contains green pencil markings with
                      regard to timings. Recorded 25.2.55

He thinks that you should bear me on your shoulder 9.M.3

The score is written on both sides of one single sheet of 30-stave music paper, measuring 43.7 x 32 cms.

9.M.3 (13")

2 pages – p. [1]   Music Recorded 22.2.55
           p. [2]   Blank

The Princes get ready/And give Mistress Shore/Catesby's ride 9.M.4/ 9.M.5/ 10.M.1
The score is written on one double sheet of 30-stave music paper, measuring 43.7 x 31.9 cms.

The manuscript paper printer's mark is shown as 30f.11i de Marino-porticato S. Francesco di Paola-Napoli

9.M.4 (1'0") | 9.M.5 (16") | 10.M.1 (26")

4 pages – p. [i]   Title page
           p. 1   9.M.4) Music: it contains green pencil
           pp. 2-3   9.M.5)   markings with regard
                     10.M.1)   to timings. Recorded 25.2.55

They smile at me/Jane Shore shuts the door/Use my babies well 10.M.2/ 12.M.4/ 13.M.1
The score is written on one double sheet of 30-stave music paper, measuring 43.7 x 32 cms.

The manuscript paper printer's mark is shown as 30f.11i de Marino-porticato S.Francesco di Paola-Napoli

10.M.2 (44") | 12.M.4 (26") | 13.M.1 (16") to be ready for Tues morn at Shepperton

4 pages – p. [1]   10.M.2) Music: it contains red pencil
           pp. [2-3] 12.M.4)   markings with regard
           p. [4]   13.M.1)   to timings. Recorded 22.2.55

Go you to the Tower 10.M.3
The score is written on one double sheet of 24-stave music paper, measuring 35.8 x 26.2 cms.

10.M.3 (53")

4 pages – p. [1]   Title page
           pp. [1-3] Music: it contains green pencil markings with
                     regard to timings. Recorded 25.2.55

Richard holds his hand to Buckingham 12.M.1
The score is written on one double sheet of 24-stave music paper, measuring 38 x 27.3 cms.

12.M.1 (30")

4 pages – p. [i]   Title page
          pp. [1-2]   Music Recorded 30.3.55
          p. [3]   Blank

Come madam come 12.M.2
The score is written on one double sheet of 30-stave music paper, measuring 43.8 x 32 cms.

The music paper has been used upside down, the manuscript paper printer's mark is shown (in the top right hand corner) as 30f.11i de Marino-porticato S. Francesco di Paola-Napoli

12.M.2 (1'48")

4 pages – p. [i]   Title page
          pp. 1-3   Music: it contains red biro/red and green pencil markings with regard to timings. Recorded 25.2.55

Come madam come (cont.) 12.M.3
The score is written on one double sheet of 24-stave music paper, measuring 35.8 x 26.2 cms.

12.M.3 (30")

4 pages – p. [i]   Title page
          ‚pp. [1-2]   Music: it contains red pencil markings with regard to timings. Recorded 25.2.55
          p. [3]   Blank

King Richard's Coronation 13.M.2
The score is written on one double and on both sides of one single sheet of 24-stave music paper, measuring 35.3 x 25.8 cms.

13.M.2 (42") [This is crossed out in pencil]

6 pages – p. [i]   Title page
          pp. 1-5   Music. Walton's pagination is also crossed out. Muir Mathieson's score (for the Shakespeare Suite No 2) is sellotaped to parts of the original manuscript.

Anne falls at the foot of the throne 13.M.3
The score is written on one double sheet of 30-stave music paper, measuring 43.7 x 36.6 cms.

The music paper has been used upside down, the manuscript paper printer's mark is shown (in the top right hand corner) as 30f.11i de Marino-porticato S.Francesco di Paola-Napoli

13.M.3 (1'18")

4 pages –   p. [i]   Title page
           pp. [1-3]   Music: it contains red biro/red and green pencil markings with regard to timings. Recorded 24.2.55

I'm not in the vein 14.M.1
The score is written on one double and on both sides of one single sheet of 24-stave music paper, measuring 35.7 x 26.2 cms.

14.M.1 (58″)

6 pages –   p. [i]   Title page
           pp. 1-5   Music: it contains red and green pencil markings with regard to timings. Recorded 25.2.55

A cushion is pushed in Tyrell's face 14.M.2
The score is written on three double sheets of 24-stave music paper, measuring 38 x 27.4 cms.

14.M.2 (2′5″)

12 pages –   p. [i] Title page
           pp. 1-10   Music: it contains red and green pencil markings with regard to timings. Recorded 30.3.55
           p. [11]   Blank

Forget not thy son George 15.M.1
The score is written on two double sheets of 24-stave music paper, measuring 35.9 x 26.4 cms.

15.M.1 (50″)

8 pages –   p. [i]   Title page
           pp. 1-6   Music: it contains black and green pencil markings with regard to timings. Recorded 30.5.55
           p. [7]   Blank

Richard rushes out to find Richmond 15.M.2 A
The score is written on two double sheets of 24-stave music paper, measuring 36 x 26.3 cms.

15.M.2 A (1′8″)

8 pages –   p. [i]   Title page
           pp. 1-7   Music: it contains black pencil markings with regard to timings. Recorded 30.3.55

All Souls Day is my doomsday 15.M.2 B
The score is written on one double sheet of 24-stave music paper, measuring 35.9 x 26.2 cms.

15.M.2 B (20"?)

4 pages –   p. [i]   Title page
            pp. [1-2]   Music Recorded 30.3.55
            p. [3]   Blank

Good Lords conduct him to his regiment 16.M.1
The score is written on one double sheet of 24-stave music paper, measuring 38 x 27.3 cms.

16.M.1 (31")

4 pages –   p. [i]   Title page
            pp. 1-3   Music: it contains red pencil markings with
                           regard to timings. Recorded 29.3.55

Ghosts appearing to Richard 16.M.2
The score is written on five double sheets of 32-stave music paper, measuring 48 x 33 cms.

16.M.2 (5'2")

20 pages – p. [i]   Title page
            pp. 1-18   Music: it contains red pencil markings with
                           regard to timings. Recorded 31.3 55
            p. 19   Blank

Bustle, bustle 17.M.1
The score is written on two double sheets of 24-stave music paper, measuring 38 x 27.3 cms.
17.M.1 (1'36")

8 pages –   p. [i]   Title page
            pp. 1-6   Music: it contains red and green pencil mark-
                           ings with regard to timings.
                           Recorded 29.3.55
            p. [7]   Blank

(New end title) 17.M.2
The score is written on five double sheets of 28-stave music paper, measuring 43.7 x 30.5 cms.

The manuscript paper printer's mark is shown as J & W CHESTER LTD LONDON (within a circle).

17.M.2 (3'22")

20 pages – p. [i]   Title page
            pp. 1-19   Music: it contains red and blue pencil markings
                           with regard to timings.
                           Recorded 29.3.55

Advance our Standards 18.M.1
The score is written on five double sheets of 28-stave music paper, measuring 43.7 x 30.5 cms.

The manuscript paper printer's mark is shown as J & W CHESTER LTD. LONDON (within a circle).

18.M.1 (2'55")

20 pages – p. [i]   Title page
        pp. 1-18   Music: it contains red and blue pencil markings
                    with regard to timings.
                    Recorded 30.3.55
        p. [19]   Blank

Rescue my Lords or else the day is lost 18.M.2
The score is written on one double sheet of 24-stave music paper, measuring 37.8 x 27.3 cms.

18.M.2 (15")

4 pages – p. [i]   Title page
        pp. 1-3   Music: it contains green and red pencil mark-
                    ings with regard to timings.
                    Recorded 30.3.55

I have set my life upon a task 18.M.3
The score is written on two double sheets of 24-stave music paper, measuring 38 x 27.4 cms.

18.M.3 (39")

8 pages – p. [i]   Title page
        pp. 1-5   Music: it contains red pencil markings with
                    regard to timings. Recorded 30.3.55
        pp. [6-7]   Blank

Stanley and Richard clash/Richard's death 18.M.4 A and 18.M.4 B
The score is written on both sides of three single sheets of 28-stave music paper, measuring 44 x 30.5 cms.

The manuscript paper printer's mark is shown as J & W CHESTER LTD. LONDON (within a circle).

18.M.4 A (21") | and | 18.M.4 B (22")

6 pages – p. [i]   Title page (with sketches in pencil)
        pp. 1-3   Music
        p. [4]   Music. At the top of the page is 18.M.4 B (21")
                    to be recorded 'wild'! It contains black and
                    red pencil markings with regard to tim-
                    ings.
        p. [5]   Blank

End Title 18.M.4 C
The score is written on three double sheets and on both sides of one single sheet of 28-stave music paper, measuring 43.8 x 30.3 cms.

The manuscript paper printer's mark is shown as J & W CHESTER LTD. LONDON (within a circle).

18.M.4 C and End Titles (3'41")

14 pages – p. [i] Title page. There are also some instructions for the copyist.

pp. 1-12 Music: it contains number markings in green biro/black and red pencil markings with regard to timings.

p. [13] Blank: there are several pencil scribblings on this page with '393' written in black pencil – in the top right hand corner.

Muir Mathieson's score (for the printed Prelude) is sellotaped to parts of the original manuscript.

No date, place, dedication or signature of the composer apparent.

Unpublished

OTHER VERSIONS

Prelude:Richard III (C63a)
First edition [Full Score]
William Walton | PRELUDE | *RICHARD III* | FULL SCORE OXFORD UNIVERSITY PRESS | MUSIC DEPARTMENT 44 CONDUIT STREET LONDON W.1

35 pages. 251 x 177 mm
Stiff orange paper wrappers. Lettered in white. Trimmed edges.

Publication: Published 27 Febraury 1964 at 14/-

Prelude: Richard III - arranged for military band (C63b)
First edition [Piano Conductor]
No title page

9 pages. 310 x 233 mm
Stiff light and royal blue wrappers. Lettered in similar colours Trimmed edges.

Publication: Published [by Boosey & Hawkes Ltd. as QMB 291] 15 May 1973 at .50 per set.

A Shakespeare Suite: Richard III (C63c)
First edition [Score]
William Walton | A SHAKESPEARE SUITE | 'RICHARD III' |
OXFORD UNIVERSITY PRESS | MUSIC DEPARTMENT 44
CONDUIT STREET LONDON W.1

39 pages. 254 x 178 mm
Stiff red paper wrappers. Lettered in lemon. Trimmed edges.

Publication: Published 19 March 1964 at 16/-

Three Pieces for Organ from Richard III (C63e)
First edition [Score]
No title page

7 pages. 311 x 232 mm
White paper covers. Lettered in black. Trimmed edges.

Publication: 3000 copies published 6 June 1963 (in the Oxford Organ
Music Series) at 4/-

ROARING FANFARE (C93)

Holograph in pencil.

The unbound score is written on one double sheet of 24-stave music
paper, measuring 45.7 x 33 cms.

Roaring Fanfare for the inauguration of the new terrace at the Lion
House - the London Zoo, June 1976 | W W | for 3 Trpts | 5 Trb 2 Perc.

4 pages –	p. [i]	Title page
	pp. 1-2	Music. 50" - 55" appears at the end of the music after the double bar line.
	p. [3]	Blank

No place or signature of the composer apparent. Initialled on the title
page.
The date (June 1976) is given on the title page.
Dedication at the head of the music on page 1.

Present location: Lord Zuckerman

Unpublished

ROMEO AND JULIET (C18)

Ballet in two tableaux by Constant Lambert, orchestrated by Walton.
British Library Loan MS 92, 1 and 2

SALUTE TO SIR ROBERT MAYER ON HIS 100TH BIRTHDAY (C97)

For 12 trumpets in B flat (an introduction to the National Anthem)

Details from a copy:
Holograph in pencil (?)

The score is written on a single sheet of music paper, measuring 32.5 x 23.5 cms.

2 pages – p. [1]   Music
p. [2]   Blank

Present location: PML Koch manuscript 620

First edition [Score]
No title page

4 pages. 255 x 176 mm
Stiff russet paper wrappers. Lettered in white. Trimmed edges.

Publication: Published 5 June 1980 by OUP at 1.95

Also included with Walton's setting of the National Anthem (C60)

No title page

5 pages. 296 x 209 mm
Stiff white paper wrappers. Lettered in blue and black with a union flag featured in red, blue and white. Trimmed edges.

Publication: Published 3 March 1988 by OUP at 3.50

SCAPINO (C40)

Overture for Orchestra

The following is taken from a photocopy

Holograph in ink (?)

The score is written on 32-stave music paper, measuring 48 x 32.8 cms.

For | Dr. F.A. Stock and the Chicago Symphony Orchestra | in commemoration of the 50th Anniversary of its foundation | [First reproduction of an etching by Callot : Balli de Sfessania] Scapino | a | Comedy Overture | for | full orchestra (after an etching from Jacques Callot's 'Balli di Sfessania' 1622) | by | William Walton | [Second reproduction after an etching by Callot : Scapino]

76 pages – p. [i]   Title page

pp. 1-75   Music

Dedication on the title page.
Signed on the title page. Place indicated/dated thus: 'London' 28.12.40

Present location: the estate of the late Lady Clark of Saltwood

Unpublished

Revised version (1950)
Holograph in ink.

The score, bound in blue leather covers, is written on 32-stave music paper, measuring 48 x 31.6 cms.

For | Dr. F.A. Stock and the Chicago Symphony Orchestra | in commemoration of the 50th anniversary of its foundation | SCAPINO | a | Comedy Overture | for | full orchestra | (after an etching from Jacques Callot's 'Balli di Sfessania' (1622) | by | William Walton

Incomplete:	p. [i]	Instrumentation required
	p. [ii]	Title page
	pp. 1-19	–
	pp. 26-33	Music
	pp. 38-39	–

Dedication on the title page.
Signed on the tile page. Place indicated/dated thus: 'London' 28.12.40

Present location: PML Koch manuscript 625

First edition [Full Score – revised version]
SCAPINO | A COMEDY OVERTURE FOR FULL ORCHESTRA | By | WILLIAM WALTON | *(after an etching from J.Callot's 'Balli di Sfessania', 1622)* | [Rule] | SCAPINO is one of the less familiar characters of the | Commedia dell'Arte, the hero of Molière's 'Les four - | beries de Scapin,' who may figure in the complicated | ancestry of Figaro. We owe him the word 'escapade', | which is descriptive of the character's stock-in-trade. | Callot's etching, reproduced on the cover, portrays him | in his traditional costume | [Rule] | OXFORD UNIVERSITY PRESS | 44 CONDUIT STREET, LONDON, W.1

68 pages. 357 x 256 mm
Buff stiff paper covers with reproduction of Callot's etching.
Lettered in black. Trimmed edges.

Publication: Published 4 January 1951 at 42/-

SET ME AS A SEAL UPON THINE HEART (C35)

Anthem for unaccompanied mixed chorus

Whereabouts of holograph unknown

First edition [Vocal Score]
No title page. Published by Oxford University Press, London in the 'Oxford Anthems' series (A 86)

4 pages. 258 x 177 mm
White stiff paper. Lettered in black. Trimmed edges.

Publication: Published 1 December 1938 at 6d.

SIESTA (C19)

for small orchestra

Whereabouts of holograph unknown.
A printed copy of the score was used by the composer in 1962 to make minor revisions (in pencil and biro). The dedication was erased in pencil and W.T.Walton changed to William Walton.

First edition [Full Score]
No title page

12 pages. 340 x 254 mm
Stiff paper wrappers with cover designed by Severini in green and white. Lettered in black. Trimmed edges.

Publication: 250 copies published 10 October 1929 by OUP at 5/-

– – – – – [Score with minor revisions]

WILLIAM WALTON | SIESTA | FOR | SMALL ORCHESTRA | FULL SCORE OXFORD UNIVERSITY PRESS | MUSIC DEPART-MENT 44 CONDUIT STREET LONDON W.1

14 pages. 254 x 178 mm
Stiff purple paper wrappers. Lettered in white. Trimmed edges.

Publication: 1000 copies published 19 September 1963 at 7/6

– – – – – [Arranged for piano (4 hands) by the composer]

No title page

12 pages. 346 x 256 mm Stiff paper wrappers with cover designed by Severini in green and white. Lettered in black. Trimmed edges.

Publication: 250 copies published 13 July 1928 by OUP at 5/-

SINFONIA CONCERTANTE (C21)

For orchestra with piano 'continuo'

Holograph (part) in ink.

The unbound score is written on twenty-five double sheets of 30-stave music paper, measuring 44.6 x 29 cms.

SINFONIA CONCERTANTE | for | orchestra | with | PIANOFORTE (CONTINUO) | by | WILLIAM WALTON

100 pages – p. [i]   Title page
         p. [ii]   Blank
         p. [1]   Blank
         pp. [2-45] First movement (not in Walton's hand)
         pp. [46-49] Blank
         pp. [50-61] Second movement
         pp. [62-89] Third movement
         pp. [90-98] Blank

No dedication apparent.

Signed by the composer on the title page.

Present location: PML Koch manuacript 587A

First edition [Full Score]

No title page

82 pages. 346 x 257 mm

Stiff paper wrappers with cover designed by Severini in green and white. Lettered in black. Trimmed edges.

Publication: © 1928 by OUP at 21/-

– – – – – [Arranged for 2 pianos by the composer]

No title page

40 pages. 347 x 256 mm

Stiff paper wrappers with cover designed by Severini in green and white. Lettered in black. Trimmed edges.

Publication: © 1928 by OUP at 7/6d

Revised version (1943)

Holograph in pencil.

The manuscript, bound in blue cloth covers, is written on 24-stave music paper, measuring 43.5 x 30 cms.

Sinfonia Concertante | for | orchestra (with pianoforte obbligato) | William Walton | (1926-27, revised 1943)

74 pages – p. [i]   Title page
      pp. 1-35   First movement
      pp. 36-47   Second movement
      pp. 48-69   Third movement
      pp. [70-73] Blank

No dedication.
Signed by the composer on the title page.

Present location: PML Koch manuscript 587B

First edition [Full score]
Sinfonia Concertante | for Orchestra | WITH PIANO OBBLIGATO | WILLIAM WALTON | Price 15/- net | OXFORD UNIVERSITY PRESS

88 pages. 246 x 188 mm
Stiff orange paper wrappers. Lettered in grey and blue. Trimmed edges.

Publication: Published 18 June 1953 at 15/-

– – – – – [Arranged for 2 pianos by Roy Douglas]
No title page

40 pages. 304 x 236 mm
Stiff paper wrappers with cover designed by Severini in green and white. Lettered in black. Trimmed edges.

Publication: Published 4 September 1947 by OUP at 10/6

SONATA FOR VIOLIN AND PIANO (C55)

Details taken from a copy:
Holograph in pencil (?)

The score is written on ten double sheets of 12-stave music paper, measuring 34.5 x 20.6 cms.

To Diana and Griselda | SONATA | for Violin and Piano | by | William Walton | 1949

40 pages – p. [i]   Title page
      pp. 1-34   Music
      pp. 35-36 (but numbered 31-32) New manuscript
      pp. [37-39] Blank

Signed and dated on the title page.

No place apparent.

Present location: The Walton Museum, Ischia

First edition [Score]
WILLIAM WALTON | SONATA | FOR | VIOLIN and PIANO | OXFORD UNIVERSITY PRESS

42 pages. 309 x 242 mm
Stiff paper wrappers with cover designed by Severini in green and white. Lettered in black. Trimmed edges.

Publication: Published 11 May 1950 at 12/6

– – – – – [Solo violin part]

To Diana and Griselda | SONATA | for Violin and Piano | Violin part edited by | Yehudi Menuhin | WILLIAM WALTON | NOTE | WHEREVER I have marked bowings in brackets, they indicate a practical | violinist's solution of the ideal phrasing set down by the composer. Thus | (V) in the middle of a ⌒ indicates one change of bow at | that point. | I firmly believe the composer's markings should always remain available | to all interpreters. | Y.MENUHIN

14 pages. 309 x 239 mm
Stiff white paper covers. Lettered in black. Trimmed edges.

Publication: Published and included with the above.

A SONG FOR THE LORD MAYOR'S TABLE (C74)

Holograph in pencil.

1. *The Lord Mayor's Table*

The unbound score is written on two double and on both sides of one single sheet of 12-stave music paper, measuring 33.2 x 23.8 cms.

The manuscript paper printer's mark is shown as Stamp.music f.11i de Marino-Piazza Plebiscito

In Honour of the City of London | A SONG FOR THE LORD MAYOR'S TABLE | A song-cycle devised by Christopher Hassall | music by William Walton | No.I The Lord Mayor's Table Thomas Jordan

10 pages – p. [i]   Title page. The printed words of the verse were formerly sellotaped to the lower half of the title page.

pp. 1-7   Music
p. [8]   Music
p. 9   [but numbered as 8] Music

2. *Glide Gently*
The unbound score is written on one double sheet of 12-stave music paper, measuring 33.2 x 23.8 cms.

The manuscript paper printer's mark is shown as Stamp.music f.11i de Marino Napoli-Piazza Plebiscito

II | W.Wordsworth Glide Gently

4 pages –   p. [i]   Title page. The printed words of the verse are
                        sellotaped to the title page.
            pp.[1-3]   Music

3. *Wapping Old Stairs*
The unbound score is written on two double sheets of 12-stave music paper, measuring 33.2 x 26.5 cms.

The manuscript paper printer's mark is shown as G.Schirmer. Single No.9 – 12 staves with Braces. Printed in the U.S.A.

III | (Anon) Wapping Old Stairs | 1790

8 pages –   p. [i]   Title page. The printed words of the verse are
                        sellotaped to the title page.
            pp. 1-5   Music
            pp. [6-7]   Blank

4. *Holy Thursday*
The unbound score is written on one double sheet of 12-stave music paper, measuring 33.2 x 26.4 cms.

The manuscript paper printer's mark is shown as G.Schirmer. Single No.9-12 staves with Braces. Printed in the U.S.A.

No title page: No.IV Holy Thursday (William Blake) | 1789 at the head of page [1]

4 pages –   pp. [1-4]   Music

5. *The Contrast*
The unbound score is written on two double sheets of 12-stave music paper, measuring 33.8 x 25.5 cms.

The manuscript paper printer's mark is shown as Hug & Co. No.12 4 linig

The Contrast (Charles Morris 1798)
8 pages –   p. [i]   Title page. The printed words of the verse are

sellotaped to the title page.

pp.[1-7]   Music

6. *Rhyme*

The unbound score is written on two double sheets of 12-stave music paper, measuring 33.8 x 25.5 cms.

The manuscript paper printer's mark is shown as Hug & Co. No.12 4 linig

No VI Rhyme (Anon 18th century)

8 pages –   p. [i]   Title page
            pp.[1-5]   Music. At the bottom of p. [1], there is a foot-
                        note : * The vowels to be repeated ga-(a)y etc.
            pp.[6-7]   Blank

No date or place apparent.
Dedication on the first page.
Signed by the composer on the first title page.

Present location: PML Koch manuscript 602

First edition [Vocal Score]
WILLIAM WALTON | A SONG FOR THE | LORD MAYOR'S TABLE | A song cycle devised by | *CHRISTOPHER HASSALL* | OXFORD UNIVERSITY PRESS | MUSIC DEPARTMENT, 44 CONDUIT STREET, LONDON, W.1

32 pages. 308 x 242 mm
Stiff turquoise paper wrappers. Lettered in blue and white. Trimmed edges.
Also featured is a black and white reproduction of the engraving taken from a 'Panorama of London' (1749), by S and N Buck, now in the Guildhall Library, London.

Publication: 1000 copies published 4 April 1963 at 12/6

OTHER VERSIONS

Arrangement for soprano and small orchestra (1970)
Holograph in pencil.

The score, bound in a brown flimsy cover with a reinforced spine, is written on 22 double sheets of 24-stave music paper, measuring 43.2 x 30.2 cms.

The manuscript paper printer's mark is shown as G.B.T. Marchio Depositato.

A Song for the Lord Mayor's Table | a song cycle devised by | Christopher Hassall

88 pages – p. [i]   Title page
         p. [ii]   Instrumentation
         p. [iii]   Blank
         pp. 1-20   The Lord Mayor's Table (Jordan): Music
         pp. 21-26 Glide Gently (Wordsworth): Music
         pp. 27-38 Wapping Old Stairs (Anon): Music
         pp. 39-50 Holy Thursday (Blake): Music
         pp. 51-69 The Contrast (Morris): Music
         p. 70   Half title page: 'VI Rhyme' (Anon - 18th century)
         pp. 71-85 Rhyme (Anon): Music

No date, dedication or signature of the composer apparent.

Present location: PML Koch manuscript 602

Unpublished

THE STAR SPANGLED BANNER/ GOD SAVE THE QUEEN (C64)

Arranged for orchestra

Whereabouts of holograph unknown

Unpublished

SYMPHONY NO 1 (C27)

for orchestra

Holograph in ink.

The score (bound in buff coloured hard paper covers) is written on 28-stave music paper, measuring 44.7 x 31 cms (first movement) and 28-stave music paper, measuring 39.6 x 28.6 cms (second, third and fourth movements).

To Imma | Freifau Von Doernberg | Symphony | William Walton | MCMXXXIII

192 pages – p. [i]   Title page
         pp. 1-58   First movement
         pp. [ii-v] Blank
         pp. 59-105 Second movement
         pp. [vi-x] Blank

pp. 106-125 Third movement
pp. [xi-xii] Blank
— — — — — — — — — — — — — —
pp. 1-53   Fourth movement
pp. [xiii-xiv] Blank

Dedication on the title page – not in Walton's hand.
No signature nor date apparent, except that on the title page.

Present location: PML Koch manuscript 593

First edition [Full Score]
WILLIAM WALTON | SYMPHONY | FULL SCORE | OXFORD
UNIVERSITY PRESS

193 pages. 343 x 260 mm
Stiff paper wrappers with cover designed by Severini in green and
white. Lettered in black. Trimmed edges.

Publication: 100 copies published 21 May 1936 at 42/-

– – – – – [Miniature Score]

WILLIAM WALTON | SYMPHONY | MINIATURE SCORE |
OXFORD UNIVERSITY PRESS
193 pages. 180 x 130 mm
Stiff paper wrappers with cover designed by Severini in green and
white. Lettered in black. Trimmed edges.

Publication: 1000 copies published 16 April 1936 at 5/-

– – – – – [Arranged for piano duet by Herbert Murrill]

No title page 112 pages. 309 x 240 mm
Stiff paper wrappers with cover designed by Severini in green and
white. Lettered in black. Trimmed edges.

Publication: Published 2 September 1937 by OUP at 7/6

SYMPHONY NO 2 (C68)

For orchestra

Holograph in pencil.

The score, bound in blue cloth covers, is written on 32-stave music
paper, measuring 47.9 x 33 cms.

The mansucript paper printer's mark is shown as G. RICORDI & C

Symphony No.2 | William Walton | Dedicated to the Royal Liverpool
Philharmonic Society | which commissioned this work

126 pages – p. [i]   Title page
       p. [ii]   Blank
       p. [iii]   Half title page: I
       pp. 1-52   Music: First movement. At the end of the music on p.52, Walton indicates the timing of this movement thus: 8'-0"c. Also indicated is the date: Jan '59, revised Feb. March '60. Forio d'Ischia
       p. [iv]   Blank
       p. [v]   Half title page: II
       pp. 53-71   Music: Second movement. At the end of the music on p.71, Walton indicates the timing of this movement thus: 9'-45"c. Also indicated is the date: Jan-Feb '60. Forio d'Ischia
       p. [vi]   Half title page: III
       pp. 72-117 Music: Third movement. At the end of the music on p.117, Walton indicates the timing of this movement thus 8'30"c.
       p. 118   Blank
       pp. [119-120] Blank

The date and place are also indicated at the end of the third movement (on p.117) as 22.7.60: Forio d'Ischia.
Dedication on the title page.
Signed by the composer on the title page.

Present location: PML Koch manuscript 634

First edition [Full Score]
Dedicated to the Royal Liverpool Philharmonic Society | SYMPHONY NO.2 | WILLIAM WALTON | MOVEMENTS | *Allegro molto p.1* | *Lento assai p.81* | *Passacaglia: Theme, Variations,* | *Fugato, and Coda-Scherzando p.114* | OXFORD UNIVERSITY PRESS | MUSIC DEPARTMENT 44 CONDUIT STREET LONDON W.1

173 pages. 265 x 187 mm
Stiff light blue, dark blue and white paper wrappers. Lettered in dark blue and white. Trimmed edges.

Publication: Published 1 December 1960 at 30/-

TELL ME WHERE IS FANCY BRED (C2)

For soprano and tenor voices, 3 violins and piano

Holograph in ink.

The unbound score is written on two double sheets of 7-stave music paper, measuring 18 x 23.5 cms.

No title page

8 pages – pp. [1-7] Music. It is marked 'Allegro vivace' and is 47
bars in length.
        p. [8] Blank

No dedication apparent.
It is dated 'July 2nd 1916' and signed by the composer at the end of the music, after the double bar line.

Present location: Manuscript Collections, The British Library (Reference Division), Add MS 52384

Unpublished

THEME FOR ORGAN IMPROVISATION (Adagio) (No C number allocated)

Submitted to André Marchal as one of four improvised movements on the occasion of his recital to The Organ Music Society on 12 November 1936. The subject of the Fugue was written by *Alan Bush*, the theme for the Adagio by *Walton*, the theme for the Scherzo by *Benjamin Britten* and the theme for the Toccata by *Constant Lambert*.

Whereabouts of holograph unknown

Unpublished

THEME (for Variazioni) FOR 'CELLO SOLO (C85)

Details from a copy:
Holograph in pencil (?)

The score is written on a single sheet of 12-stave music paper. It was later bound with the other manuscripts in red leather for presentation to the Prince of Wales.

2 pages – p. [1] Music
        p. [2] Blank

Signed by the composer below the double bar line and dated '25.4.70'
No place apparent.

Present location: The Prince of Wales

Unpublished

THREE SISTERS (C83)

Music for the film

Holograph in pencil

1. The unbound score is written on two double sheets of 24-stave music paper, measuring 42 x 30 cms.

Opening titles

8 pages –   p. [i]   Title page
            pp. 1-7   Music (Duration: 2'30")

2. The unbound score is written on five double sheets of 24-stave music paper, measuring 42 x 30 cms.

Dream Sequence

20 pages –   p. [i]   Title page
             pp. 1-18   Music (Duration: 2'43")
             p. [19]   Blank

3. The unbound score is written on one double sheet of 24-stave music paper, measuring 42 x 30 cms.

End Titles

4 pages –   p. [i]   Title page
            pp. 1-2   Music (Duration: 55")
            p. [3]   Blank

No date, place, dedication or signature of the composer apparent.

Present location: British Lion Films Ltd.

Unpublished

THREE SONGS (1918) (No C number allocated)

Details taken from a copy:

1. *Child Song*

Holograph in pencil (?)

The unbound score is written on one double sheet of 12-stave music paper, measuring 32.5 x 23.5 cms.

4 pages –   p. [i]   Title page (?)
            pp. [1-3]   Music

Signed by the composer at the top of p. [1]

No place apparent and the date is given as 'July 1918'

2. *A Lyke Wake Song*

Holograph in pencil (?)

The unbound score is written on one double sheet of 14-stave music paper, measuring 34.5 x 27.5 cms.

4 pages –   p. [i]   Title page (?)
            pp. [1-3]   Music

Signed by the composer at the top of p. [1]
No place given and the date is given as 'July 1918'

3. *Song*

Holograph in pencil (?)

The unbound score is written on one double sheet of 12-stave music paper, measuring 30.5 x 23 cms.

4 pages –   p. [i]   Title page (?)
            pp. [1-3]   Music

No signature or place apparent.
The date is given as 'July 1918'

Present location: unable to trace

Unpublished

THREE SONGS (1932) (C26)

Whereabouts of holograph unknown

First edition [Vocal Score]
No title page

18 pages. 310 x 243 mm
Stiff paper wrappers with cover designed by Severini in green and white. Lettered in black. Trimmed edges.

Publication: Published 13 October 1932 by OUP at 4/6

TITLE MUSIC FOR THE BBC TV SHAKESPEARE SERIES (C96)

Details taken from a copy:
Holograph in black felt-tipped pen (?)

The unbound score is written on one single sheet of 12-stave music paper, measuring 43.5 x 30 cms.

2 pages – p. [1]   Music
         p. [2]   Blank

No signature, place or date apparent.

Present location: PML Koch manuscript 619

Unpublished

TOCCATA FOR VIOLIN AND PIANO (C13)

Holograph in ink.

The unbound score is written on nine double sheets of 12-stave music paper, measuring 31.3 x 23.3 cms.

The manuscript paper printer's mark is shown as R.C.1 with a ship within a circle underneath it.

TOCCATA | for | Violin and pianoforte | W.T.Walton (Also in the top right of the title page is written: Return to | The British Music Society | 3 Berners Street | LONDON W1)

36 pages – p. [i]   Title page
         pp. 1-28   Music
         pp. [29-35] Blank

No dedication apparent.
Signed by the composer on the title page and initialled ('WTW') at the foot of page 28.

Present location: PML Koch manuscript 592

Unpublished

TRITONS (C8)

Song for voice and piano

Holograph in ink.

The unbound score is written on both sides of two single sheets of 12-stave music paper, measuring 30.1 x 24.1 cms.

No title page

4 pages – pp. [1-3]   Music. There are alterations in red ink.
         p. [4]   Music (in Walton's hand but erased)

No dedication apparent.
Signed and dated ('1920') by the composer at the top of page [1]

Present location: PML Koch manuscript 589

First edition [Vocal Score]
No title page.

7 pages. 310 x 235 mm
White stiff paper wrappers. Lettered in black. Trimmed edges.

Publication: © 1921 by J & W Curwen at 2/-

Republished by Oxford University Press in 1985

No title page

4 pages. 306 x 232 mm
Stiff black, grey and white paper wrappers. Lettered in black and white.
Trimmed edges.

Publication: © 1985 at 1.95

THE TRIUMPH OF NEPTUNE (C20)

Numbers of this Sitwell/Berners ballet orchestrated by Walton
British Library Loan MS 75, 12 and 13

TROILUS AND CRESSIDA (C62)

Opera in three acts

Holograph in pencil.

The score (each act is bound separately in blue cloth covers) is written
on

Act I –   32-stave music paper,
Act II –   32-stave music paper,
Act III –   32-stave music paper,

measuring 47 x 31 cms.

Troilus and Cressida | by | William Walton | Act I

184 pages – p. [i]   Title page
               p. [ii]   Characters and details of the action for Act I
               pp. 1-182 Music: Act I
_ _ _ _ _ _ _ _ _ _ _ _ _ _

Act II
172 pages – p. [i]   Title page
               pp. 1-171 Music: Act II
_ _ _ _ _ _ _ _ _ _ _ _ _ _

No title page

166 pages - pp. 1-166 Music: Act III

– – – – – – – – – – – – – –

Dated '13.9.54' at the end of the score.
No place indicated.
Dedicated 'To my wife' at the end of the score.
Signed by the composer on the first title page.

Present location: PML Koch manuscript 580

First edition [Vocal Score]
TROILUS AND | CRESSIDA | *Opera in Three Acts* | Libretto by |
CHRISTOPHER HASSALL | German translation by ERNST ROTH |
Music by | WILLIAM WALTON | Vocal Score, Price 3.3s.0d.net|
OXFORD UNIVERSITY PRESS | MUSIC DEPARTMENT | 44 Con-
duit Street, London W.1 | NEW YORK TORONTO | 114 Fifth Avenue

360 pages. 310 x 242 mm
Stiff grey and white paper wrappers with a photograph (taken by
Wilfred Newton), on the front cover, of the first meeting of Troilus
and Cressida in Act I, showing Magda Lazlo and Richard Lewis in the
original production of the opera in London. Lettered in white and
blue. Trimmed edges.

Publication: Published 15 December 1955 at 63/-

– – – – – [Libretto]

WILLIAM WALTON | TROILUS AND | CRESSIDA | OPERA IN
THREE ACTS | *LIBRETTO BY* | CHRISTOPHER HASSALL |
OXFORD UNIVERSITY PRESS | 1954

71 pages. 182 x 124 mm
Stiff light and royal blue paper wrappers. Lettered in light and royal
blue. Trimmed edges.

Publication: Published 25 November 1954 at 3/6

– – – – – [Libretto in Italian]

WILLIAM WALTON | TROILO E CRESSIDA | OPER IN TRE
ATTI | LIBRETTO DI | CHRISTOPHER HASSALL | VERSIONE
RITMICA ITALIANA DI | EUGENIO MONTALE | PROPRIETA
PER L'IMPERO BRITANNICO, U.S.A. E CANADA | OXFORD
UNIVERSITY PRESS | PER TUTTI GLI ALTRI PAESI | BOOSEY
AND HAWKES LONDON | RAPPRESTANTI PER L'ITALIA |
CARISCH S.p.A. - MILANO

68 pages. 188 x 142 mm
Stiff grey paper wrappers. Lettered in dark blue and grey.
Trimmed edges.

Publication: unable to trace

– – – – – [Vocal Score: revised edition]

Troilus and Cressida | [treble rule] | Opera in three acts | [rule] Libretto by Christopher Hassall | German translation by Ernst Roth | Italian translation by Eugenio Montale | [treble rule] | Music by William Walton | [treble rule] | Vocal score (revised version) | Oxford University Press | Music Department, 37 Dover Street London W1X 4AH

315 pages. 310 x 232 mm
Stiff blue wrappers. Lettered in red, gold and green. Trimmed edges.

Publication: © 1980 at 30.00

– – – – – [Libretto: revised edition]

WILLIAM WALTON | TROILUS & CRESSIDA | Opera in three acts | *Libretto by* | CHRISTOPHER HASSALL| Oxford University Press

52 pages. 208 x 145 mm
Stiff maroon and white paper wrappers. Lettered in white. Trimmed edges.

Publication: Published 4 November 1976 at 1.25

Derived publication
Put off the Serpent Girdle
Song for 3-part unaccompanied female voices, taken from Act II

First edition [Vocal Score]
No title page. Published by Oxford University Press, London in the 'Oxford Choral Songs' series (no. W74)

3 pages. 255 x 178 mm
White stiff paper. Lettered in black. Trimmed edges.

Publication: 3000 copies published 28 September 1967 at 10d.

THE TWELVE (C77)

Anthem for mixed chorus and organ

Holograph in pencil.

The unbound score is written on eight double sheets of 16-stave music paper, measuring 34 x 23.7 cms.

The manuscript paper has been used upside down, the manuscript paper printer's mark is shown (in the top right hand corner) as 16 Stamp. music f.11i de Marino-Napoli-Porticato S.Francesca di Paola.

32 pages – p. [i] For not less than: 16 Trebles | 4 Altos | 4 Tenors | 4 Basses | and | Organ
p. [ii] Title page: To Christ Church Oxford | The Twelve | An Anthem | words by W.H. Auden | music by William Walton
pp.1-21)
p. 21 [sic]) Music
pp.22-29)

Present location: The Bodleian Library, Oxford

First edition [Vocal Score]
William Walton | THE TWELVE | *Words by* W.H.AUDEN | [Bar] | ORCHESTRATION | Double woodwind Tuba | 4 Horns Timpani | 2 Trumpets Percussion | 3 Trombones Harp | Strings | Duration 11 minutes | Full scores and orchestral parts are on hire | The work was given its first performance (with organ) | on 16 May 1965 by the choir of Christ Church, Oxford, | directed by Sidney Watson. | [Bar] | OXFORD UNIVERSITY PRESS | MUSIC DEPARTMENT 44 CONDUIT STREET LONDON W.1

30 pages. 254 x 176 mm
Stiff brown paper wrappers. Lettered in lemon. Trimmed edges.

Publication: Published 20 January 1966 at 6/-

OTHER VERSIONS

Orchestral version of the organ part (C77a)
Holograph in pencil.

The unbound score is written on both sides of 23 single sheets of 24-stave music paper, measuring 40 x 30 cms.

The manuscript paper printer's mark is shown as GBT MARCHIO DEPOSITATO

The Twelve | An anthem for the feast of any Apostle | words by W.H.Auden | music by William Walton

46 pages – p. [i] Title page
pp.1-45 Music

No date, place or dedication apparent.
Signed by the composer on the title page.

Present location: PML Koch manuscript 599

Unpublished

TWO PIECES FOR VIOLIN AND PIANO (C56)

Whereabouts of holograph unknown

First edition [Score]
TWO PIECES | FOR VIOLIN AND PIANO | Duration: 5 minutes |
WILLIAM WALTON

13 pages. 310 x 230 mm
Stiff paper wrappers with cover designed by Severini in green and
white. Lettered in black. Trimmed edges.

Publication: 1500 copies published 22 March 1951 by OUP at 5/-

– – – – – [Solo violin part]

No title page

3 pages. 309 x 239 mm
Stiff white paper wrappers. Lettered in black. Trimmed edges.

Publication: Published and included with the above

VALSE IN C MINOR (C5)

for solo piano

Holograph in ink

The unbound score is written on one side of a single sheet of music
paper, measuring 44 x 30 cms.

2 pages – p. [1] Music
p. [ii] Blank

No dedication or place apparent.
Signed by the composer at the top of and at the end of the music and
dated 'Feb 2nd 1917'.

Present location: Christ Church College Library, Oxford

Unpublished

VARIATION ON AN ELIZABETHAN THEME (SELLINGER'S ROUND) (C61)

Holograph in pencil.

The score is written on four double sheets of 16-stave music paper,
measuring 33 x 23 cms.

The whole manuscript, consisting of 7 items, is unbound and kept in a folder.

Finale to a set of variations on 'Sellinger's Round' | William Walton.

In the top right hand corner, in ballpoint pen, is written: 'Please return to | Festival Manager | 11 High Street | ALDEBURGH | Suffolk'
In the top left hand corner, in pencil, is written 'VARIATION 6'.
Neither is in Walton's hand.

16 pages – p. [i]	Title page
pp. 1-13	Music
pp. 14-15	Blank

No dedication. Only the first variation is dated: '1953'.
No place given.
Signed by the composer on the title page.

Present location: The James Marshall and Marie-Louise Osborn Collection, Yale University Library, New Haven, Connecticut, U.S.A.

Unpublished

VARIATIONS ON A THEME BY HINDEMITH (C76)

For orchestra

Holograph in pencil.

The score, bound in blue cloth covers, is written on 32-stave music paper, measuring 47.6 x 32.5 cms.

The manuscript paper printer's mark is shown as G.RICORDI & C

To | Paul and Gertrud Hindemith | Variations on a Theme by Hindemith | written in honour of the 150th Anniversary of the Royal Philharmonic Society | by William Walton

112 pages –p. [i]	Title page
p. [ii]	Blank
p. 1	Tema
p. [2]	Blank
pp. 1-4	Tema (1'48"c. indicated as its timing). Page 1 is a new, substituted page, with an indication at the foot (in Walton's hand) that the *theme* is taken 'from the 2nd movement of Hindemith's Concerto for Violoncello and Orchestra (1940). By permission of Edition Schott, Mainz.'
pp. 5-16	I (1.45c.)

pp. 17-28	II (1.37)
pp. 29-34	III (1.43c.)
pp. 35-42	IV (45c.)
pp. 43-48	V (1.57c.)
pp. 49-59	VI (1.2c.)
pp. 60-68	VII (3.0c.) Towards the bottom of p.66, written in Walton's hand on the top line of the 27th stave, is: '* quotation from the opera Mathis der Maler'
pp. 69-74	VIII (40)
pp. 75-77	IX (40c.)
pp. 77-96	Finale
pp. 96-103	Coda
pp. [104-108]	Blank

Date and place indicated as thus: 'Forio 6.2.63' – it is written under the last bar on p.103 on the top of the 32nd stave.

Dedication on the title page.
Signed by the composer on the title page.

Present location: PML Koch manuscript 600

First edition [Full Score]
To Paul and Gertrud Hindemith | VARIATIONS | ON A THEME BY HINDEMITH | Written in honour of the 150th Anniversary | of the Royal Philharmonic Society | *by* William Walton | OXFORD UNIVERSITY PRESS | MUSIC DEPARTMENT 44 CONDUIT STREET LONDON W.1

134 pages. 253 x 175 mm
Stiff blue paper wrappers. Lettered in white. Trimmed edges.

Publication: Published 31 October 1963 at 30/-

WENT THE DAY WELL? (C47)

Music for the film

Whereabouts of holograph unknown.
A sketch for the main and end titles [A March] in short score is held by the present author.

Holograph in pencil.

The sketch is written on one side of a single sheet of 14-stave music paper, measuring 36.4 x 27 cms.

No date or signature apparent.

Unpublished

WHAT CHEER? (C73)

Christmas carol for unaccompanied mixed chorus

Whereabouts of holograph unknown

First edition [Vocal Score]
The Oxford Choral Songs | OXFORD UNIVERSITY PRESS.MUSIC
DEPARTMENT. 44 CONDUIT STREET. LONDON, W.1 | X90
S.A.T.B. (Unacc.) 8d net | *WILLIAM WALTON* | WHAT CHEER? |
A CHRISTMAS CAROL | for unaccompanied mixed voices | Words
from Richard Hill's Commonplace Book (*16th C.*)

4 pages. 254 x 177 mm
White stiff paper wrappers. Lettered in black. Trimmed edges.

Publication: 3000 copies published 24 August 1961 in *Carols for Choirs I*
at 8/6
Published 23 August 1962, separately, at 8d.

WHERE DOES THE UTTERED MUSIC GO? (C52)

For unaccompanied mixed chorus

Holograph in pencil.

The score is written on two double and one single sheet of 16-stave
music paper, measuring 34.29 x 27.30 cms.
The manuscript is not bound but kept in a green card cover.

The manuscript paper printer's marks at the foot of the title page are
shown as follows:

(on the left)	SCHIRMER
	Imperial Brand
	No. 4-16 staves
	Printed in U.S.A.
(on the right)	A.G.Schirmer crest with the words
	LABORUM DULCE LENIMEN

For the Henry Wood Memorial Fund | Sir Henry Wood | a setting for
mixed voices of a poem by | John Masefield | to music | by William
Walton

Also on the title page is 'Prom 18/9/46 7.5 minutes' which is circled, and *'First Performed'* at the Sir Henry Wood *Memorial Service*, St. Sepulchre's Church, *26.4.46*, BBC Chorus (with Theatre Revue Chorus), Leslie Woodgate - Conductor (Timing - 8'20") in the bottom right hand corner. Neither are in Walton's autograph.

10 pages – p. [i]   Title page
         pp. 1-9   Music

Dedication on the title page.
Signed by the composer on the title page.

Present location: Royal Academy of Music, London (MS 320)

First edition [Vocal Score]
No title page

16 pages. 257 x 177 mm
White stiff paper wrappers. Lettered in black. Trimmed edges.

Publication: 1000 copies published 23 January 1947 by OUP at 1/4d

THE WINDS (C6)

Song for voice and piano

Whereabouts of holograph unknown

First edition [Vocal Score]
No title page

9 pages. 312 x 236 mm
White stiff paper wrappers. Lettered in black. Trimmed edges.

Publication: © 1921 by J & W Curwen at 2/-

Republished by OUP in 1985
No title page

7 pages. 306 x 232 mm
Black, grey and white stiff paper wrappers. Lettered in black and white.
Trimmed edges.

Publication: © 1985 at 1.95

THE WISE VIRGINS (C38)

Ballet in one act

Whereabouts of holograph unknown

First edition [Full Score of a suite from the ballet] (C38a)
No title page

68 pages. 266 x 189 mm
Stiff paper wrappers with cover designed by Severini in green and
white. Lettered in black. Trimmed edges.

Publication: Published 17 December 1942 by OUP at 17/6

– – – – – No 5 - Sheep may safely graze (C38c) [Full score - available
separately]

No title page

15 pages. 257 x 177 mm
Stiff paper wrappers with cover designed by Severini in green and
white. Lettered in black. Trimmed edges.

Publication: © 1942 by OUP at 5/6

OTHER VERSIONS

– – – – – No 4 - *Ah! how ephemeral:* arr. for 2 pianos (C38d)

No title page

9 pages. 309 x 230 mm
Stiff paper wrappers with cover designed by Severini in green and
white. Lettered in black. Trimmed edges.

Publication: Published 29 September 1960 by OUP at 7/6

Letters

Walton always maintained that he never wrote or collected letters. The situation is, however, very different. A rich, virtually unknown and untapped source exists which reveals many new facets and paints a further in-depth and fascinating picture of the composer.

This is therefore a first attempt to detail the whereabouts of these scattered collections which are arranged alphabetically by location. Notes are provided in some cases to describe certain collections.

Arts Council, London
Letters to John Denison, Music Director about *Orb and Sceptre* (C59)

British Broadcasting Corporation
Letters, memos, etc. about the commissioning of several works, including *Belshazzar's Feast* (C23), *Crown Imperial* (C32) and *Christopher Columbus* (C46)
Now at the BBC Written Archives Centre, Caversham

British Council, London
Letters to Arthur Bliss/ Ernest Makower about the *Violin Concerto* (C37)
Now at the Public Record Office, Kew

British Library, London
Letters to Adrian Boult
    (Manuscript Collections, Add. MS 60499)
Letters to Edward Clark
    (Manuscript Collections, Add. MS 52257)
Letters to Cecil Gray
    (Manuscript Collections, Add. MS 57787: Volume XIV)
Letters to the Royal Philharmonic Society
    (Manuscript Collections, Loan 48.13/38 (b))
Letters to Sir Henry and Lady Jessie Wood
    (Manuscript Collections, Add. MS 56422)

Britten-Pears Library, Aldeburgh
Letters to Benjamin Britten and Peter Pears

Craggs, Stewart, Sunderland
Letters to S R Craggs, 1966–1982

Drachman, Mrs D., USA
Letters to Gregor Piatigorsky about the *Cello Concerto* (C65)
(Copies deposited in the Library of Congress, Washington, DC)

Fleischmann, Professor Aloys, Ireland
Letters about the commissioning of *Cantico del Sole* (C90) and the 1974
Cork International Festival

Frank, Alan C., London
Private correspondence with the former Head of the Music Department at Oxford University Press

Humanities Research Center, University of Texas at Austin, USA
Letters to John Masefield and John Lehmann

Library of Congress, Washington DC, USA
Letter to Jascha Heifetz, dated 15 October 1939 about the *Violin Concerto* (C37)

Lutyens, Elisabeth, London
Letters to the late Elizabeth Lutyens

Marriner, Neville, London
Letters to Neville Marriner about the *Sonata for String Orchestra* (C53a)

Oxford University Press, Oxford
Various files of business letters between Walton and Hubert Foss,
Alan Frank, Norman Peterkin and Christopher Morris

Queen's University, Belfast
Letter to Leonard Hirsch, dated 23 May 1975 with a contribution to
his book on *Sir Hamilton Harty*

Rix, Diana, London
Letters to Diana Rix of Harold Holt, Ltd.

Sparkes, Diana, Southampton
Letters to her late father and mother, Hubert and Dora Foss

University of Missouri-Kansas City, USA
Postcard to Paul Creston, dated 30 September 1967

Westminster Abbey, London
Letters to William McKie about the *Coronation Te Deum* (C58) and other Coronation music
(Deposited in the Muniment Room and Library)

William Walton Museum, Ischia
A large collection of letters and other material exists at the Walton Museum. Included are original letters from:
    Peter Andry (EMI)
    Malcolm Arnold : volume 1 - 1954 to 1974
                     volume 2 - 1974 to 1978
    Adrian Boult
    Dallas Bower
    Stewart Craggs : volume 1 - General correspondence
                    volume 2 - Typed copy of vol 1 of SRC's thesis
                            on Walton and his music
    Paul Dehn
    Roy Douglas
    William Ferris
    Colin Graham
    Christopher Hassall: Original and carbon copied correspondence between Walton, Hassall and others including Alice Wimborne, Ernest Newman, Wystan Auden and Neville Cardus. In 23 volumes
    Edward Heath
    Harold Holt Ltd
    Elgar Howarth
    Walter Hussey
    Oliver Knussen
    Kevin McBeath
    Angus Morrison
    Laurence Olivier
    André Previn
    Queen Elizabeth II
    Karl Rickenbacher
    Mstislav Rostropovich
    Siegfried Sassoon

Lillias Sheepshanks
Edith Sitwell
Osbert Sitwell
Reresby Sitwell
Sacheverell Sitwell
George Szell
Michael Tippett
Alec Walton (brother)
Jo Walton (sister-in-law)
Louise Turner Walton (mother): volume 1 - 1910 to 1918
                                volume 2 - October 1918 to
                                1937
Susana Walton: original handwritten correspondence between
               Lady Walton and her family in Argentina -
               volume 1 - April 1972 to December 1976 vol-
               ume 2 - January 1977 to February 1983

Yale University, USA
Letters to Leonard Burkett, Artistic Director of the Boston Symphony
Orchestra
Letters to Bruce Simonds, Dean of the Yale School of Music

Recordings

This section about the recorded works is divided into the following:

I – A list of Walton's recorded works (arranged alphabetically by title), conducted by the composer, both 78 and 33rpm. Recording venues and dates are also supplied.

II – Walton as speaker. Details of interviews (arranged by date) which I have been able to trace from various sources. An indication is given of their whereabouts if copies still exist.

I. WORKS CONDUCTED BY WALTON

Belshazzar's Feast (C23)

1. Dennis Noble (bar.), Huddersfield Choral Society and the Liverpool Philharmonic Orchestra.

   Recorded in Philharmonic Hall, Liverpool, 3 and 10 January 1943

   HMV C 3330-4 (78 rpm: non-automatic)
   HMV C 7572-6 (78 rpm: automatic) Released March 1943
   VICTOR (USA) VM 974 (5) (78 rpm: automatic)

   Reissued in HMV ALP 1089 (mono, 33 rpm) Released December
   1953
   EMI ED 29 0715 1 (mono)
   ED 29 0715 4 (cassette) Released August 1986
   CDH7 63381–2 Released March 1992

2. Donald Bell (bar.), Philharmonia Chorus and Orchestra.

   Recorded in Kingsway Hall, London, 2, 3, 4 and 5 February 1959

   COLUMBIA CX 1679 (mono, 33 rpm) Released December 1959
   SAX 2319 (stereo, 33 rpm) Released March 1961
   ANGEL (USA) 35681
   ANGEL (USA) S 35681 Released c. September
   1960

   Reissued in EMI SXLP 30236 Released March 1977
   EMI SLS 5246 (stereo) Released 1982

Capriccio Burlesco (C80)

1. London Symphony Orchestra.
   Recorded in Walthamstow Assemby Hall, 13 April 1970
   LYRITA SRCS 49 (stereo, 33 rpm) Released June 1971
   SRCD 224 Released June 1992

Concerto for Viola and Orchestra (C22)

1. Frederick Riddle (viola) and the London Symphony Orchestra.

   Recorded in Kingsway Hall, London, 6 December 1937

   DECCA X199-201 (78 rpm) Released January 1938

2. William Primrose (viola) and the Philharmonia Orchestra.

Recorded in Abbey Road Studios, London, 22 and 23 July 1946

HMV DB 6309-11 (78 rpm: non-automatic)
DB 9036-8 (78 rpm: automatic) Released October 1946

Reissued in EMI EH 29 1276-1 (mono, 33 rpm)
EH 29 1276-4 (cassette)
CDH7 63828-2 (mono)

3. Yehudi Menuhin (viola) and the New Philharmonia Orchestra.

Recorded in Abbey Road Studios, London, 9 and 11 October 1968

HMV ASD 2542 (stereo, 33 rpm) Released March 1970
ANGEL (USA) 36719 Released c. April 1971

Concerto for Violin and Orchestra (C37)
1. Jascha Heifetz (violin) and the Philharmonia Orchestra.

Recorded in Abbey Road Studios, London, 26 and 27 June 1950

HMV DB 21257-9 (78 rpm: non-automatic)
DB 9611-13 (78 rpm: automatic) Released May 1951

Reissued in HMV BLP 1047 (mono, 33 rpm) Released July 1954
RCA LSB 4102 Released August 1973
RCA GK 87966 (cassette)
GD 87966 (compact disc) Released November
. 1988

2. Yehudi Menuhin (violin) and the London Symphony Orchestra.

Recorded in No 1 Studio, Abbey Road, London, 12-15 July 1969

HMV ASD 2542 (stereo, 33 rpm) Released March 1970
ANGEL (USA) 36719 Released c. April 1971

Crown Imperial (C32)
1. The Philharmonia Orchestra.

Recorded in Kingsway Hall, London, 18 March 1953

COLUMBIA 33C 1016 (mono, 33 rpm)
Reissued in (45) COLUMBIA SEL 1504 (mono) Released April
  1954
  EMI HQM 1006 (mono) Released Dec 1965
  ANGEL (USA) 35639 (mono)
  EMI SLS 5246 (stereo) Released 1982

Façade (C12)

1. 11 items with Edith Sitwell and Constant Lambert as reciters and instrumental ensemble.

   Recorded in the Chenil Galleries, London, 28 November 1929

   DECCA T 124-5 (78 rpm)
   AMERICAN DECCA 25632/3 (78 rpm) Released February 1930

   Reissued in (45) OUP 110 (mono) Released March 1972 as part of the de-luxe edition of the score of *Façade*

2. Complete 1951 version, with Peggy Ashcroft and Paul Scofield as reciters and the London Sinfonietta.

   Recorded in Decca Studio No 3, 156 Broadhurst Gardens, London 5-7 May 1969 (the music was recorded first, with the voices added some months later).

   ARGO ZRG 649 (stereo) Released March 1972

Façade: Suites No 1 (C12c) and No 2 (C12e)

1. *Nos 1-8 + 10* with the London Philharmonic Orchestra.

   Recorded in No 1 Studio, Abbey Road, London, 5 March 1936

   HMV C 2836-7 (78 rpm) Released May 1936

   Nos 9 and 11 with the London Philharmonic Orchestra.

   Recorded in No 1 Studio, Abbey Road, London, 25 October 1938

   HMV C 3042 (78 rpm) Released January 1939

   Reissued in EMI ED 29 0715 1 (mono, 33 rpm)
     CDH7 63381–2 Released March 1992

2. The Philharmonia Orchestra.

Recorded in Kingsway Hall, London, 20 April 1955 and 26 March 1957

COLUMBIA 33C 1054 (mono) Released March 1958

Reissued in COLUMBIA SED 5556 Released November 1958
EMI HQM 1006 (mono) Released December 1965
ANGEL (USA) 35639 (mono)
EMI SLS 5236 (stereo) Released 1982

Hamlet: Funeral March (C54a)

1. The Philharmonia Orchestra.

Recorded in Abbey Road Studios, London, 15 October 1963

COLUMBIA 33CX 1883 (mono, 33 rpm)
SAX 2527 (stereo) Released April 1964
Tape C 33CX 1883 (mono)
VICTOR (USA) 36198 (mono)
    S 36198 (stereo) Released May 1964
Reissued in WORLD RECORD CLUB T 656 (mono, 33 rpm)
    ST 656 (stereo) Released November 1967
    HMV Concert Classics SXLP 30139 (stereo) Released
    April 1972

Henry V (C50)

1. Laurence Olivier with the Philharmonia Orchestra.

Recorded in Abbey Road Studios, London, 27 and 28 August, and 12 and 13 October 1946
(with an extra session on 13 November 1946)

HMV C 3583-6 (78 rpm: non-automatic)
    C 7678-81 (78 rpm: automatic) Released July 1947
VICTOR (USA) 11-9600/3 (non-automatic)
    VM 1128 (automatic)

Reissued in HMV ALP 1375 (mono, 33 rpm) Released September
    1956
    RCA RB 16144 (mono, 33 rpm) Released May 1959
    RCA LSB 4104 (mono, 33 rpm) Released August 1973
    VICTOR (USA) LM 1926

Henry V: Suite (arr Mathieson) (C50b)
1. The Philharmonia Orchestra.

Recorded at Abbey Road Studios, 15 October 1963

COLUMBIA 33CX 1883 (mono, 33 rpm)
SAX 2527 (stereo) Released April 1964
Tape C 33CX 1883 (mono)
VICTOR (USA) 36198 (mono)
S 36198 (stereo) Released May 1964

Reissued in WORLD RECORD CLUB T 656 (mono, 33rpm)
Released
ST 656 (stereo) November 1967
HMV Concert Classics SXLP 30139 (stereo) Released
April 1967
EMI SLS 5246 (stereo) Released 1982

Henry V: Two Pieces for Strings (C50e)
1. The Philharmonia String Orchestra.

Recorded at Abbey Road Studios, 12 October 1945

HMV C 3478-3480 (78 rpm: non-automatic)
C 7635/7 (78 rpm: automatic) Released January 1946
Reissued in HMV ALP 1375 (mono, 33 rpm) Released September
1956
EMI ED 29 0715 1 (mono)
ED 29 0715 4 (cassette) Released August 1986
CDH7 63381–2 Released March 1992

Johannesburg Festival Overture (C66)
1. The Philharmonia Orchestra.

Recorded at Kingsway Hall, 26 March 1957

COLUMBIA 33C 1054 (mono, 33 rpm) Released March 1958
ANGEL (USA) 35639 (mono)

Reissued in EMI HQM 1006 (mono, 33 rpm) Released December
1965

EMI SLS 5246 (stereo) Released 1982

Music for Children (C39a)
(Nos 1 - 10)
1. London Philharmonic Orchestra.

Recorded at Walthamstow Assembly Hall, London 15 April 1970

LYRITA SRCS 50 (stereo, 33 rpm) Released June 1971
SRCD 224 Released June 1992

Orb and Sceptre (C59)
1. The Philharmonia Orchestra.

Recorded at Kingsway Hall, London, 18 March 1953

COLUMBIA LX 1583 (mono, 78 rpm) Released June 1953

Reissued in COLUMBIA 33C 1016 (mono, 33 rpm) Released June 1953
COLUMBIA SEL 1504 (mono, 45 rpm) Released April 1954
EMI HQM 1006 (mono, 33 rpm) Released December 1965
EMI SLS 5246 (stereo) Released 1982

Partita for Orchestra (C67)
1. The Philharmonia Orchestra.

Recorded at Kingsway Hall, London, 6 and 16 February 1959

COLUMBIA   33CX 1679 (mono, 33 rpm) Released December 1959
SAX 2319 (stereo) Released March 1961
ANGEL (USA) 35681 (mono)
S 36681 (stereo)

Reissued in EMI SXLP 30236 (stereo) Released March 1977
EMI SLS 5246 (stereo) Released 1982

Portsmouth Point (C17)
1. The Philharmonia Orchestra.

Recorded at Kingsway Hall, London, 18 and 21 March 1953

COLUMBIA 33C 1016 (mono, 33 rpm) Released June 1953

Reissued in COLUMBIA SEL 1506 (mono, 45 rpm) Released May 1954
ANGEL (USA) 35639 (mono) Released c. December 1958
COLUMBIA SEG 8217 (mono, 45 rpm) Released February 1963
EMI HQM 1006 (mono, 33 rpm) Released December 1965
EMI SLS 5246 (stereo) Released 1982

2. The London Philharmonic Orchestra.

Recorded at Walthamstow Assembly Hall, London, 15 April 1970

LYRITA SRCS 47 (stereo) Released August 1971
SRCD 224 Released June 1992

Reissued in VIRGIN CLASSICS VC 790715 1 (stereo)
VC 790715 4 (cassette)
VC 790715 2 (compact disc)
Released July 1988

The Quest: Suite from The Ballet (C49a)

1. The London Symphony Orchestra.

Recorded at Walthamstow Assembly Hall, London, 14 April 1970

LYRITA SRCS 49 (stereo) Released June 1971
SRCD 224 Released June 1992

Richard III: Prelude (C63a) and Suite (C63c)

1. The Philharmonia Orchestra.

Recorded at Abbey Road Studios, London, 15 and 16 October 1963

COLUMBIA 33CX 1883 (mono, 33 rpm))
SAX 2527 (stereo) Released April 1964
Tape 33CX 1883 (mono)
VICTOR (USA) 36198 (mono)
S 36198 (stereo) Released May 1964

Reissued in WORLD RECORD CLUB T 656 (mono) Released

ST 656 (stereo) November 1967
HMV Concert Classics SXLP 30139 (stereo) Released
April 1972
EMI SLS 5246 (stereo) Prelude only Released 1982

Scapino (C40)

1. The Philharmonia Orchestra.

Recorded Abbey Road Studios, London, 19 October 1951

HMV DB 21499 (78 rpm) Released August 1952

Reissued in EMI ED 29 0715 1 (mono, 33 rpm)
ED 29 0715 4 (cassette) Released August 1986
CDH7 63381–2 Released March 1992

2. The London Symphony Orchestra.

Recorded Walthamstow Assembly Hall, London, 13 April 1970

LYRITA SRCS 49 (stereo, 33 rpm) Released June 1971
SRCD 224 Released June 1992

Siesta (C19)

1. The London Philharmonic Orchestra.

Recorded at No 1 Studio, Abbey Road, London, 25 October 1938

HMV C 3042 (78 rpm) Released January 1939
VICTOR (USA) 12532

Reissued in EMI ED 29 0715 1 (mono, 33 rpm)
ED 29 0715 4 (cassette) Released August 1986

2. The London Philharmonic Orchestra.

Recorded at Walthamstow Assembly Hall, London, 15 April 1970

LYRITA SRCS 47 (stereo) Released August 1971
SRCD 224 Released June 1992

Sinfonia Concertante (C21)

1. Phyllis Sellick (piano) and the City of Birmingham Orchestra.

Recorded in Dudley Town Hall, 8 August 1945

HMV C 3478-80 (78 rpm: non-automatic)
C 7635/7 (78 rpm: automatic) Released January 1946

Reissued in WORLD RECORD CLUB SH 128 (mono, 33 rpm)
Released May 1970
EMI EH 29 1276 1 (mono, 33 rpm)
EH 29 1276 4 (cassette) Released October 1987
EMI CDH7 63828-2 (mono) Released August 1991

2. Peter Katin (piano) and the London Symphony Orchestra.

Recorded in Walthamstow Assembly Hall, London, 14 April 1970

LYRITA SRCS 49 (stereo) Released June 1971
SRCD 224 Released June 1992

Spitfire Prelude and Fugue (C45a)

1. The Hallé Orchestra with Laurance Turner (violin).

Recorded at Houldsworth Hall, Manchester, 24 June 1943

HMV C 3359 (78 rpm) Released August 1943

Reissued in HMV 7P 312 (mono, 45 rpm) Released February 1963
EMI ED 29 0715 1 (mono, 33 rpm)
ED 29 0715 4 (cassette) Released August 1986
CDH7 63381–2 Released March 1992

2. The Philharmonia Orchestra.

Recorded at the Abbey Road Studios, London, 16 October 1963

EMI SXLP 30139 (stereo, 33 rpm) Released April 1972

Reissued in EMI SLS 5246 (stereo) Released 1982

Symphony No 1 (C27)

1. The Philharmonia Orchestra.

Recorded at Abbey Road Studios, London, 17-19 October 1951

HMV ALP 1027 (mono, 33 rpm)
VICTOR (USA) LHMV 1041 (mono)
Victor set WHMV 1041 (automatic sequence) Released February 1953

Reissued in EMI SLS 5246 Released 1982

Troilus and Cressida (C62)
Excerpts

1. Elisabeth Schwarzkopf (sop), Richard Lewis (ten.) and the Philharmonia Orchestra.

    Recorded in Kingsway Hall, London, 18-20 April 1955

    COLUMBIA 33CX 1313 (mono, 33 rpm)
    ANGEL (USA) 35278   Released
    QCX (ITALY) 1073   November 1955
    Tape CAT 283

    Reissued in WORLD RECORD CLUB OH 217 (mono, 33 rpm)
    Released September 1968

2. Excerpt from Act II
    Marie Collier (sop.), Peter Pears (ten.) and the Covent Garden Orchestra.

    Recorded in Kingsway Hall, London, in February and July 1968

    DECCA MET 392-3 (mono)
    SET 392-3 (stereo) Released October 1968

The Wise Virgins: Suite (C38a)
1. The Sadler's Wells Orchestra.

    Recorded at the Abbey Road Studios, London :
    Sides 1 and 2 - 24 July 1940
    Sides 3 and 4 - 8 August 1940
    HMV C3178-9 (78 rpm)
    VICTOR (USA) Set M 817(2)
    VICTOR (USA) 18752/3 Released September 1940

The Wise Virgins: Excerpt (C38c)
Sheep may safely graze

1. The Philharmonia Orchestra.

    Recorded in Kingsway Hall, London, 21 March 1953

    COLUMBIA 33C 1016 (mono) Released June 1953

Reissued in COLUMBIA SEL 1504 (mono, 45rpm) Released April 1954

II. WALTON AS SPEAKER

14 August 1951:	Interviewed by Spike Hughes in the series *Records I Like* LP. 16731 BBC Sound Archives
15 January 1956:	Interviewed by Felix Aprahamian (for ABC) on *Troilus and Cressida* No details
18 February 1959:	Interviewed on his life and work in the series *The Composer Speaks* LP. 25903 BBC Sound Archives
26 March 1959:	Interviewed by Lance Sieveking in a talk on broadcasting at Savoy Hill LP. 24912 BBC Sound Archives
2 April 1962:	Interviewed by Dilys Powell and Anthony Hopkins in the series *Frankly Speaking* LP. 27281 BBC Sound Archives
March 1964:	Talking with Berl Senovsky Broadcast on ABV-2 (ABC)
July 1965:	Interviewed by Bernard Palmer in *This is Britain* programme
22 July 1965:	Interviewed by Roy Plomley in *Desert Island Discs*
3 September 1965:	Interviewed by Hans Keller on contemporary music, its problems and its future LP. 30545 BBC Sound Archives
24 September 1965:	Interviewed by Eric Roseberry on his First Symphony LP. 34332 BBC Sound Archives
19 January 1966:	Interviewed by Martin Dalby about his work M 724 R NSA Tape

11 June 1966:	Talking about *Constant Lambert (1905-1951): a portrait* T. 30368 (tape) BBC Sound Archives
1 January 1968:	Talking to Felix Aprahamian M 1180 W NSA Tape
12 March 1968:	Interviewed by Hans Keller on contemporary music, in the series *Talking about Music* LP. 31959 BBC Sound Archives
28 April 1968:	Interviewed by Geoffrey Skelton on Paul Hindemith LP. 34820 BBC Sound Archives
26 May 1968:	Interviewed by John Warrack in the BBC2 series *Workshop*
10 March 1969:	Recalls the composer in *Portrait of Paul Hindemith* LP. 32961 BBC Sound Archives
16 August 1971:	Interviewed on the first 24 years of the Edinburgh International Festival in retrospect T. 33992 (tape) BBC Sound Archives
18 February 1972:	Interviewed by John Amis on his work, with references to Paul Hindemith LP. 34276 BBC Sound Archives
March 1972:	Interviewed by Joseph Cooper as the guest in the BBC2 series *Face the Music*
16 March 1972:	Interviewed by Kevin Byrne on aspects of his career, with reference to the critics LP. 34404 BBC Sound Archives
21 March 1972:	Interviewed by Hans Keller on the occasion of his 70th birthday, with references to composing, Stravinsky, broadcasting and recording LP. 34404 BBC Sound Archives

| 29 March 1972: | Interviewed by Sue MacGregor on his 70th birthday, with references to living in Italy and film music
LP. 34404   BBC Sound Archives |
| --- | --- |
| 29 March 1972: | Interviewed by Tony Thomas. Broadcast by ABC on Walton's 70th birthday (Includes an interview with Walton recorded during a visit to Los Angeles, 1963) |
| 11 June 1973: | Interviewed by Bernard Keeffe on the *Façade Affair*
MT 41111   BBC Sound Archives |
| 2 July 1974: | Interviewed by David Munroe about *Belshazzar's Feast* and his life as a composer
T 52122 (tape)   BBC Sound Archives |
| 18 October 1975: | Interviewed by Russell Harty in *Sir William and our Gracie* ('Aquarius' – ITV) |
| 19 October 1975: | Interviewed with Owain Arwel Hughes about *Belshazzar's Feast* (BBC2) |
| 5 November 1976: | Interviewed by John Amis on *Troilus and Cressida*
LP. 37509   BBC Sound Archives |
| 29 March 1977 | (recorded Autumn 1976): Interviewed by Richard Pyatt in *The Life and Music of Sir William Walton*, a programme written and produced by G Millais for the British Information Services, New York, in co-operation with the Municipal Broadcasting System |
| 4 June 1977: | Interviewed in *A Portrait of William Walton* (Originally made for the BBC Transcription Service) |

| 18 November 1977: | Interviewed by Arthur Jacobs about his work |
| | LP. 38004   BBC Sound Archives |

18 November 1977: Interviewed by Arthur Jacobs about his work
LP. 38004   BBC Sound Archives

13 November 1978: Interviewed by John Pearson on Edith, Osbert and Sacheverell Sitwell
T. 38610 (tape)   BBC Sound Archives

14 April 1981: Interviewed by John Amis on the *Violin Concerto*
LP. 48502   BBC Sound Archives

19 April 1981: Interviewed by Tony Palmer in *At the Haunted End of the Day* (ITN)

25 March 1982: Interviewed by Russell Harty during a musical celebration of Walton's 80th birthday (BBC2)
5866W   National Sound Archive

27 March 1982: Interviewed by Roy Plomley in the series *Desert Island Discs*
T 082283 (tape)   BBC Sound Archives

28 March 1982: Interviewed in *Music Weekly* (introduced by Michael Oliver): a portrait in words and music on the eve of his 80th birthday

Bibliography

This bibliography presents writings relating to William Walton and his music from the earliest years to the present day.

All articles, theses, books and record sleeve notes are collected under the relevant headings of Walton's works if they are specifically concerned with those works. The category GENERAL deals mainly with biographical aspects of the composer's life and general mention of his works. All items are listed in alphabetical order of author's name. Reprints and programme notes are not included in view of the exigencies of space.

ALL THIS TIME (C84)
A C FRANK Sleeve note for Argo ZRG 725 (1972)

ANNIVERSARY FANFARE (C89)
J CHISSELL [EMI Birthday Concert]
The Times, 1 December 1973, p. 13g-h
E GREENFIELD [EMI Birthday Concert]
Gramophone, 51 (1974), pp. 1364 + 1369

ANON IN LOVE (C71)
J AMIS 'Aldeburgh Festival'
The Guardian, 23 June 1960, p. 9e
ANON. 'Walton's new Love Songs'
The Times, 22 June 1960, p. 7f-g
R TEAR Sleeve note for Argo ZK 39 (1978)

ANON IN LOVE: ORCHESTRAL VERSION (C71a)
C PALMER Sleeve note for CHANDOS CHAN 8824/ ABTD 1449 (1990)

AS YOU LIKE IT (C31)
B BRITTEN 'As You Like It: Walton's music'
World Film News, 1, no 7 (October 1936), p. 46

AS YOU LIKE IT: SUITE ARR. DAVIS (C31a)
C PALMER Sleeve note for EMI EL 27 0591 1/ EL 27 0591 4/
CDC 7 47944 2 (1987)

AS YOU LIKE IT: SUITE ARR. PALMER (C31b)
C PALMER Sleeve note for CHANDOS CHAN 8842/ ABTD 1461 (1990)

BACH BOOK FOR HARRIET COHEN (C25)
ANON. 'Harriet Cohen at Queen's Hall'
Musical Opinion, 56 (1932), p. 235
ANON. 'Recitals of the Week: Miss Harriet Cohen'
The Times, 21 October 1932, p. 12d
H COHEN [Bach Book] in 'A Bundle of Time: memoirs'
London, Faber, 1969, p. 183

BATTLE OF BRITAIN (C81)
S DAY LEWIS 'Walton's anger at film snub'
The Daily Telegraph, 23 June 1969, p. 15a
L GEDDES-BROWN [Battle of Britain score]
The Sunday Times, 13 March 1983, p. 42a-b
L GEDDES-BROWN [Battle of Britain score]
The Sunday Times, 27 March 1983, p. 39c
E GREENFIELD 'Sounds of Dog-Fights'
The Guardian, 29 April 1969, p. 10b-d
E GREENFIELD 'Spring Laugh-in'

HiFi/Musical America, 19 (August 1969), p. 16
K NURSE 'Heath ends Walton music row'
The Daily Telegraph, 30 March 1972, p. 1e
K PEARSON [The Battle of Britain; film music]
The Sunday Times, 19 January 1969, p. 55e
K ROSE 'Film-makers scorn Walton's score'
The Sunday Telegraph, 22 June 1969, p. 2f-g
J T TAYLOR 'Laurence Olivier as Dowding'
The Times, 16 September 1969, p. 7a

BATTLE OF BRITAIN: SUITE (C81a)
J HUNTLEY Sleeve note for EMI ASD 3797 (1979)
N LEBRECHT [Battle of Britain Suite]
The Sunday Times, 5 May 1985, p. 3a-b
C PALMER Sleeve note for CHANDOS CHAN 8870/ABTD 1485 (1990)
C PALMER Sleeve note for EMI EL 27 0591 1/ EL 27 0591 4/
                                CDC 7 47944 2 (1987)

THE BEAR (C79)
E CHAPMAN 'New One-Act Operas by Berkeley and Walton'
Musical Events, 22 (August 1967), pp. 33-34
M COOPER 'Two One-Act Operas make debut'
The Daily Telegraph, 5 June 1967, p. 15a
W DEAN 'Music in London: English Opera Group'
The Musical Times, 108 (September 1967), pp. 821-822
P DEHN 'New operas for Aldeburgh'
About the House, 2 (1967), pp. 35-37
P DEHN Sleeve note for EMI SAN 192 (1967)
N GOODWIN 'Vaudeville for the Vienna Boys'
Music and Musicians, 15 (August 1967), pp. 20-21
E GREENFIELD 'Britten and the Aldeburgh Festival'
HiFi/Musical America, 17 (September 1967), pp. 24-26
E GREENFIELD 'Three new operas at the Aldeburgh Festival'
The Guardian, 5 June 1967, p. 5a-d
B HADDAH 'Aspen'
Opera News, 33 (12 October 1968), p. 26
A JACOBS 'London Opera Diary'
Opera, 18 (September 1967), pp. 772-774
A JACOBS 'Other Student Performances
Opera, 20 (September 1969), p. 816
W MANN 'Three new operas in a day'
The Times, 5 June 1967, p. 6c-e
A PORTER 'Festivals: Aldeburgh'
The Musical Times, 108 (July 1967), p. 632

H ROSENTHAL 'English Opera Group'
Musical Opinion, 90 (August 1967), pp. 617-618
H ROSENTHAL 'London Opera Diary'
Opera, 23 (December 1972), pp. 1116-1117
H ROSENTHAL 'The 1967 Aldeburgh Festival'
Opera, 18 (Autumn 1967), pp. 24-25
H ROSENTHAL 'On Television'
Opera, 21 (April 1970), pp. 368-369
S SADIE 'English Opera Group: Sadler's Wells'
The Times, 13 July 1967, p. 8e
S SADIE 'Well wrought opera by Berkeley'
The Times, 13 July 1967, p. 8e
E SENIOR 'Three-Way Link'
Music and Musicians, 15 (July 1967), p. 43
D SHAWE-TAYLOR 'Aldeburgh and Bath'
The Sunday Times, 11 June 1967, p. 50a-c
E TELLINI 'The Bear'
Opera, 35 (July 1984), p. 790
J WARRACK 'Operatic Wit'
The Sunday Telegraph, 11 June 1967, p. 11a-b
K-H WOCKER 'Protest gegen die Routine'
Opern Welt, 9 (September 1967), pp. 17-18
A YOUNG 'Walton's Bear, Susskind's Diversity'
HiFi/Musical America, 18 (November 1968), p. 25

BELSHAZZAR'S FEAST (C23)
ANON. 'Composer at Leeds rehearsal'
The Yorkshire Post, 14 September 1931, p. 4a
ANON. 'Leeds Music Festival'
The Yorkshire Post, 9 October 1931, p. 5a
ANON. 'Leeds Music Festival: a contrast of religions'
The Times, 10 October 1931, p. 10b
ANON. 'Leeds Musical Festival: new choral works'
The Times, 9 October 1931, p. 10b-c
ANON. 'Novelties at the Evening Concert'
The Yorkshire Post, 9 October 1931, p. 5b
ANON. 'A Yorkshire Poet's Biblical Mosaic'
Yorkshire Evening Post, 7 October 1931, p. 6c-f
I BARTLETT 'Set works for O-level, 1983'
Music Teacher, 61 (March 1982), pp. 20-21
E BRADBURY 'Belshazzar's Feast: for chorus, baritone solo and orchestra'
Music and Letters, 38 (October 1957), p. 407
R CAPELL ['Belshazzar's Feast']
Monthly Musical Record, LXII (June 1932), pp. 13-14

N CARDUS 'Leeds Music Festival'
The Manchester Guardian, 10 October 1931, p. 13e
R CAVALIERO 'Settling an old score'
The Sunday Times, 18 October 1987, p. 24
J.D. 'Walton re-records Belshazzar's Feast'
American Record Guide, 27 (October 1960), pp. 156-158
L EAST 'Modern British'
Music and Musicians, 20 (July 1972), p. 66
J H ELLIOT 'William Walton's Belshazzar's Feast'
The Sackbut, 12 (January 1932), pp. 84-86
A H FOX-STRANGWAYS 'Music and Musicians - Belshazzar's Feast'
The Observer, 29 November 1931, p. 10d-e
S GODDARD 'Contemporary British Music'
Canon, 12 (February 1959), p. 228
N GOODWIN Sleeve note for COLUMBIA 33CX 1679 (1959)/
SAX 2319 (1961)
N GOODWIN Sleeve note for EMI ALP 1628 (1958)
H GRACE 'William Walton's new choral work'
The Listener, VI (18 November 1931), pp. 860-861
E GREENFIELD Sleeve note for EMI SAN 324 (1972)
F S HOWES 'The Leeds Festival novelties'
Monthly Musical Record, LXI (October 1931), pp. 298-299
B JAMES Sleeve note for NIXA NLP 904 (1954)
N LEBRECHT 'Walton's choral masterpiece lost in Argentina'
The Sunday Times, 11 October 1987, p. 1a-f
A.H.M. 'From Red-Hot Conception to Red-Hot Expression'
The Boston Evening Transcript, 104, 30 March 1933, p. 13a-e
W McNAUGHT 'Belshazzar's Feast'
The Musical Times, 73 (January 1932), p. 68
B MAINE 'Walton's Feast'
Spectator, 147 (12 December 1931), pp. 808-809
C PALMER Sleeve note for CHANDOS CHAN 8760/ ABTD 1398 (1989)
V PILKINGTON 'Stravinsky and Walton'
The London Mercury, 25 (January 1932), pp. 300-301
B L SCHERER 'Royal Philharmonic debuts on its own label'
The New York Times, 28 June 1987, Section 2, p. 21h
K R SCHWARZ 'English Music: tradition individualized'
The New York Times, 30 August 1987, Section 2, p. 21h
A T SHAW 'The Opening Concert'
Berrow's Worcester Journal, 6 September 1957, p. 6g
H THOMPSON 'Novelties at the evening concert: Belshazzar's Feast'
The Yorkshire Post, 9 October 1931, p. 5b-c
W J TURNER 'The Content of Music'
New Statesman and Nation, 5, 21 June 1933, p. 73

THE BOY DAVID (C30)

ANON. 'The Boy David: audience on best behaviour'
The Glasgow Herald, 23 November 1936, p. 10d-e

ANON. 'The Boy David: Elisabeth Bergner's elfin production'
Weekly Scotsman, 28 November 1936, p. 5a-g

ANON. 'The Boy David: a play by Sir James Barrie'
The Times, 15 December 1936, p. 14b-c

ANON. 'The Boy David Premiere in Edinburgh'
The Glasgow Herald, 23 November 1936, pp. 11e-f & 12f-g

ANON. 'Edinburgh: The Boy David'
The Times, 23 November 1936, p. 10b

ANON. 'Editorial Diary: The Boy David'
The Glasgow Herald, 23 November 1936, p. 10d-e

ANON. 'His Majesty's Theatre: The Boy David'
The Stage, 17 December 1936, p. 10a

ANON. 'Premiere of Sir J M Barrie's new play'
The Weekly Scotsman, 77, 28 November 1936, p. 5a-g

C ASQUITH [The Boy David] *in* 'Portrait of Barrie'
London, Barrie, 1954, pp. 201-216

P BULL [The Boy David] *in* 'I know the face, but ....'
London, Davies, 1959, pp. 128-134

C B COCHRAN [The Boy David] *in* 'Cock-a-Doodle-Do'
London, Dent, 1941, pp. 1-33

J DUNBAR [The Boy David] *in* 'JMB: the man behind the image'
London, Collins, 1970, pp. 291-298

GALLERYITE 'Canned music at Barrie premiere'
Weekly Scotsman, 77, 28 November 1936, p. 7c

S HEPPNER [The Boy David] *in* 'Cockie'
London, Frewin, 1969, pp. 190-201

D MACKAIL [The Boy David] *in* 'The Story of J.M.B.'
London, Davies, 1941, pp. 663-707

CANTICO DEL SOLE (C90)

C ACTON 'Cork'
The Musical Times, 115 (August 1974), pp. 682-683

ANON. 'First Performance'
World of Music, 16, no.4 (1974), p. 62

F APRAHAMIAN 'Cork Festival'
The Times, 5 May 1974, p. 37e-f

W MANN 'The five thousand voices of Cork'
The Times, 1 May 1974, p. 12g-h

G PROTHEROE Sleeve note for ABBEY LPB 798 (1979)

J SHERIDAN 'Icelandic Charms in Cork'
The Irish Press, 26 April 1974, p. 3a-d

CAPRICCIO BURLESCO (C80)
ANON. 'Royal Philharmonic Society'
Musical Events, 24 (March 1969), p. 27
ANON. 'Walton Overture not ready for the Proms'
The Times, 5 August 1968, p. 5d
ANON. 'Walton's new work'
The Times, 26 November 1968, p. 6e
M COOPER 'Clarinet work packed with ideas'
The Daily Telegraph, 6 February 1969, p. 21f
P DAVIS 'Walton's new work'
The Times, 10 December 1968, p. 7a-b
A C FRANK Sleeve note for COLUMBIA TWO 272 (1969)
A C FRANK Sleeve note for LYRITA SRCS 49 (1971)
H JOHNSON 'Kostelanetz plays new Capriccio'
The New York Post, 768, 9 December 1968, p. 72a-b
W MANN 'Philharmonic's cheerful novelties'
The Times, 6 February 1969, p. 13b
C PALMER Sleeve note for CHANDOS CHAN 8968/ ABTD 1560 (1991)
D SIMMONS 'London Music'
Musical Opinion, 92 (March 1969), pp. 287-288

CHRISTOPHER COLUMBUS (C46)
D BOWER 'Columbus'
The Radio Times, 77, 9 October 1942, p. 1
A DENT 'Critic on the Hearth: Christopher Columbus'
The Listener, XXVIII, 15 October 1942, p.508
R HILL 'Composers and Craftsmen'
The Radio Times, 9 October 1942, p. 4
F LAWS (Ed) [Christopher Columbus] in 'Made for Millions'
London, Contact Publications, 1947, p.54
L MacNEICE [Incidental music] in 'Christopher Columbus:
a radio play' London, Faber, 1944, p.9
C PALMER 'Radio'
The Musical Times, 114 (June 1973), pp. 631-632

CHRISTOPHER COLUMBUS: SUITE (C46a)
C PALMER Sleeve note for CHANDOS CHAN 8824/ ABTD 1449 (1990)

CONCERTO FOR CELLO AND ORCHESTRA (C65)
ANON. 'Boston hears new Walton concerto'
The Daily Telegraph, 26 January 1957, p. 9f
ANON. 'Editorial Notes'
Strad, 67 (March 1957), p. 406
ANON. 'Grisha and Sir William'

Time, 69, 13 May 1957, pp. 59-60
ANON. 'Sir William Walton's New Concerto'
The Times, 14 February 1957, p. 5c-d
ANON. 'Walton Cello Concerto and overture issued'
Musical America, 78 (June 1958), p. 22
ANON. 'Walton's cello concerto: Boston première'
The Times, 1 February 1957, p. 3e
C.B. 'Royal Philharmonic Society'
Musical Opinion, 80 (May 1957), p. 455
J N BURK Sleeve note for RCA RB 16027 (1959)
M COOPER [Walton Cello Concerto]
The Daily Telegraph, 23 February 1957, p. 8f
S S DALE 'Contemporary Cello Concerti'
The Strad, 83 (August 1972), pp. 171-175
D DREW 'London'
Musical Courier, 155 (April 1957), pp. 39-40
C DURGIN 'First Symphony by Smit has Boston première'
Musical America, 77 (March 1977), pp. 16 + 18
A C FRANK 'Walton's Cello Concerto'
London Musical Events, 12 (May 1957), pp. 19-20
A C FRANK 'Walton's new concerto: warm and lyrical'
Music and Musicians, 5 (February 1957), p. 9
R FREED 'Superb British Concertos from Ma and Previn'
Stereo Review, October 1985, pp. 71-72
P HEYWORTH [Walton's Cello Concerto]
The Observer, 17 February 1957, p. 11g
I KEYS 'Reviews of Music: Concerto for Violoncello'
Music and Letters, 39 (April 1958), pp. 199-200
R KROKOVER 'Walton Concerto'
Saturday Review, 40, 18 May 1957, p. 37
G.M. 'William Walton: Concerto per violoncello e orchestra'
Rassegna Musicale, 28 (September 1958), pp. 240-241
C MASON 'A giant refreshed'
The Spectator, 22 February 1957, p. 254
C MASON 'Walton's new cello concerto'
The Manchester Guardian, 15 February 1957, p. 9e-f
I NEWTON [Walton's Cello Concerto] in 'At the Piano: the world of an
   accompanist' London, Hamilton,1966, pp.128-129
C PALMER Sleeve note for CHANDOS CHAN 8959/ ABTD 1551 (1991)
A PORTER 'Notes Abroad'
High Fidelity, 7 (July 1957), p. 16
H RUTLAND 'Walton's new Cello Concerto'
The Musical Times, 98 (February 1957), pp. 69-71
H RUTLAND 'Walton's Cello Concerto'

The Musical Times, 98 (April 1957), p. 213
R.S. 'Piatigorsky plays Walton Cello Concerto'
Musical America, 77 (June 1957), p. 18
M B STANFIELD 'Silhouettes from Britain'
Violins, 18 (May-June 1957), p. 100
L TIMBLE 'Current Chronicle: New York'
Musical Quarterly, 43 (July 1957), pp. 383-384
F WALTER ['Walton's new Cello Concerto and other recent events in London]
Melos, 24 (May 1957), pp. 149-150

CONCERTO FOR VIOLA AND ORCHESTRA (C22)
ANON. 'Editorial Notes'
Strad, 72 (February 1962), p. 377
ANON. 'Musical tribute to Walton'
The Times, 19 January 1962, p. 13
ANON. 'Promenade Concert: New works by Bax and Walton'
The Times, 4 October 1929, p. 12c
E BLOM 'London Concerts: Promenade Concerts: Novelties'
The Musical Times, 71 (1929), pp. 1029-1030
D DALTON [Walton Viola Concerto] *in* 'Playing the Viola: conversations with William Primrose' Oxford OUP 1988, pp.197-201
S FLEMING 'Menuhin plays Walton - a brilliant show'
Hi/Fi Musical America, 21 (May 1970), p. 80
A C FRANK Sleeve note for EMI ASD 2542 (1970)
R HILL (Ed) [Walton Viola Concerto] *in* 'The Concerto'
Harmondsworth, Penguin Books, 1962, pp. 392-396
L HUGHES-JONES 'Sir Malcolm Sargent's programme with the LPO'
Music and Musicians, 11 (March 1962), p. 41
G F KNIGHT 'Walton and the Viola Concerto'
Hallé, no 42 (November 1951), pp. 8-10
C LAMBERT 'Viola and Orchestra'
The Listener, 17 February 1937, p. 335
B MAINE [Walton Viola Concerto] *in* 'Twang with our music'
London, Epworth Press, 1957, pp. 112-113
W PRIMROSE [Walton Viola Concerto] *in* 'Walk on the North Side: memoirs of a violist' Provo (Utah), Brigham Young University Press, 1978, pp. 89,99,101,113,115,182,185,186
D PUFFETT 'Letters to the Editor: Walton, Hindemith, Schoeck'
The Musical Times, 123 (June 1982), p. 392
L TERTIS [Walton Viola Concerto] *in* 'Cinderella no more' London, Nevill, 1953, pp. 38, 66-67
D F TOVEY [Walton Viola Concerto] *in* 'Essays in Musical Analysis: Volume III - Concertos' London, OUP, 1936, pp. 220-226

A VEINUS [Walton Viola Concerto] *in* 'The Victor Book of Concertos' New York, Simon and Schuster, 1948, pp. 414-419

CONCERTO FOR VIOLIN AND ORCHESTRA (C37)

ANON. 'Corigliano Soloist with Philharmonic'
Musical America, 79 (February 1959), p. 211
ANON. 'The new concerto - William Walton'
The Times, 7 November 1941, p. 6f
ANON. 'Mr Walton's new Violin Concerto'
The Times, 28 March 1939, p. 12d
ANON. [Walton Violin Concerto]
The New York Herald Tribune, 17 December 1939, p. 6e
E BLOM [Walton Violin Concerto]
The Birmingham Post, 27 October 1941, p. 2h
L.B.D. [Walton Violin Concerto]
The (Wolverhampton) Express and Star, 17 January 1944, p. 3e-f
S S DALE 'Twentieth Century Violin Concertos'
The Strad, 91 (December 1980), pp. 571-572
J DIETHER 'This one is not for the vaults'
American Record Guide, 31 (January 1965), p. 464
S FLEMING 'Menuhin plays Walton - a brilliant show'
HiFi/Musical America, 21 (May 1970), p. 80
H J FOSS 'The new Walton concerto'
The Listener, XXVI, 30 October 1941, p. 609
A C FRANK Sleeve note for EMI ASD 2542 (1970)
E GREENFIELD 'Behind the Scenes: Return of the Virtuoso'
HiFi/Musical America, 19 (October 1969), pp. 30-31
R HILL [Walton Violin Concerto] *in* 'The Concerto' Harmondsworth, Penguin Books, 1962, pp. 396-399
D HUSSEY 'Walton's Violin Concerto'
The Spectator, 167 (7 November 1941), p. 446
W G KING 'William Walton writes a concerto for Heifetz'
The New York Sun, 106 (1 July 1939), p. 14a-b
W McNAUGHT 'London Concerts: Walton's Violin Concerto'
The Musical Times, 82 (December 1941), pp. 443-444
F MERRICK 'Walton's Concerto for Violin and Orchestra'
Music Review, 2 (November 1941), pp. 309-318
H.M.P. 'BBC Symphony Orchestra: William Walton's Violin Concerto'
The Bedfordshire Times and Standard, 14 November 1941, p. 7g
R J PIPKIN 'An Analysis of William Walton's Concerto for Violin and Orchestra' M.Mus Thesis. North Texas State College, 1957
E SACKVILLE-WEST 'Walton's Violin Concerto'
New Statesman and Nation, 22 (8 November 1941), p. 408
A VEINUS [Walton Violin Concerto] in 'The Victor Book of Concertos' New York, Simon and Schuster, 1948, pp. 414-417

CORONATION TE DEUM (C58)
ANON. 'Coronation Music: The Abbey Service'
The Times, 24 April 1953, p. 3g
ANON. 'Coronation Score for British Museum'
The Times, 16 May 1953, p. 6c
ANON. 'Coronation Te Deum'
Musical Opinion, 76 (July 1953), p. 609
ANON. 'The Music in the Abbey'
The Times, 3 June 1953, p. 15g
ANON. 'Promenade Concert: Coronation music'
The Times, 29 July 1953, p. 2c
ANON. 'Song of Praise'
The Times, 3 June 1953, p. 15g
ANON. 'Te Deum Laudamus'
Musical Opinion, 80 (January 1957), p. 241
J CHISSELL 'Miscellaneous First Performances'
Musical Opinion, 77 (November 1953), p. 73
A B CREIGHTON 'Te Deum Laudamus in Twentieth Century Coronation
    Services' DMA Thesis, University of Southern California, 1966
A C FRANK Sleeve note for EMI ASD 3348 (1977)
I KEYS 'Coronation Te Deum'
Music and Letters, 34 (July 1953), p. 269
C MASON 'The Coronation Service Music'
The Guardian, 3 June 1953, p. 8b
C PALMER Sleeve note for CHANDOS CHAN 8760/ABTD 1398 (1989)
H E REDLICH 'New Music: A Critical Interim Report'
Music Review, 16 (August 1955), pp. 264-266

CROWN IMPERIAL (C32)
ANON. 'Crown Imperial'
Making Music, 16 (Spring 1950), p. 27
ANON. 'March Steps: a reflection of the week'
The Times, 15 May 1937, p. 10b
ANON. 'William Walton's latest triumph'
The Oldham Evening Chronicle, 5 April 1937, p. 5d-e
A H ASHWORTH 'New works at Leeds Festival'
The Yorkshire Post, 8 October 1937, p. 5b
T ECKERT 'Elgar and Walton Marches'
Christian Science Monitor, 22 September 1980, p. 18
A C FRANK Sleeve note for COLUMBIA 33C 1016 (1953)
A C FRANK Sleeve note for COLUMBIA TWO 272 (1969)
A C FRANK Sleeve note for EMI ASD 3348 (1977)

ESCAPE ME NEVER: SUITE (no C number assigned)
C PALMER Sleeve note for CHANDOS CHAN 8870/ ABTD 1485 (1990)
C PALMER Sleeve note for DECCA PFS 4363 (1976)

FAÇADE (C12)
G.A. 'New Music'
Monthly Musical Record, 81 (November 1951), p. 245
C ABERCONWAY [Façade] *in* 'A Wiser Woman'
London, Hutchinson, 1966, pp. 90-91
ANON. 'Façade'
The Daily Telegraph, 13 June 1923, p. 6e
ANON. 'Façade'
The Era, 86, 20 June 1923, p. 6d
ANON. 'Façade'
The Morning Post, 13 June 1923, p. 10f
ANON. 'Façade' *Musical Opinion*, 75 (October 1951), p. 29
ANON. 'Façade: Miss Sitwell's poems through a megaphone'
The Times, 29 April 1926, p. 14d
ANON. 'Futuristic Music and Poetry'
The Manchester Guardian, 13 June 1923, p. 12e
ANON. 'London Concerts: Façade'
The Daily Telegraph, '13 June 1923, p. 6a
ANON. 'Mask and Megaphone'
The Daily Mail, 13 June 1923, p. 7f
ANON. 'Poems through a megaphone'
The Times, 14 June 1923, p. 12b
ANON. 'Poetry through a megaphone: one note concert by Miss Sitwell'
The Daily Express, 13 June 1923, p. 7b
D L BOONE [Façade] *in* 'The treatment of the trumpet in 6 published chamber
    works composed between 1920 and 1929'
    Dissertation, University of Illinois (Urbana-Champaign), 1972
R CAPELL 'The Sienna Festival'
Monthly Musical Record, LVIII (1 October 1928), p. 300
J CAREWE Sleeve notes for FONTANA STL 5449 (1968)
G A CEVASCO [Façade] *in* 'The Sitwells : Edith, Osbert and Sacheverell'
    Boston, Twayne Publishers, 1987, pp. 26,27,33,59,133
S R CRAGGS 'Façade and the Music of Sir William Walton'
The Library Chronicle of the University of Texas at Austin, nos 25/26 (1984), pp.
    100-117
S R CRAGGS 'Façade and the Music of Sir William Walton' *in Perspectives in
    Music: Essays on Collections at the HRC*, ed by D Oliphant and T Zigal. HRC,
    University of Texas, 1985, pp.100-117
G CUMBERLAND 'Façade: a new entertainment'
Vogue, 62 (early July 1923), pp. 36 and 70
E EVANS 'Façade: first performance in public'

The Pall Mall Gazette, 13 June 1923, p. 3e
W N FLOWER (ed) [Façade] *in* 'The Journals of Arnold Bennett:1921-28' London, Cassell, 1933, p. 130
H J FOSS 'The Siena Festival of modern music'
The Musical Times, 69 (October 1928), p. 937
R FULLER 'Façade'
The Listener, 89, 7 June 1973, p. 773
B GOODEN 'The Siena Festival: an impression'
Monthly Musical Record, LVIII (November 1928), p, 331
K K 'Metrics through the megaphone'
The Evening Standard, 13 June 1923, p. 3a-b
I KEYS 'Façade: an entertainment with poems by Edith Sitwell'
Music and Letters, 33 (January 1952), p. 90
P KRESH 'Two new Façades to celebrate Walton's birthday'
Stereo Review, 29 (September 1972), p. 104
J LEHMANN [Façade] *in* 'A Nest of Tigers' London, Macmillan, 1988, pp. 1-11
J LYONS 'No-Nonsense Nonsense'
HiFi/Musical America, 22 (July 1922), pp. 67-68
R MEGROZ [Façade] *in* 'The Three Sitwells' London, The Richards Press, 1927, pp. 69-78
P L MILLER 'Façade: An Entertainment with poems by Edith Sitwell'
Notes, 9 (June 1952), p. 502
E NEWMAN 'Façade'
The Sunday Times, 2 May 1926, p. 7b
C OSBORNE 'Sitwell and Walton'
London Magazine, 2 (December 1962), pp. 60-62
C PALMER Sleeve notes for CHANDOS CHAN 8869/ ABTD 1484 (1990)
T W RAND 'The Letters of Edith Sitwell to Siegfried Sassoon' Dissertation, Washington State University, 1986
D RICHARDS 'Records: Two-faced Façade'
Music and Musicians, 28 (August 1980), pp. 32-33
R SABIB 'Façade in First American hearing'
Musical America, 69 (February 1949), p. 279
P A SCHOLES 'Façade'
The Observer, 17 June 1923, p. 10d
E SITWELL [Façade] *in* 'Taken Care of' London, Hutchinson, 1965, pp. 122-125
O SITWELL [Façade] *in* 'Laughter in the Next Room' London Macmillan, 1949, pp. 168-198
S SITWELL 'Façade' London, OUP, 1972. pp. XIII-XV
S WIKNER Sleeve notes for OUP 201 (1980)
ZOETE, B de 'Façade' *The Music Bulletin*, 8 (May 1926), p. 142

FAÇADE 2
ANON. 'Façade 2 by Walton is recorded'
Billboard, 92 (3 May 1980), p. 32

R CRICHTON [Façade 2]
The Financial Times, 29 March 1977, p. 3g
P DRIVER 'Façade Re-visited'
Tempo, nos 133-134 (September 1980), pp. 3-9
E GREENFIELD [Façade 2]
The Guardian, 26 March 1977, p. 10e
D SHAWE-TAYLOR [Façade 2]
The Sunday Times, 3 April 1977, p. 38d
S WIKNER Sleeve note for OUP 201 (1980)

FAÇADE: ORCHESTRAL SUITES (C12c and C12e)
ANON. 'The Promenade Concerts'
The Musical Times, 79 (1938), pp. 780-781
ANON. 'A Second Façade Suite'
The Times, 12 September 1938, p. 10c
ANON. 'The Triumph of Neptune'
The Times, 6 December 1926, p. 12b
N DEMUTH Sleeve note for COLUMBIA 33SX 1003 (1953)
L GILMAN 'Music: a Philharmonic Symphony audience enjoys itself hilariously'
The New York Herald Tribune, 31 March 1938, p. 11a-b
H OTTAWAY Sleeve note for EMI ASD 3317 (1977)
M ROSE Sleeve note for EMI HQM 1006 (1965)
H THOMPSON 'Variety of works for last day'
The Yorkshire Post, 8 October 1928, p. 8b

FAÇADE: BALLETS (C12a, C12b and C12d)
ANON. 'The Camargo Society'
The Times, 27 April 1931, p. 10c
ANON. 'The Chamber Ballet Dancing Theatre'
De Brucke, 1 (September/October 1929), p. 2
ANON. 'Façade'
The Dancing Times, 20 (1930), pp. 700-702
ANON. 'Façade (ballet)'
The Dancing Times, 21 (January 1931), p. 212
ANON. [Façade ballet]
The Hagener Journal, no 218 (17 September 1928), p. 2
ANON. 'Taking Steps' (Diary Note)
The Times, 15 February 1983, p. 12a
F ASHTON 'The Ballet Façade' London, OUP, 1972, p.XIX
C W BEAUMONT [Façade Ballet] *in* 'Complete Book of Ballets' London, Putman, 1937, pp. 990-991
C W BEAUMONT [Façade Ballet] *in* 'The Sadler's Wells Ballet' London, Beaumont, 1946, pp. 140-143

P BRINSON and C CRISP [Façade Ballet] in 'Ballet and Dance' London, David and Charles, 1980, pp. 98,100-101
Z DOMINIC and J S GILBERT [Façade Ballet] in 'Frederick Ashton: a choreographer and his ballets', London, Harrap, 1971, pp. 232-237
D DREW (ed) [Façade Ballet] in 'The Decca Book of Ballet' London, Muller, 1958, pp. 384-388
E EVANS [Façade Ballet] in 'Music and Dance' London, Jenkins, 1948, pp. 98-101
A HASKELL [Façade Ballet] in 'Balletomania Then and Now' New York, Knopf, 1977, p. 142
B HASTINGS [Façade Ballet] in 'Choreographer and Composer' Boston, Twayne Publishers, 1983, p. 163
R HENDERSON 'Entertaining tribute to Walton'
The Dancing Times, 11 October 1972, p. 15a-b
O KARENSKY [Façade Ballet] in 'The World of Ballet' New York, Coward-McCann, 1970, pp. 43-44
R LAWRENCE [Façade Ballet] in 'The Victor Book of Ballets and Ballet Music' New York, Simon and Schuster, 1950, pp. 167-168
J PERCIVAL [Façade Ballet] in 'Theatre in my blood: a biography of John Cranko' London, Herbert Press, 1983, pp. 143-144
H SEARLE [Façade Ballet] in 'Ballet Music' London, Cassell, 1958, pp. 142-144
D VAUGHAN [Façade Ballet] in 'Frederick Ashton and his ballets' London, Adam and Charles Black, 1977, pp. 54-55,127-128, 456-458

FAÇADE: TWO PIANO ARRANGEMENTS (C12n)
ANON. 'Tarantella and Sevillana from Façade'
Canon, 4 (November 1950), pp. 216-217
ANON. 'Tarantella Sevillana'
Musical Courier, 143, no 9 (1 May 1951), p. 29
W S NEWMAN 'Tarantella Sevillana from Façade'
Notes, 8 (June 1951), p. 578

FANFARE FOR THE NATIONAL (C92)
M BILLINGTON [ITV Programme on the National Theatre]
The Guardian, 23 August 1976, p. 6e

THE FIRST OF THE FEW (C45)
R HOWARD [The First of the Few] in 'In Search of My Father' London, Kimber, 1981, pp. 104-120
W WHITEBAIT 'The Movies'
New Statesman and Nation, 29 August 1942, p. 140

THE FIRST SHOOT (C29)
J E AGATE [The First Shoot] in 'Immoment Toys' London, Cape, 1945, pp. 173-176

ANON. 'Adelphi Theatre: Follow the Sun'
The Times, 5 February 1936, p. 10b
ANON. 'Clever Mr Cochran – the panto and the circus'
The Manchester Evening News, 24 December 1935, p. 4d
ANON. 'Follow the Sun'
The Dancing Times, March 1936, p. 752
ANON. 'News Section'
Tempo, no 137 (June 1981), p. 57
ANON. 'Sitwellian Satire'
The Manchester Evening News, 24 December 1935, p. 4d
C BEATON [The First Shoot] *in* 'Ballet' London, Wingate, 1951, pp. 43- 44
C B COCHRAN [The First Shoot] *in* 'Cock-a-doodle Do' London, Dent, 1941, pp. 20 + 317
C B COCHRAN [The First Shoot] *in* 'Showman looks on' London, Dent, 1945, p. 217
S HEPPNER [The First Shoot] *in* 'Cockie' London, Frewin, 1969, pp. 264-265
J NAGLEY 'Orchestral'
The Musical Times, 122 (November 1981), p. 764
P PAGE 'Drama of the Week'
The Sphere, 15 February 1936, p. 304
C PALMER Sleeve note for CHANDOS CHAN 8968/ ABTD 1560 (1991)

THE FIRST SHOOT: ARRANGEMENT FOR BRASS BAND (C29b)
E GREENFIELD [The First Shoot]
The Guardian, 9 September 1981, p. 10e-f
P GRIFFITHS [The First Shoot]
The Times, 9 September 1981, p. 9a-f
P HEYWORTH [The First Shoot]
The Observer, 13 September 1981, p. 26f-i

FIVE BAGATELLES FOR GUITAR (C86)
M DONLEY 'Walton's Five Bagatelles'
Classical Guitar, May 1990, pp. 35-36 + 38
                June 1990, pp. 35-36 + 38-39
                July 1990, pp. 35-36 + 38 + 40
T EASTWOOD Sleeve note for RCA SB 6876 (1973)
E GREENFIELD 'England: Davies' Tavener and Festival Highlights'
HiFi/Musical America, 22 (November 1972), pp. 27-28
E GREENFIELD 'Walton first performances at Bath'
The Guardian, 29 May 1972, p. 6e-f
S SADIE 'Bath Festival'
The Times, 29 May 1972, p. 5g-h
P STADLEN 'Walton Sonata re-written for Orchestra'
The Daily Telegraph, 29 May 1972, p. 10a
E M WEBSTER 'Bath: Prestige or Parasols'

Musical Opinion, 95 (July 1972), pp. 519 + 521

THE FOREMAN WENT TO FRANCE (C44a)
C PALMER Sleeve note for CHANDOS CHAN 8870/ ABTD 1485 (1990)

GALOP FINALE (C39b)
R BUCKLE [Galop Finale]
Ballet, January 1950, p. 20
C PALMER Sleeve note for CHANDOS CHAN 8968/ ABTD 1560 (1991)

GENERAL
ANON. 'Background, Middleground and Foreground'
Musical Opinion, 78 (September 1955), p. 729
ANON. 'Beyond the façade ... the reluctant Grand Old Man'
The Times, 29 March 1982, p. 5a-h
ANON. 'From 'Willie of Chelsea' into Musical Knight'
Music and Musicians, 5, no 6 (1957), p. 7
ANON. 'Living British Composers'
Hinrichsen's Musical Yearbook, 6 (1949-1950), p. 125
ANON. 'A major composer'
The Periodical, Summer 1957, pp. 64-66
ANON. 'Memorial Services: Sir William Walton, OM'
The Times, 21 July 1983, p. 12d
ANON. 'Meteoric Rise: Career of Mr W T Walton'
The Oldham Chronicle, 1 May 1926, p. 9c-d
ANON. 'The Music of William Walton'
Music Review, 27, no 2 (1966), pp. 144-146
ANON. 'Music on Record: Sir William Walton'
Audio Record Review, 8 (1968), pp. 180-181
ANON. 'Musical Britain 1951', London, OUP, 1951, pp. 8, 25, 70, 82, 86, 106,
    107, 113, 116, 117, 197 and 218
ANON. 'Musician of the Year'
The Times, 29 March 1977, p. 18c
ANON. 'Portrait'
Illustrated London News, 218 (6 January 1951), p. 15
ANON. 'Portrait'
Illustrated London News, 222 (3 January 1953), p. 7
ANON. 'Portrait'
Tempo, no 145, June 1983, p. 19
ANON. 'Sir William Walton'
The Sunday Times, 25 April 1954, p. 3c-d
ANON. 'Sir William Walton'
Musical Events, 17 (April 1962), p. 27
ANON. ['Sir William and our Gracie']
The Sunday Times, 19 October 1975, p. 40e-f
ANON. 'Sir William Walton on the musical schisms of today'

The Times, 29 August 1960, p. 12a-e

ANON. 'Sir William Walton's four concertos: composer content to be himself'
The Times, 22 February 1957, p. 3b-c

ANON. 'The teasing inconsistencies of William Walton'
The Times, 23 March 1962, p. 17e-g

ANON. 'Times Arts Diary: Walton's wish'
The Times, 10 October 1987, p. 21h

ANON. 'The Touch of the Master'
The Times, 3 April 1977, p. 38

ANON. 'William Walton'
The Observer, 12 February 1950, p. 9c-f

ANON. [Untitled]
B'lgarska Muziska 33 (June 1982), p. 109

F APRAHAMIAN 'Walton Retrospective'
Music and Musicians, 20 (July 1972), pp. 22-26

A ARAD 'Walton as Scapino'
The Strad, 100 (February 1989), pp. 137, 139-141

T ARMSTRONG 'The Ear is the Judge'
The Oxford Mail, 28 November 1955, p. 6f-h

K AVERY 'William Walton'
Music and Letters, 28 (January 1947), pp. 1-11

L AYRE [William Walton] in 'The Proms' London, Frewin, 1968, pp. 119,129, 132, 145 and 153

A L BACHARACH [William Walton] in 'British Music of our time' Harmondsworth, Penguin Books, 1946, pp. 134-146 and 254-255

S BAYLISS 'Walton'
The Musical Times, 106 (August 1965), pp. 600-601

G BEECHEY 'William Walton, Adrian Boult and Herbert Howells: an appreciation'
Musical Opinion, 106 (May 1983), pp. 236-237

L BERKELEY 'Walton yesterday'
Performing Right, 7 (May 1972), pp. 18-19

E BLOM 'The later William Walton'
The Listener, 20 September 1945, p. 333

A BLYTH [Sir William Walton]
Radio Times, 25-31 March 1973, p. 15

A BLYTH 'Walton at 70'
The Times, 30 March 1972, p. 11g-h

A C BOULT [William Walton] *in* 'My Own Trumpet' London, Hamilton, 1973, pp. 105-107, 113, 136, 137

E BRADBURY 'Sir William Walton at 60'
The Yorkshire Post, 28 March 1962, p. 6d-e

E BRADBURY 'Walton at seventy'
The Yorkshire Post, 28 March 1972, p. 6a-g

E BRADBURY 'Walton's Ham, Lamb and Jam'
The Yorkshire Post, 28 April 1964, p. 4g-h
T BRAY 'William Walton: his life and music' [review]
Music and Letters, 66, no 3 (1985)' pp. 279-280
W R BROMME 'An analysis of the sacred choral works of William Walton'
 Music Dissertation, Southwestern Baptist Theological Seminary, 1981
D BROOK 'William Walton' in 'Composer's Gallery' London, Rockliff, 1946,
 pp. 106-111
J BURN 'Sir William Walton'
Musical Opinion, 100 (November 1976), pp. 64-65, 67 and 69

N CARDUS 'The rebel's detractors'
The Guardian, 29 March 1962, p. 6e
J CHURCHILL 'The Church Music of William Walton'
Music (AGO), 11 (May 1977), pp. 40-41
A CLEMENTS 'Walton at 80'
New Statesman, 26 March 1982, pp. 27-28
H COLE 'Walton in retrospect'
The Listener, 25 March 1982, p. 35
M COOPER 'The Age of Walton'
The Daily Telegraph, 25 March 1972, p. 12c-e
M COOPER 'The unpredictable Walton'
The Listener, 25 July 1957, p. 146
M COOPER (ed) [William Walton] in 'The Modern Age: 1890-1960' London,
 OUP, 1974, pp. 523-539
M COOPER [William Walton] in 'Les Musiciens anglais d'aujourd'hui' Paris,
 Librarie Plon, 1952, pp. 95-123
K CORDEN 'The genius of Green Island'
Radio Times, 25-31 May 1968, p. 33
S R CRAGGS 'Sir William Walton: a catalogue, annotated bibliography and
 discography of his musical works' Fellowship of the Library Association
 thesis, 1973
S R CRAGGS 'A Walton Pot-Pourri'
The Musical Times, 113 (March 1972), pp. 253-254
S R CRAGGS 'William Walton: a catalogue' Oxford, OUP, 1990
S R CRAGGS 'William Walton: a thematic catalogue of his musical works'
 London, OUP, 1977
S R CRAGGS 'William Turner Walton: his Life and Music' M A Thesis,
 University of Strathclyde (Glasgow), 1978 (3 volumes)
A CRUFT 'Book Reviews: The Music of William Walton' *Composer*, 17
 (October 1965), pp. 20-21

J.D. 'Sir William Walton's Shakespeare film scores'
American Record Guide, 30 (May 1964), pp. 881-883
J C DECKER 'A comparative textual analysis of selected orchestral works of

Sir William Walton and Paul Hindemith' DMA dissertation, University of Missouri-Kansas City, 1971

N DEMUTH [William Walton] in 'Musical trends in the 20th century' London, Rockcliff, 1952, pp. 167, 168-179, 315, 317, 321 and 323

J DIETHER 'A Meticulous Study of the Meticulous Sir William'
American Record Guide, 32 (December 1965), p. 385

G DORRIS 'Copland and Walton'
Dance Chronicle, 9, no 1 (1986), pp. 148-154

O DOWNES 'Visiting composer'
The New York Times, 102, 16 August 1953 (Section 2), p. 7a-b

J DUNSFORD 'His tune at 15 set the theme for fame'
The Manchester Evening News, 24 March 1962, p. 4f-i

Q EATON 'Book: a simple opera'
Opera News, 30 (29 January 1966), p. 33

T ECKERT 'Walton on Record'
Christian Science Monitor, 75 (23 March 1983), p. 18

E EVANS 'Modern British Composers I: William Walton'
The Musical Times, 85 (1944), pp. 329-332 and 364-368

E EVANS 'Walton and Lambert'
Modern Music, 7, no 2 (1930), pp. 26-31

M EVANS [William Walton] in 'Soundtrack: the music of the movies' New York, Hopkinson and Blake, 1975, pp. 50, 82, 85-87, 89, 228, 268

P EVANS 'The Music of William Walton by F Howes'
Music and Letters, 47 (1966), pp. 52-55

P EVANS 'Sir William Walton's manner and mannerism'
The Listener, 62 (20 August 1959), p. 297

B A FERRIS 'Style, development and achievement: a survey of the music of William Walton' MA thesis, University of Bristol, 1969

E FORBES 'Seven English composers'
About the House, 5, no 10 (1979), p. 70

C FORD 'A tremendous time in the 30s'
The Times, 29 March 1982, p. 5

C FORD 'William Walton'
The Guardian, 30 July 1976, p. 10a-d

L FOREMAN 'The recorded works of Sir William Walton'
Tempo, no 137 (June 1981), pp. 45-46

H J FOSS 'The music of William Walton'
The Listener, 17 May 1945, p. 557

H J FOSS 'William Walton'
The Chesterian, 11 (1930), pp. 175-181

H J FOSS 'William Walton'
Musical Quarterly, 26 (1940), pp. 456-466

H J FOSS 'William Walton'

Hallé, December 1946-January 1947, pp. 9-12
A C FRANK 'Contemporary Portraits: William Walton'
Music Teacher, 31 (March 1952), pp. 135-136
A C FRANK 'The music of William Walton'
The Chesterian, 20 (1939), pp. 153-156
A C FRANK 'Sir William Walton' *in* 'Modern British Composers' London,
Dobson, 1953, pp. 58-63
A C FRANK 'Sir William Walton'
Canon, 15 (May 1962), pp. 6-7
A C FRANK 'Sir William Walton'
Res Musicae, 8, no 4 (1962), pp. 9-10
A C FRANK 'Sir William Walton' (Performing Right Society Profile 7)
Performing Right Gazette, 47 (April 1967), pp. 14-15
W K FULTON 'Selected choral works of William Walton' PhD thesis, Texas
Technical University, 1981
W K FULTON 'William Walton's Choral Style: a birthday offering'
Choral Journal, 22, no 7 (March 1982), pp. 5-9

G GILBERT 'Walton on trends in composition'
The New York Times, 4 June 1939 (Section IX), p. 5b-d
P GLANVILLE-HICKS 'Willie has a silver spoon'
Hi-Fi Music at Home, 12 (January-February 1956), pp. 24-25,55-56
V GLENDINNING 'Behind Façade'
Harpers and Queen, February 1988, pp. 88-92
V GLENDINNING 'Edith Sitwell: A Unicorn among Lions' London, Wei-
denfeld and Nicholson, 1981, pp. 51, 56, 106, 128, 130, 227, 256, 264, 268,
271, 294, 302, 304
S GODDARD 'Interpreting the age'
The Listener, 15 May 1940, p. 341
S GODDARD 'William Walton'
The Listener, 12 September 1946, p. 357
A GOLDBERG 'A Bourgeois Chord? Idea baffles Walton'
The Los Angeles Times, 9 August 1953 (Section IV), pp. 1g-h and 5a-b
C GRAY [William Walton] *in* 'Musical Chairs', London, Home and Van Thal,
1948, pp. 107, 179, 239, 242-243, 258-289, 314
E GREENFIELD 'Here and There: Sir William Walton at 80'
Gramophone, 59 (March 1982), p. 1239
E GREENFIELD 'The Impact of Pierre Boulez'
HiFi/Musical America, 22 (August 1972), pp. 30-31
E GREENFIELD 'The lady who became a lady'
The Guardian, 19 May 1971, p. 11a-c
E GREENFIELD 'Sir William Walton at 80'
Gramophone, 59 (March 1982), p. 1239
E GREENFIELD 'Walton by Walton: a 70th birthday tribute'
Gramophone, 49 (May 1972), pp. 1865-1866

E GREENFIELD 'William Walton'
The Guardian, 29 February 1972, p. 10a-f
E GREENFIELD 'Woman behind the Façade'
The Guardian, 6 February 1988, p. 13a-f

A.H. 'Frank Howes: The Music of William Walton'
Recorded Sound, 19 (July 1965), p. 370
I.H. 'Recording on Ischia'
Gramophone, 68 (March 1991), p. 1753
F HALL [William Walton] in 'Modern English Ballet' London, Melrose, 1950, pp. 197 and 202
G E HANSLER 'Stylistic characteristics and trends in the choral music of five 20th century composers' PhD Thesis, New York University, 1957
R HARTY 'Just William'
The Sunday Times Magazine, 7 November 1976, pp. 54-56 and 59
B HESFORD 'Early Days'
Musical Opinion, 100 (November 1976), pp. 56-57 and 59
B HESFORD 'William Walton and the Organ'
Musical Opinion, 100 (November 1976), pp. 68-69
F HIRSCH [William Walton] in 'Laurence Olivier' Boston, Twayne Publishers, 1979, pp. 69,85 and 97
H HOLLANDER 'Frank Howes: The Music of William Walton' [Review]
Neue Zeitschrift fur Musik, 135 no 10 (1974), p. 658
H HOLLANDER 'Sir William Walton: Siebzigjahrig'
Neue Zeitschrift fur Musik, June 1972, p. 323
H HOLLANDER 'Stewart R Craggs: William Walton – A Thematic Catalogue' [Review]
Das Orchester 27 (January 1979), p. 49
P HOWARD 'The Queen invites her most meritorious'
The Times, 18 November 1977, p. 4
F S HOWES 'Features of Walton's style' *Monthly Musical Record*, 72 (1942), pp. 126-129
F S HOWES 'The Music of William Walton' (The Musical Pilgrim Series), London, OUP, Volume 1 1942, Volume 2, 1943
F S HOWES 'The Music of William Walton' London, OUP 1965; London, OUP 1973
F S HOWES 'VW und Walton'
Musica, 12 (July-August 1958), pp. 405-408
F S HOWES 'Walton's formative years at Oxford'
The Oxford Mail, 2 April 1962, p. 6a-c
F S HOWES [William Walton] in 'The English Musical Renaissance' London, Secker and Warburg, 1966, pp. 270-272, 304-306
P C HUGHES 'Nobody calls him Willie now'
High Fidelity, 10 (September 1960), pp. 43-46 and 116-117
S HUGHES [William Walton] in 'Opening Bars' London, Pilot Press, 1946, pp. 314-319, 355, 363, 365-366

J HUNTLEY 'Music in Film'
The Musical Times, 98 (December 1957), pp. 662-663
M HURD 'The music of William Walton'
Music in Education, 30, no 317 (1966), pp. 36-37
M HURD 'The music of William Walton'
Music in Education, 38, no 366 (1974), p. 80

A JACOBS 'A cult and a recluse'
The Times Literary Supplement, 19-25 February 1988, p. 181
A JACOBS 'Passing notes'
Gramophone, 39 (January 1962), p. 373
A JACOBS 'William Walton'
Musical America, 72 (February 1952), pp. 18 + 83
A JACOBS (ed) [William Walton] in 'Choral Music' Harmondsworth, Penguin Books, 1963, pp. 332, 339-341, 389
A JEFFERSON 'The Music of William Walton'
Music and Musicians, 14 (October 1965), p. 54
A JEFFERSON 'Walton, Man and Music'
Music and Musicians, 13 (March 1965), pp. 16-21
W JOSEPHS 'Foreign honours for Sir William Walton'
Musical Events, 19 (January 1964), p. 7

H KELLER & W WALTON 'Contemporary Music: its problems and its future'
Composer, 20 (1966), pp. 2-4
M E KENDRICK 'The Music of William Walton'
American Music Teacher, 24 no 1 (1974), p. 35
M KENNEDY 'Enigmatically eclipsed: Neil Tierney, William Walton: His Life and Music' [Review]
The Times Literary Supplement, 4276 (1985), p. 291
M KENNEDY 'New flowers in a scented garden'
The Sunday Telegraph, 29 September 1991, p. XIV
M KENNEDY 'Portrait of Walton' Oxford, Oxford University Press, 1989
M KENNEDY 'Sturdy genius of William Walton'
The Daily Telegraph, 26 March 1977, p. 9c-f
M KENNEDY 'Walton in perspective'
The Listener, 11 August 1983, p. 30
J W KLEIN 'Walton as a musical dramatist'
Musical Opinion, 84 (December 1960), p. 155ff

C LAMBERT 'Fresh hand, new talent, vital touch'
The Boston Evening Transcript, 27 November 1926 (Section IV), p.5a-f
C LAMBERT 'Some angles of the compleat Walton'
Radio Times, 7 August 1936, p. 13
C LAMBERT 'Some recent works by William Walton'
The Dominant, 4 (1928), pp. 16-19

J W LAMBERT 'Imp and Sceptre'
The Sunday Times, 25 March 1962, p. 39

Z LAWRENCE-CURREN 'Dynamism and lyricism in selected works of William Walton, 1929-1939' BA (Music) Dissertation, University of Durham, 1987

R LAYTON 'Walton and his critics'
The Listener, 29 March 1962, p. 577

P LEWIS 'Sir William Walton, just like his music, a joke here, a little acid there ...'
The Daily Mail, 28 March 1972, p. 7a-g

R S LICHTENBERGER 'The film music of Sir William Walton'
The Max Steiner Journal, 7 (1973), pp. 6-9

J McCABE 'Twentieth Century Melodist'
Records and Recordings, 13, no 7 (1970), pp. 18-19

J McCABE 'Well composed at 70'
Records and Recordings, 15, no 8 (1972), pp. 32-36

C McCARTY 'William Walton'
Film and TV Music, 16 (Fall 1956), pp. 12-13

B MAINE 'The Music of William Walton'
Musical Opinion, 60 (1937), pp. 492 + 686-687

A MAITLAND 'Sir William Walton'
This England, 15 (Spring 1982), pp. 38-39

W MANN 'BBCSO/Colin Davis'
The Times, 31 March 1977, p. 9b

W MANN 'Sir William Walton: music for super professionals'
The Times, 16 March 1972, p. 10d-g

J MARTIN 'Walton's Instrumental output and style' BA Dissertation, University of Durham, 1968

W MARTIN 'The vocal works of William Walton'
NATS Bulletin, 33, no 3 (1977), pp. 30-35 + 38

B MASON 'The genial life: an interview with Sir William Walton'
New Zealand Listener, 13 March 1964, pp. 5 + 21

C MASON 'The music of William Walton'
Canon, 16, no 11 (1963), pp. 7-8

C MASON 'The Musical Achievement'
The Gramophone, 29 March 1962, p. 6a-d

C MASON 'William Walton' in A L Bacharach (ed) 'British music of our time'
Harmondsworth, Pelican Books, 1946, pp. 137-149

E MASON 'Walton for the Wells?'
Music and Musicians, 11 (June 1963), p. 18

W MELLERS 'Recent trends in British Music'
Musical Quarterly, 38 (April 1952), pp. 194-196

W MELLERS 'Sir William Walton and 20th century *Opera*'
The Listener, 25 November 1954, p. 933

H MENDL-SCHRAMA 'Lady Walton and her plans for a Summer Festival in Ischia'
Music and Musicians, August 1986, pp. 8-9
H MENDL-SCHRAMA 'Lady Walton and the William Walton Trust'
Music and Musicans International, 39 (September 1990), p. 8
D MITCHELL 'The Modernity of William Walton'
The Listener, 7 February 1957, p. 245
D MITCHELL 'Revaluations'
Musical Opinion, 78 (July 1955), pp. 601-603
D MITCHELL 'Some observations on William Walton'
The Chesterian, 26 (January 1952), pp. 35-38
C MOOREHEAD 'Beyond the Façade ... the reluctant Grand Old Man'
The Times, 29 March 1982, p. 5
C MOOREHEAD 'Composer in residence'
Radio Times, 19-25 March 1977, pp. 13-15
A MORRISON 'Willie: the young Walton and his four masterpieces'
The Royal College of Music Magazine, 80 (1984), pp. 119-127

C NORRIS 'Frank Howes: The Music of William Walton'
Music and Musicans, 22 (February 1974), p. 28
B NORTHCOTT 'In search of Walton'
The Musical Times, 123 (March 1982), pp. 179-184
B NORTHCOTT 'Opening Up: British Concert Music since the War'
Musical Newsletter, 5 no 3 (1975), pp. 3-4

M OLIVER 'After the Renaissance'
The Gramophone, 61 (August 1983), p. 222
M OLIVER 'Bookshelf'
The Gramophone, 62 (March 1985), p. 1136
A ORGA 'Sir William Walton: some thoughts'
Composer, 68 (Winter 1979/1980), pp. 11-14
A ORGA 'Sir William Walton: some thoughts on his 70th birthday'
Musical Events, 27 (March 1972), pp. 7-10 + 32
B ORR 'Awards and Appointments'
Composer, 27 (Spring 1968), p. 36
H OTTAWAY 'Music on Record: Sir William Walton'
HiFi News and Record Review, 22, no 6 (1977), pp. 109 + 111
H OTTAWAY 'Walton and his critics'
The Listener, 83, 25 June 1970, p. 869
H OTTAWAY 'Walton and the 1930s'
Monthly Musical Record, 81 (January 1951), pp. 4-9
H OTTAWAY 'Walton at 75'
Halle, 2, no 7 (1977), pp. 2-3 + 32
H OTTAWAY 'Walton Revisited?'
The Musical Times, 115 (January 1974), p. 42
H OTTAWAY 'William Walton' Sevenoaks, Novello, 1972/ 2nd ed 1977

C PALMER 'Symphonies of the Silver-Screen'
Gramophone, 68 (June 1990), pp. 31-32
C PALMER 'The uncollected Walton'
The Musical Times, cxxxi (May 1990), pp. 247-252
C PALMER 'Walton Birthday'
The Musical Times, 113 (May 1972), p. 475
C PALMER 'Walton in Focus'
The Musical Times, 113 (December 1972), p. 1185
C PALMER 'Walton's Church Music'
Church Music, 3, no 12 (February 1973), pp. 10-13
C PALMER 'Walton's Film Music'
The Musical Times, 113 (March 1972), pp. 249-252
A PERCHANSKY 'Barber, Copland, Walton win'
Billboard, 91 (27 October 1979), p. 82
P PETERS 'Duet for One'
The Sunday Telegraph Magazine, 31 January 1988, pp. 16-18
P J PIRIE 'Book reviews: The Recorded Works of William Walton'
Music Review, 42, no 2 (May 1981), pp. 152-154
P J PIRIE 'Scapino: the development of William Walton'
The Musical Times, 105 (April 1964), pp. 258-259
P J PIRIE 'Walton at 70'
Music and Musicians, 20 (March 1972), pp. 16 + 18
R PONSONBY 'Moving South'
The Listener, 90 (5 July 1973), p. 26
A PORTER '*Musical Events*'
New Yorker, 58 (26 April 1982), p. 112
A POULTON 'Sir William Walton: a discography' Kidderminster, Bravura
    Publications, 1980
A PREVIN 'Happy Birthday, Sir William'
Radio Times, 27 March - 2 April 1982, pp. 6-7

B.R. 'The Music of William Walton'
Musical Opinion, 89 (March 1966), p. 351
M RATCLIFFE 'Mischief in the Master Musician'
The Times, 20 April 1981, p. 7c
H RAYNOR 'The 1968 Promenade Concerts'
Music Review, 30, no 2 (1969), p. 152
C B REES 'Impressions: Sir William Walton'
London Musical Events, 6 (March 1951), pp. 15-16
C B REES 'Musical Roundabout'
The Music Teacher, 30 (February 1951), p. 77
C B REES 'Walton's 60th Birthday'
Musical Events, 17 (May 1962), pp. 6-7
C B REES and R HILL 'William Walton'
Radio Times, 18 May 1945, p. 5

C REID '60 years of William Walton'
Music and Musicians, 10 (March 1962), pp. 19 + 27
J RENNERT '235 this year'
World of Church Music, 1982, pp. 43-58
D RICHARDS 'Proms: Walton night'
Music and Musicians, 17 (October 1968), pp. 45-46
D RICHARDS 'William Walton: a survey'
Musical Opinion, 100 (November 1976), pp. 60-61
J ROOK 'Making beautiful music together'
The Daily Express, 19 November 1976, p. 5a-h
K ROSE 'Albany at large'
The Sunday Telegraph, 25 March 1974, p. 2
H ROSENWALD 'Speaking on Music ...'
Music News 42 (December 1950), pp. 6-7
F ROUTH 'William Walton' *in* 'Contemporary British Music' London, Mac-
donald, 1972, pp. 25-42
E RUBBRA 'William Walton's 70th birthday'
The Listener, 87 (23 March 1972), pp. 394-395
T RUSSELL 'William Walton'
London Philharmonic Post, 2 (1942), pp. 4,5.8 and 11

E SALZMAN 'View from Ischia'
The New York Times, 110, 12 February 1961, (Section 2), p. 11h
M SCHAFER 'William Walton' *in* 'British Composers in Interview' London,
Faber, 1963, pp. 18-23, 72-82 + 151
E SECKERSON 'Walton won'
Gramophone, 66 (August 1988), pp. 264 + 267
H G SEER 'English Music'
Philharmonic Post, 7 (May-June 1954), p. 32
E SENIOR 'Music Man's Diary'
Music and Musicians, 16 (January 1968), p. 50
D SHAWE-TAYLOR 'The Challenge of Walton'
The Sunday Times, 26 March 1972, p. 37f-h
D SHAWE-TAYLOR 'The Touch of the Master'
The Sunday Times, 3 April 1977, p. 38d-h
D SHAWE-TAYLOR 'Walton: a feast of affection'
The Sunday Times, 4 April 1982, p. 38e-h
B SHORE 'William Walton'
Music Digest, 10 (1950), pp. 51-53
D SIMMONS 'London Music'
Musical Opinion, 91 (October 1968), p. 7
D SIMMONS 'London Music'
Musical Opinion, 95 (May 1972), p. 398
D SIMMONS '20th Century English composers'
Instrumentalist, 23 (November 1968), p. 50

292 · WILLIAM WALTON

E SITWELL 'Young William Walton comes to town'
The Sunday Times, 18 March 1962, p. 40f-h
J SMALL 'The eclectic Walton'
Prospect, 7, no 2 (1964), pp. 22-23
J SMALL 'Walton reconsidered'
Bulletin, 9 May 1964, p. 43
C J SMITH 'William Walton: a bio-bibliography' Westport (Conn), Greenwood Press, 1988
E SMITH 'The Music of William Walton'
Music Teacher, 53 (August 1974), p. 23
D J SORIA 'Artist Life'
HiFi/Musical America, 19 (April 1969), pp. 6-7
D J SORIA 'Artist Life'
HiFi/Musical America, 25 (December 1975), pp. 8-9
D J SORIA 'Sir William Walton, OM'
HiFi/Musical America, 18 (February 1968), pp. 4ff
J SOUTHWORTH 'Garden of Love'
The Daily Mail, 2 April 1988, p. 9
K SPENCE 'Television'
The Musical Times, 111 (October 1970), p. 1025
K SPENCE 'Television'
The Musical Times, 113 (May 1972), p. 486
J SPRAGUE 'Sir William talks to J Sprague'
The Oldham Chronicle, 12 September 1959, p. 12a-e
P STANFORD 'Sir William Walton and his English public'
Musical Opinion, 100 (November 1976), pp. 55-56
M STOTT 'The Walton Idyll'
The Guardian, 18 May 1965, p. 9b-e
S STOTT 'Festival's Quiet Guest of Honour'
The Advertiser (Adelaide), 11 March 1964, pp. 1 + 3
C STUART 'William Walton at Huddersfield'
The Yorkshire Observer, 21 October 1942, p. 2d-f

J TALBOT 'The Works of William Walton: a critical analysis' BA Dissertation, University of Queensland, 1963
P TAYLOR 'The Operas of William Walton'
Musical Opinion, 100 (November 1976), pp. 61, 63-64
S de B TAYLOR 'William Walton: a brief survey of some of his works'
Musical Opinion, 54 (1931), pp. 593-594
B TEMPLE 'The Music of William Walton' BMus Dissertation, University of Birmingham, 1971
D W THORNTON 'A Survey of the music of William Walton' Music Dissertation, University of Melbourne, 1965
N TIERNEY 'Making music on Ischia'
The Daily Telegraph, 19 September 1990, p. 12

N TIERNEY 'William Walton: his life and music' London, Hale, 1984
M TREND [William Walton] in 'The Music Makers' London, Weidenfeld
and Nicholson, 1985, pp. 136,165-172 and 230

J.S.W. 'Frank Howes: The Music of William Walton'
Musical Events, 21 (January 1966), pp. 33-34
D R WALKER 'Sonata form in the music of William Walton' MA Disser-
tation, University College of South Wales, 1975
M WALKER 'Recorded works of Sir William Walton'
The Musical Times, 122 (June 1981), pp. 380-381
S WALSH 'The Music of William Walton'
Tempo, no 74 (Autumn 1965), pp. 29-31
S WALTON 'Behind the Façade: conduct unbecoming'
The Times, 30 December 1987, p. 12a-f
S WALTON 'Behind the Façade: the feeding of a hungry genius'
The Times, 28 December 1987, p. 12a-g
S WALTON 'Behind the Façade: underscoring Olivier'
The Times, 29 December 1987, p. 12a-e
S WALTON 'The Making of Memories'
Expression, July 1988, pp. 38-39
S WALTON 'Musical Enchantment'
Country Homes and Interiors, September 1991, pp. 90-93
S WALTON 'William Walton: Behind the Façade' Oxford, Oxford Univer-
sity Press, 1988
S WALTON 'William Walton Trust'
The Times, 15 September 1984, p. 9e
W WALTON 'My life in music'
The Sunday Telegraph, 25 March 1962, p. 8c-h
W WALTON 'Preface' to 'Alan Rawsthorne', Volume 3 (ed. A. Poulton)
Hindhead, Bravura, 1986
J O WARD 'Glimpses of William Walton'
HiFi/Musical America, 33 (November 1983), pp. 19-21 + 24
J WARRACK 'A silence with voices'
The Daily Telegraph Magazine, 24 May 1968, pp. 45-46
J WARRACK 'Sir William Walton talks to John Warrack'
The Listener, 8 August 1968, pp. 176-178
J F WEBER 'The Recorded Works of Sir William Walton'
Association for Recorded Sound Collections Journal, 13, no 2 (1981), pp. 112-113
E W WHITE 'William Walton'
Life and Letters, 16 (1937), pp. 111-114
F WHITSEY 'A Paradise out of disaster'
The Daily Telegraph (Weekend), 21 October 1989, p. III
F WHITSEY 'Plants for a Music Maker'
Country Life, 171 (April 1982), pp. 890-892
A WHITTALL 'England, Italy and Spain'

Musical Opinion, 88 (August 1965), p. 663
G WIDDICOMBE 'Behind Walton's Façade'
The Observer Magazine, 7 February 1982, pp. 28-29, 31 + 33
G WIDDICOMBE 'Grand old man of British music'
The Observer, 28 March 1982, p. 32a-e
G WIDDICOMBE 'Sir William Walton' *in* 'Philharmonia Orchestra', 1981/1982, pp. 22-23
G WIDDICOMBE 'Walton Revived'
The Observer Magazine, 21 November 1976, pp. 13-14
S WILLIAMS 'An English Composer'
The Evening Standard, 5 November 1935, p. 7a-b
A WILLIAMSON [William Walton] *in* 'Contemporary Ballet' London, Rockliff, 1946, pp. 54, 69-70, 78-80
C WILSON 'Self-effacing composer'
The Scotsman, 11 March 1963, p. 4a-c
J WISER 'Walton's Walton'
Asoociation for Recorded Sound Collectors Journal, 14, (1982), pp. 91-92
A W WOLF 'Concert Reviews'
Music of the West Magazine, 9 (October 1953), p. 6
A WOODHOUSE 'Growing in harmony'
Homes and Gardens, July 1988, pp. 105-109
R WRIGHT 'A Walton Discography'
Composer, Winter 1980-1981, p. 32

A M de ZEEUW 'Tonality and the Concertos of William Walton' Music Dissertation, University of Texas at Austin, 1983
B de ZOETE 'William Walton'
Monthly Musical Record, 59 (1929), pp. 321 - 323 + 356
V ZORIAN 'Freedom for a composer'
Lancashire Life, 9, no 1 (1961), pp. 28-29

GLORIA (C72)

ANON. 'Gloria'
Music Review, 23, no 1 (1962), pp. 83-84
ANON. 'New work by Sir William Walton'
The Times, 26 September 1961, p. 14d
ANON. 'Sir William Walton's new Gloria'
The Times, 25 November 1961, p. 4a
E BRADBURY 'Choir celebrates with première'
The Yorkshire Post, 25 November 1961, p. 9a-c
E CHAPMAN 'A Walton Programme'
Musical Events, 17 (March 1962), p. 30
A C FRANK Sleeve note for EMI ASD 3348 (1977)
L HUGHES-JONES 'Gloria'
Music and Musicians, 10 (January 1962), p. 40

L HUGHES-JONES 'Sir Malcolm Sargent programme with the LPO'
Music and Musicians, 11 (March 1962), p. 41
A JACOBS 'Walton's Gloria at Huddersfield'
The Musical Times, 103 (January 1962), p. 24
C MASON 'First hearing at Huddersfield'
The Guardian, 25 November 1961, p. 5e
E MASON 'Walton's Gloria'
The Choir, 53 (April 1962), p. 70
D MITCHELL 'Stirred by his text: quality in Walton's Gloria'
The Daily Telegraph, 25 November 1961, p. 10f
R H MYERS 'News from Britain'
Canon, 15 (January-February 1962), pp. 9-10
R H MYERS 'New from Britain'
Canon, 15 (March 1962), p. 16
C PALMER Sleeve note for CHANDOS CHAN 8760/ ABTD 1398 (1989)
J E REYES 'Gloria'
Notes, 20 (1963), p. 568
J.S.W. 'Gloria'
Musical Events, 17 (January 1962), p. 24

GRANADA PRELUDE (C75a)
C PALMER Sleeve note for CHANDOS CHAN 8968/ ABTD 1560 (1991)

HAMLET (C54)
ANON. 'Excerpts from the score of Hamlet'
Film Music Notes, 9 (November-December 1949), pp. 7-15
ANON. 'Hamlet'
Photoplay, 33 (November 1948), pp. 54-55
ANON. 'Hamlet'
Woman's Home Companion, 75 (October 1948), pp. 10-11
ANON. 'The new play Hamlet'
Vogue, 112, 15 September 1948, p. 148
ANON. 'Sir Laurence Olivier's new film'
The Times, 5 May 1948, p. 7d
ANON. 'The Tragedy of Hamlet'
Life, 24, 15 March 1948, pp. 117-127
E BRANDEN 'Hamlet'
Photoplay, 33 (October 1948), p. 22
J M BROWN 'Seeing Things'
Saturday Review, 31, 21 October 1948, pp. 26-28
C CHAPPELL 'Hamlet'
Kinematograph Weekly, 375, 6 May 1948, p. 6
W A CHISLETT Sleeve note for LYRITA SRCS 71: Funeral March (1978)
B CROSS (ed.) [William Walton's music for Hamlet] in 'The film Hamlet'
London, The Saturn Press, 1948, pp. 61-64

A DENT (ed.) 'Hamlet: the film and the play' London, World Film Productions Ltd., 1948
S GODDARD 'Music for the film'
Penguin Music Magazine, 8 (February 1949), pp. 86-89
V GRAHAM 'Contemporary Arts: The Cinema'
The Spectator, 180, 7 May 1948, p. 553
R HATCH 'Movies: Olivier's Hamlet'
New Republic, 119, 4 October 1948, pp. 28-30
A HOPKINS 'Hamlet and Olivier'
Theatre Arts, 32 (Fall 1948), pp. 30-31
J HUNTLEY 'The music of Hamlet and Oliver Twist'
The Penguin Film Review, 8 (January 1949), pp. 110-116
H KELLER 'Music for the film (Hamlet)'
Film Monthly Review, April 1948, pp. 10-11 and 13
H KELLER 'Walton's (music) for Hamlet'
Music Review, 9 (August 1948), pp. 197-198
M MATHIESON 'Note on Hamlet'
Film Music, 13, no 3 (January-February 1954), p. 19
M MATHIESON Sleeve note for EMI 33CX 1883/ SAX 2517: Funeral March (1964)
C PALMER Sleeve note for CHANDOS CHAN 8842/ ABTD 1461 (1990)
L PARSONS 'Cosmopolitan's citation for the best production of the month'
Cosmopolitan, 125 (September 1948), pp. 12-13 and 159
H RAWLINSON 'A movie maker's notebook'
The British Journal of Photography, XCVI, 9 December 1949, p. 590
W WALTON 'Excerpts from the score for Hamlet'
Film Music Notes, 9 (November/December 1949), pp. 7-15
W WHITEBAIT 'Hamlet at the Odeon'
The New Statesman, 35, 8 May 1948, p. 373

HENRY V (C50)
ANON. 'Film Music'
The Times, 15 December 1944, p. 8b
ANON. 'Henry V: Shakespeare in technicolour'
The Times, 23 November 1944, p. 6c-d
ANON. 'New Music: Organ'
The Musical Times, 90 (April 1949), p. 120
ANON. 'Reviews for Showmen: Henry V'
Kinematograph Weekly, 30 November 1944, p. 28
H CLIFFORD 'Walton's Henry V Music'
Tempo, no, 9 (December 1944), pp. 13-14
H FINCH 'Walton: Shakespeare well served'
The Times, 14 May 1990, p. 16
H M GEDULD [Walton's music for Henry V] *in* 'Filmguide to Henry V'
Bloomington, Indiana University Press, 1973, pp. 63-65, 81-82

E GREENFIELD 'A late score from Agincourt'
The Guardian, 14 May 1990, p. 37
M HAYES 'Blast of war blows in our ears'
The Daily Telegraph, 14 May 1990, p. 14
J HUNTLEY 'British film music' *Penguin Film Review*, 6 (April 1948), pp. 91-96
J HUNTLEY 'Music in current British film'
Film Music Notes, 8, no 3 (January-February 1949), pp. 15-16
J HUNTLEY [Walton's music for Henry V] *in* 'British Film Music'
London, Skelton Robinson, 1947, pp. 171-176, 224-225
M MATHIESON Sleeve note for EMI 33CX 1883/ SAX 2527 (1964)
R MAYCOCK 'Setting an old score'
The Independent, 14 May 1990, p. 13
C PALMER Sleeve note for CHANDOS CHAN 8892/ ABTD 1503 (1990)
C PALMER Sleeve note for EMI EL 27 0591 1/ EL 27 0591 4/ CDC 7 47944 2
(1987)

THE HISTORY OF THE ENGLISH SPEAKING PEOPLES: MARCH
(C70)
ANON. [A History of the English Speaking Peoples]
The Daily Telegraph, 10 February 1959, p. 10c
C PALMER Sleeve note for CHANDOS CHAN 8968/ ABTD 1560 (1991)
C PALMER Sleeve note for EMI EL 27 0591 1/ EL 27 0591 4/CDC 7 47944 2
(1987)

IMPROVISATIONS ON AN IMPROMPTU OF BENJAMIN BRITTEN
(C82)
ANON. 'Concert-Goers' News'
Musical Events, 25 (June 1970), p. 27
ANON. 'Editorial Notes'
Strad, 80 (February 1970), p. 445
ANON. 'Notes - Commissions'
Composer, 35 (Spring 1970), pp. 34 ff
ANON. 'Sir William Walton's new work'
The Times, 8 December 1969, p. 11c
F APRAHAMIAN 'Captivating Walton'
The Sunday Times, 5 July 1970, p. 25c
A BLOOMFIELD 'Krips conducts a great Beethoven's 8th'
San Francisco Examiner, 105, 15 January 1970, p. 23a-c
J CHISSELL 'LPO: Festival Hall'
The Times, 21 October 1970, p. 15a
N GOODWIN 'Rebuilding the House'
Music and Musicians, 18 (August 1970), pp. 18-19
E GREENFIELD 'Aldeburgh'
The Musical Times, 111 (August 1970), p. 820
E GREENFIELD Sleeve note for EMI SAN 324 (1972)

E GREENFIELD 'Walton's Improvisations at Aldeburgh'
The Guardian, 29 June 1970, p. 4e-f
J D KRAMER 'Improvisations on an Impromptu of Benjamin Britten'
Performing Arts, 4 (January 1970), pp. 27 and 29
C PALMER Sleeve note for CHANDOS CHAN 8959/ ABTD 1551 (1991)
A E PAYNE 'Walton's leisurely air in Improvisations'
The Daily Telegraph, 29 June 1970, p. 12a-b
S SADIE 'Bang on ...'
The Times, 29 June 1970, p. 11d
G WIDDICOMBE 'Walton'
The Financial Times, 30 June 1970, p. 3a-b
G WIDDICOMBE 'Walton: Festival Hall'
The Financial Times, 22 October 1970, p.3a-b

IN HONOUR OF THE CITY OF LONDON (C33)
ANON. 'BBC Orchestra: Two significant choral works'
The Times, 2 December 1937, p. 12c
ANON. 'Rossini Mass at Leeds Festival'
The Yorkshire Observer, 7 October 1937, p. 6a-c
A H ASHWORTH 'Success of Leeds Festival'
The Yorkshire Post, 7 October 1937, p. 5b
A H ASHWORTH 'William Walton's Choral Ode'
The Yorkshire Post, 7 October 1937, p. 5b
W McNAUGHT 'London Concerts: Ireland and Walton'
The Musical Times, 79 (January 1938), p. 57
C PALMER Sleeve note for EMI EL 7 49496 4/ CDC 7 49496 2 (1989)
C SPERO 'Cathedral Haze'
Music and Musicians, 11 (September 1962), p. 38
J R WILLIAMS 'Spectacular choral works at Leeds Musical Festival'
The Yorkshire Evening News, 6 October 1937, p. 7c-d

JOHANNESBURG FESTIVAL OVERTURE (C66)
ANON. 'Johannesburg Festival Overture'
Canon, 10 (September 1956), p. 73
ANON. 'London'
Musical Courier, 155, 1 March 1957, p. 31
ANON. 'Sir Malcolm Sargent introduces Festival Overture'
The Cape Argus, 27 September 1956, p. 5b-c
ANON. 'Sir William Walton'
London Musical Events, 11 (September 1956), p. 18
ANON. 'Sir William Walton's new overture'
The Times, 7 July 1956, p. 8e
ANON. 'Three city men are main planners of Rand festival'
The Cape Argus, 6 March 1956, p. 9a-b
M COOPER 'Brilliant New Walton Work'
The Daily Telegraph, 24 January 1957, p. 10d

A C FRANK Sleeve note for COLUMBIA TWO 272 (1969)
C PALMER Sleeve note for CHANDOS CHAN 8968/ ABTD 1560 (1991)
P J PIRIE 'Johannesburg Festival Overture'
Music and Letters, 39 (July 1958), p. 318-319
M ROSE Sleeve note for EMI HQM 1006 (1965)
D RYCROFT 'Melodic Imports and Exports'
British Institute of Recorded Sound Bulletin, 3 (Winter 1956), pp. 19-21
D.L.S. '8 minutes – but they were a big part in city's festival'
The Rand Daily Mail, 26 September 1956, p. 11g-h
R SABIN 'Munch introduces overture by Walton'
Musical America, 77 (April 1957), p. 25

JUBILATE (C87)
H COLE 'Walton's Jubilate in Oxford'
The Guardian, 24 April 1972, p. 8e-f
A C FRANK Sleeve note for ARGO ZRG 725 (1972)
M.J.H. 'Fine performance for composer'
The Oxford Mail, 24 April 1972, p. 8a-c
W MANN 'Walton'
The Times, 25 April 1972, p. 8g-h
G WIDDICOMBE 'Bach and Walton'
The Financial Times, 25 April 1972, p. 3g-h

A LITANY (C1)
A C FRANK Sleeve note for ARGO ZRG 725 (1972)
C TILNEY Sleeve note for ARGO RG 340/ ZRG 340 (1963)

MACBETH (C43)
ANON. 'Macbeth'
Theatre World, XXXVII, September 1942, pp. 9-17
ANON. 'Macbeth'
The Times, 9 July 1942, p. 6b
ANON. 'The Piccadilly: Macbeth'
The Stage, 16 July 1942, p. 5a-b
H.H. 'Mr Gielgud's Macbeth'
The Observer, 12 July 1942, p. 2c
R HAYMAN [Macbeth] *in* 'John Gielgud' London, Heinemann, 1971, pp. 134-138
C PALMER Sleeve note for CHANDOS CHAN 8841/ ABTD 1460 (1991)

MAGNIFICAT AND NUNC DIMITTIS (C91)
W HUSSEY [Magnificat and Nunc Dimittis] *in* 'Patron of Art' London, Weidenfeld and Nicholson, 1985, pp. 132-137
N ROBERTSON Sleeve note for ABBEY LPB 770 (1976)

MAJOR BARBARA (C41)
C PALMER Sleeve note for CHANDOS CHAN 8841/ ABTD 1460 (1991)

MAKE WE JOY NOW IN THIS FEST (C24)
ANON. 'Make we joy'
The Daily Dispatch, 24 December 1931, pp. 1e and 5c-e
A C FRANK Sleeve note for ARGO ZRG 725 (1972)

MEMORIAL FANFARE FOR HENRY WOOD (C48a)
ANON. 'Sir Henry Wood Memorial Concert'
The Times, 5 March 1945, p. 8c
F BONAVIA 'Noble music of three orchestras'
The Daily Telegraph, 5 March 1945, p. 3d
A DICK 'Massed Orchestras pay tribute to Sir Henry Wood'
The Daily Telegraph, 5 March 1945, p. 3c

MISSA BREVIS (C78)
A C FRANK Sleeve note for ARGO ZRG 725 (1972)
D McVEAGH 'Music in London'
The Musical Times, 108 (June 1967), p. 524

MUSIC FOR CHILDREN (C39a)
ANON. 'Music for Children'
Musical America, 69, 1 January 1949, p. 30
ANON. 'Walton's Music for Children'
The Times, 18 February 1941, p. 6e
F BONAVIA 'Walton's new suite'
The Daily Telegraph, 17 February 1941, p. 3c
G CRANKSHAW Sleeve note for LYRITA SRCS 50 (1971)
E MEYERS 'Music for Children'
Notes, 7 (June 1950), p. 450
C PALMER Sleeve note for CHANDOS CHAN 8968/ ABTD 1560 (1991)

THE NEXT OF KIN (C42)
A ALDGATE & J RICHARDS [The Next of Kin] *in* 'Britain can take it'
    Oxford, Blackwell, 1986, pp. 96-114
ANON. 'The Next of Kin'
The Times, 14 May 1942, p. 6e
B CROWTHER [The Next of Kin]
The New York Times, 6 May 1943, p. 7b-c
C A LEJEUNE [The Next of Kin]
The Observer, 17 May 1942, p. 7e
C PALMER Sleeve note for CHANDOS CHAN 8870/ ABTD 1485 (1990)
D POWELL [The Next of Kin]
The Sunday Times, 17 May 1942, p. 2e
J RICHARDS [The Next of Kin] *in* 'Thorold Dickinson: the Man and his
    Films' London, Croom Helm, 1986, pp. 84-108

OBITUARIES
ANON. 'Britsky Skladatel Sir William Walton'
Huderii Razhledy, 36, no 7 (1983), p. 318

ANON. 'De laatste Eer: William Walton'
Mens en Melodie, 38 (April 1983), p. 170
ANON. 'In Memoriam'
Neue Zeitschrift fur Musik, 5 (1983), p. 51
ANON. 'Last Chorus'
Crescendo International, 22 (February-March 1984), p. 25
ANON. 'Milestones: Died. William Walton'
Time, 21 March 1983, p. 82
ANON. 'Music of a master: leader'
The Guardian, 9 March 1983, p. 10d
ANON. 'Music with a purpose: leader'
The Times, 9 March 1983, p. 13a-e
ANON. 'Notiziaro: William Walton (Forio d'Ischia, 8 March 1983)'
Nova Rivista Musicale Italiana, 17 (1983), p. 179
ANON. 'Obituaries'
HiFi/Musical America, 33 (August 1983), p. 40
ANON. 'Obituaries'
Opera News, 48 (September 1983), p. 67
ANON. 'Obituaries: Sir William Walton'
Central Opera Service Bulletin, 25, no 2 (1983), p. 20
ANON. 'Obituaries: Sir William Walton'
Variety, 310, 16 March 1983, p. 196
ANON. 'Obituaries: Sir William Walton'
Ballet News, 5 (July 1983), p. 42
ANON. 'Obituary: Sir William Walton'
The Times, 9 March 1983, p. 14f-h
ANON. 'Sir William, the rebel who wrote for the Queen ... '
The Daily Mail, 9 March 1983, p. 13a-e
ANON. 'Sir William Walton'
Newsweek, 21 March 1983, p. 82
ANON. 'Sir William Walton'
Opera, 34 (May 1983), p. 499
ANON. 'Sir William Walton'
Opera News, 48, no 3 (September 1983), p. 67
ANON. 'Sir William Walton'
Soundboard, 10 (Summer 1983), p. 123
ANON. 'Sir William Walton: 1902-1983'
Instrumentalist, 37 (May 1983), p. 84
ANON. 'Sir William Walton: central figure in modern British music'
The Times, 9 March 1983, p. 14f
ANON. 'Sir William Walton, OM: an obituary'
Performing Right News, no. 17 (September 1983), p. 16
ANON. 'Walton finished ballet score just before his death'
The Daily Telegraph, 9 March 1983, p. 21a-b
ANON. 'William Walton dies at 80'

Billboard, 95, 19 March 1983, p. 70
D BARKER 'Sir William Walton dies at island home'
The Guardian, 9 March 1983, p. 1d-g + 26f
L BELLINGARDI 'William Walton (d. 8 March 1983) - in memoriam'
Nuova Rivista Musicale Italiana, 17, no 1 (1983), p. 179
H COLE 'Walton in Retrospect'
Country Life, 173, 31 March 1983, p. 766
R CRIGHTON 'Obituary: Sir William Walton'
The Financial Times, 9 March 1983, p. 13e-h
B FORD 'Walton's last chord'
The Spectator, 250, 26 March 1983, pp. 18-19
E GREENFIELD 'Distant trumpets'
The Guardian, 9 March 1983, p. 9g-h
E GREENFIELD 'Sir William Walton (1902-1983)'
Gramophone, 60 (May 1983), p. 1244
A K HELLER 'Sir William Walton 1902-1983'
Journal of Church Music, 25 (September 1983), p. 40
J JONES 'Versatile British Composer Sir William Walton dies'
The Los Angeles Times, 102, 9 March 1983, Section I, p. 3
A LAWRENCE 'William Walton: 1902-1983'
Diapason, 74 (May 1983), p. 3
B NORTHCOTT 'William Walton'
The Sunday Telegraph, 13 March 1983, p. 17b-c
D OWENS 'William Walton's musical legacy of pomp - and quiet, lyrical movements'
Christian Science Monitor, 75, 18 March 1983, p. 19
C PALMER 'Sir William Walton: an obituary'
The Musical Times, 124 (May 1983), p. 316
D SHAWE-TAYLOR 'Angry young men in Elgar's line'
The Sunday Times, 13 March 1983, p. 42c-g
M St. 'In Memoriam: William Walton'
Musikhandel, 34 (1983), p. 135
G WIDDICOMBE 'The quiet musician of Ischia'
The Observer, 13 March 1983, p. 7a-e

OLD SIR FAULK (Façade): arr for piano (C12l)
C PALMER Sleeve note for POLYDOR Super 2383 391 (1976)

ORB AND SCEPTRE (C59)
ANON. 'Eighth Coronation Concert'
The Times, 8 June 1953, p. 3f
ANON. 'New Coronation March'
The Times, 13 April 1953, p. 10d
ANON. 'Sir William Walton to write Coronation March'
The Times, 15 December 1952, p. 9c

F V DUNN Sleeve note for EMI CSD 1562 (1964)
T ECKERT 'Elgar and Walton Marches'
Christian Science Monitor, 22 September 1980, p. 18
A C FRANK Sleeve note for COLUMBIA 33C 1016 (1953)
A C FRANK Sleeve note for COLUMBIA TWO 272 (1969)
A C FRANK Sleeve note for EMI ASD 3348 (1977)
A C FRANK Sleeve note for EMI HQM 1006 (1965)
P.K. 'Pops on the March'
Stereo Review (July 1981), pp. 88-89
I KEYS 'Orb and Sceptre'
Music and Letters, 35 (January 1954), p. 76
W MARGRAVE 'Orb and Sceptre, Coronation March, 1953'
Notes, 13 (March 1956), p. 352
H F REDLICH 'New Music: A Critical Interim Report'
Music Review, 16 (August 1955), pp. 264-266

PARTITA (C67)
ANON. 'New work by Sir William Walton'
The Times, 6 December 1957, p. 5e
ANON. 'Sir William Walton: another commission from America'
The Times, 6 December 1956, p. 14d
ANON. 'Sir William Walton's new US commission'
Canon, 10 (January 1957), p. 197
ANON. 'Sir William Walton's new work'
The Musical Times, 99 (January 1958), p. 26
ANON. 'Sir William Walton's Visit'
Canon, 11 (June 1958), p. 332
ANON. 'Walton's new Partita'
The Times, 5 May 1958, p. 5e
C.B. 'Royal Philharmonic Society'
Musical Opinion, 81 (June 1958), p. 569
H ELWELL 'Partita is filled with blasts of colour and sly satire'
The Cleveland Plain Dealer, 31 January 1958, p. 17d-h
A C FRANK Sleeve note for COLUMBIA 33 CX 1816/ SAX 2459 (1962)
N GOODWIN Sleeve note for COLUMBIA 33 CX 1679/ SAX 2319 (1959)
G LEE 'Premiers and Commissions'
Musical Courier, 157 (March 1958), p. 5
B MURRAY 'Cleveland Orchestra's 40th Anniversary'
The Musical Times, 99 (October 1958), p. 559
C PALMER Sleeve note for CHANDOS CHAN 8959/ ABTD 1551 (1991)
R SABIN 'Walton writes brilliant showpiece for orchestra'
Musical America, 78, 15 December 1958, p. 28
M TILLIS [Walton's Partita] *in* 'Chords and Discords' London, Phoenix House, 1960, pp. 128-134

PASSACAGLIA FOR CELLO (C98)

A BLYTH [Passacaglia for cello]
The Daily Telegraph, 18 March 1982, p. 15a
A CLEMENTS [Passacaglia for cello]
The Financial Times, 18 March 1982, p. 21a-b
P GRIFFITHS [Passacaglia for cello]
The Times, 18 March 1982, p. 11f-g
C PALMER Sleeve note for CHANDOS CHAN 8959/ ABTD 1551 (1991)
D SHAWE-TAYLOR [Passacaglia for cello]
The Sunday Times, 21 March 1982, p. 38b
S WALSH [Passacaglia for cello]
The Observer, 21 March 1982, p. 32h-i

PORTSMOUTH POINT (C17)

ANON. 'Contemporary Music: An International Festival'
The Times, 30 June 1926, p. 14b
ANON. 'The Russian Ballet'
The Times, 30 June 1926, p. 14c
R BAGAR and L BIANCOLLI [Portsmouth Point] in 'The Concert Companion' New York, Whittlesey House, 1947, pp. 830-832
W A CHISLETT Sleeve note for LYRITA SRCS 47 (1971)
N DEL MAR 'Confusion and Error'
Score (London) 1 (October 1957), p. 29
A EAGLEFIELD-HULL 'International Festival at Zurich'
Monthly Musical Record, 56 (1926), pp. 227-229
A C FRANK Sleeve note for COLUMBIA 33C 1016 (1953)
A C FRANK Sleeve note for EMI HQM 1006 (1965)
? ISLER 'International Music Festival'
Neue Zurcher Zeitung, 24 June 1926, [p.1]
C PALMER Sleeve note for CHANDOS CHAN 8968/ ABTD 1560 (1991)

PRELUDE AND FUGUE ('THE SPITFIRE') (C45a)

A C FRANK Sleeve note for COLUMBIA TWO 272 (1969)
P.K. 'Digital-space: spectacular music from films'
Stereo Review, (April 1980), p. 141
C PALMER Sleeve note for CHANDOS CHAN 8870/ ABTD 1485 (1990)

PROLOGO E FANTASIA (C100)

ANON. 'Many Happy Returns - Musically'
The Times, 28 January 1982, p. 12a
ANON. 'Prologo e Fantasia'
Symphony Magazine, 33 (1982), p. 130
F APRAHAMIAN [Prologo]
The Sunday Times, 28 February 1982, p. 39b-c
A CLEMENTS [Prologo]
The Observer, 28 February 1982, p. 29b-c

M HARRISON 'NSO/Rostropovich'
The Times, 22 February 1982, p. 7b-d
R HENDERSON [Prologo]
The Daily Telegraph, 22 February 1982, p. 11d-e
R JOSEPH [Prologo]
The Financial Times, 23 February 1982, p. 15a-b
J NAGLEY 'Orchestral'
The Musical Times, 123 (April 1982), p. 275
C PALMER Sleeve note for CHANDOS CHAN 8968/ ABTD 1560 (1991)
P J PIRIE 'Prologo e Fantasia'
The Musical Times, 126 (March 1985), p. 164

QUARTET FOR PIANO AND STRINGS (C7)
ANON. 'Carnegie United Kingdon Trust'
The Music Bulletin, VI (1924), p. 179
ANON. 'London Concerts: Gordon Bryan'
Musical Opinion, 53 (December 1929), p. 230
ANON. 'Recital of the Week'
The Times, 1 November 1929, p. 14d
E BLOM 'Mr Gordon Bryan's Concert'
The Musical Times, 71 (December 1929), pp. 1124-1125

QUARTET FOR STRINGS [NO 1] (C11)
ANON. 'The British Music Society'
The Musical Times, 64 (August 1923), p. 571
ANON. 'Contemporary Music. The Serious Composers'
The Times, 7 July 1923, p.8a
ANON. [First ISCM Festival]
Salzburger Volksblatt, 6 August 1923, p. 3b
ANON. 'International Society for Contemporary Music'
The Music Bulletin, V (July 1923), p. 225
ANON. 'The Salzburg Festival'
The Times, 14 August 1923, p. 11e
ANON. 'Salzburg International Music Festival'
Monthly Musical Record, LIII (October 1923), p. 290
H ANTCLIFFE 'The Congress'
The Music Bulletin, V (July 1923), p. 214
E J DENT 'ISCM: The Salzburg Festival'
The Music Bulletin, V (June 1923), p. 194
A EAGLEFIELD HULL 'The performance and the music at Salzburg'
Musical Opinion, 47 (1923), pp. 52-53
E EVANS 'The Salzburg Festival'
The Musical Times, 64 (September 1923), p. 633
E GREENFIELD [First String Quartet]

Gramophone, 69 (October 1991), p. 137
M KENNEDY 'The silence is ended'
The Daily Telegraph (Weekend), 21 September 1991, p. XXV
W LYLE 'London Concerts and Recitals'
The Musical Standard, XXII, 14 July 1923, p. 10
B NORTHCOTT 'Closet modernist'
The Independent, 31 August 1991, p. 29
H.P. 'London Contemporary Music Centre'
The British Music Bulletin, III (April 1921), p. 96
C PALMER Sleeve note for CHANDOS CHAN 8944/ ABTD 1540 (1991)
'SFORZANDO' 'The British Music Society Congress'
Monthly Musical Record, LIII (August 1923), pp. 226-227
VARIOUS 'ISCM: Letter to the Hon.President'
The Musical Times, 64 (August 1923), p. 549
A WEISSMANN 'The Salzburg Festival'
Musical News and Herald, LXV, 1 September 1923, p. 154

QUARTET FOR STRINGS [NO 2] (C53)
ANON. 'Walton's new quartet: first public performance'
The Times, 6 May 1947, p. 6d
E BRADBURY 'Out of sight - and out of mind'
The Yorkshire Post, 9 July 1968, p. 7e-h
P EVANS Sleeve note for ARGO RG 329/ ZRG 5329 (1964)
W MANN Sleeve note for CHANDOS ABRD 1185 (1986)
C PALMER Sleeve note for CHANDOS CHAN 8944/ ABTD 1540 (1991)
D SHAWE-TAYLOR 'William Walton's New Quartet'
New Statesman and Nation, 33, 10 May 1947, p. 334

THE QUEST (C49)
ANON. 'Sadler's Wells Ballet: The Quest'
The Times, 7 April 1943, p. 6c
C W BEAUMONT [The Quest] *in* 'The Sadler's Wells Ballet' London, Beaumont, 1946, pp. 170-178
D DREW [The Quest] *in* 'The Decca Book of Ballet' London, Muller, 1958, pp. 384-388
E EVANS 'The Music of The Quest'
The Dancing Times, 34 (June 1943), pp. 404-406
E EVANS [The Quest] *in* 'Music and the Dance' London, Jenkins, 1948, pp. 106-108
F HALL [The Quest] *in* 'Modern English Ballet' London, Melrose, 1950, pp. 197 + 202
C PALMER Sleeve note for CHANDOS CHAN 8871/ ABTD 1486 (1990)
D VAUGHAN [The Quest] *in* 'Frederick Ashton and his ballets' London, A & C Black, 1977, pp. 196-200; 428-430

THE QUEST: ORCHESTRAL SUITE (C49a)
ANON. 'First Prom of the Season'
The Times, 23 July 1962, p. 14g
A C FRANK Sleeve note for LYRITA SRCS 49 (1971)

RICHARD III (C63)
ANON. 'Sir Laurence Olivier's film of Richard III'
The Times, 29 May 1954, p. 8d
ANON. 'Richard III on the screen'
The Times, 14 December 1955, p. 5a-b
E CONNOR 'The Sound Track'
Films in Review, 7, no 3 (March 1956), pp. 134-136
H KELLER 'Film music and beyond'
Music Review, 17 (May 1956), pp. 154-156
F LEWIN 'Richard III'
Film and TV Music, 16, no 1 (Fall 1956), pp. 11-13
J LEYDON 'The evil that men do ... '
Film Culture, 2 (1956), pp. 21-23
M MATHIESON Sleeve note for COLUMBIA 33CX 1883/ SAX 2527 (1964)
J A MOORE [Walton's score] *in* 'Richard III: an annotated bibliography' New
   York, Garland Press, 1986
C PALMER Sleeve note for CHANDOS CHAN 8841/ ABTD 1460 (1991
G PRATLEY 'The Sound Track'
Films in Review, 7 (May 1956), pp. 229-231

SALUTE TO THE RED ARMY (C48)
ANON. 'The Warrior City'
The Times, 22 February 1943, p. 4d
B DEAN [Salute to the Red Army] *in* 'Mind's Eye' London, Hutchinson, 1973,
   pp. 283-286
B DEAN [Salute to the Red Army] *in* 'The Theatre at War' London, Harrop,
   1956, pp. 304-310
W GLOCK [Red Army Celebrations]
The Observer, 28 Febraury 1943, p. 2e

SALUTE TO SIR ROBERT MAYER (C97)
P STADLEN [Robert Mayer's 100th Birthday Concert]
The Daily Telegraph, 7 June 1979, p. 15h

SCAPINO (C40)
ANON. 'London Philharmonic Orchestra: Walton's Overture'
The Times, 15 December 1941, p. 8c
ANON. 'Reviews of new music: Scapino'
Musical Opinion, 74 (April 1951), pp. 345 + 347
ANON. 'Scapino, a Comedy Overture'

Canon, 4 (May 1951), p. 505

R BAGAN and L BIANCOLLI [Scapino] *in* 'The Concert Companion' New York, Whittlesey House, 1947, pp. 830-832

E BERRY 'Auditors thrill to intensity of great soprano'
The Chicago Daily Tribune, 4 April 1941, p. 26d

A C FRANK Sleeve note for COLUMBIA TWO 272 (1969)

A C FRANK Sleeve note for LYRITA SRCS 49 (1971)

W McNAUGHT 'London Concerts: Walton's Scapino'
The Musical Times, 83 (1942), p. 28

C PALMER Sleeve note for CHANDOS CHAN 8968/ ABTD 1560 (1991)

E STINSON 'Music Views: The Symphony'
The Chicago Daily News, 4 April 1941, p. 26d-e

SET ME AS A SEAL (C35)

C FRANK Sleeve note for ARGO ZRG 725 (1972)

D LUMSDEN Sleeve note for EMI CLP 3588/ CSD 3588 (1966)

SIESTA (C19)

ANON. 'A Chamber Concert: Mr Guy Warrack's concert'
The Times, 26 November 1926, p. 12a

W A CHISLETT Sleeve note for LYRITA SRCS 47 (1971)

SIESTA: BALLETS (C19c and C19d)

ANON. 'Sadler's Wells Ballet: Walton's Siesta'
The Times, 25 January 1936, p. 8a

ANON. 'Sadler's Wells: Siesta'
The Times, 26 January 1936, p. 13c

ANON. 'Siesta: Frederick Ashton's latest ballet'
About the House, 4, no 1 (1972), pp. 44-45

E NEWMAN 'Sadler's Wells'
The Sunday Times, 26 January 1936, p. 5e

J PERCIVAL 'Siesta'
The Times, 31 July 1972, p. 8d-f

D VAUGHAN [Siesta] *in* 'Frederick Ashton and his Ballets' London, A & C Black, 1977, pp. 380-381

SINFONIA CONCERTANTE (C21)

ANON. [Sinfonia Concertante]
The Times, 7 January 1928, p. 8c

R CAPELL [Sinfonia Concertante]
Monthly Musical Record, LVIII, (February 1928), p. 43

F BONAVIA 'London Concerts'
The Musical Times, 85 (June 1944), p. 189

A C FRANK Sleeve note for LYRITA SRCS 49 (1971)

R HILL [Sinfonia Concertante] *in* 'The Concerto' Harmondsworth, Penguin books, 1962, pp. 389-392

M ? 'William Walton's Sinfonia Concertante'

The Musical Times, 69 (February 1928), p. 165
C PALMER Sleeve note for CONIFER MCFC 175/ CDCF 175 (1989)

A SON OF HEAVEN (C16)
ANON. 'The Scala: The Son of Heaven'
The Stage, 16 July 1925, p. 16b-c
ANON. 'The Son of Heaven'
The Curtain, July 1925, p. 113
ANON. 'The Son of Heaven: Mr Lytton Strachey's play'
The Times, 14 July 1925, p. 12c
M HOLROYD [A Son of Heaven] *in* 'Lytton Strachey : a critical biography,
  volume II'. London, Heinemann, 1968, pp. 508-512
G SIMSON 'Eminent Chinese: Lytton Strachey as dramatic herald from the
  Court of Peking'
Etudes Anglaises, 33, no 4 (1980), pp. 440-452

SONATA FOR STRING ORCHESTRA (C53a)
F APRAHAMIAN 'Bath Festival: 1972'
The Sunday Times, 4 June 1972, p. 37e
A C FRANK Sleeve note for ARGO ZRG 711 (1973)
E GREENFIELD 'England: Davies' Tavener and Festival Highlights'
HiFi/Musical America, 22 (November 1972), pp. 27-28
E GREENFIELD 'Walton first performances at Bath'
The Guardian, 29 May 1972, p. 6e-f
A PORTER 'Bath Festival'
The Financial Times, 31 May 1972, p. 3g-h
S SADIE 'Bath Festival'
The Times, 29 May 1972, p. 5g-h
P STADLEN 'Surprising revision by Walton'
The Daily Telegraph, 29 May 1972, p. 10a
M TANNOCK 'Ensemble displays polished technique'
The Western Australian, 3 March 1972, p. 10
S WALSH 'Bath novelties'
The Observer, 4 June 1972, p. 31e-f
E M WEBSTER 'Bath: Prestige or Parasols'
Musical Opinion, 95 (July 1972), pp. 512 + 521

SONATA FOR VIOLIN AND PIANO (C55)
ANON. 'Current Chronicle - England'
Musical Quarterly, 36 (April 1950), p. 289
ANON. 'Menuhin and Kentner'
The Times, 6 February 1950, p. 4d
ANON. 'New Music: William Walton'
Canon, 4 (August 1950), pp. 42-43
ANON. 'Sonata for Violin and Piano'
Musical Opinion, 73 (July 1950), p. 587

ANON. 'Sonata for Violin and Piano'
Strad, 61 (September 1950), p. 172
ANON. 'Sonata for Violin and Piano'
Musical Courier, 143, no 5, 1 March 1951, p. 27
ANON. 'William Walton's new Violin and Piano Sonata'
Canon, 3 (June 1950), p. 668
R CAPELL 'The new Walton Violin Sonata'
The Daily Telegraph, 6 February 1950, p. 5c
M COOPER 'Walton's Violin Sonata'
The Spectator, 10 February 1950, p. 178
R FISKE 'Walton: Sonata for Violin and Piano'
American Record Guide, (July 1984), pp. 27-28
H J FOSS 'William Walton's Violin Sonata'
Making Music, no 17 (Autumn 1951), pp. 9-11
S GODDARD 'Walton's Sonata for Violin and Piano'
The Chesterian, XXIV (April 1950), pp. 96-98
B HARVEY 'Walton Violin Sonata: A Comparative Record Review'
Strad, 94 (1984), pp. 890-891
B JACOBSON 'British Music: the pastoral tradition'
Stereo Review, 43 (September 1979), p. 108
H KELLER 'First performances: Their Pre- and Reviews'
Music Review, 11 (May 1950), pp. 146-150
E LOCKSPEISER 'Sonata for Violin and Piano'
Musical America, 70 (April 1950), p. 6
C MASON [Walton's Sonata for Violin and Piano] in 'Cobbett's Cyclopedic
Survey of Chamber Music, volume iii' London, Oxford Uinversity Press,
1963 (2nd ed), pp. 86-87
H MURRILL 'Walton's Violin Sonata'
Music and Letters, XXXI (July 1950), pp. 208-215
A NOTCUTT 'London greets new scores and debuts in concerts and operas'
Musical Courier, 141, 1 April 1950, p. 6
R.S. 'New Music Reviews: Walton's Sonata for Violin published'
Musical America, 71 (August 1951), p. 30
D SHAWE-TAYLOR 'Walton's Violin Sonata'
The New Statesman, XXXIX, 11 February 1950, p. 159
M B STANFIELD 'Silhouettes from Britain'
Violins and Violinists, 11 (March-April 1950), pp. 98-99
W VON SCHUH 'Konzerte'
Neue Zurcher Zeitung, 5 October 1949

A SONG FOR THE LORD MAYOR'S TABLE (C74)
ANON. 'New works at the Festival of the City of London'
Musical Events, 17 (July 1962), p. 15
ANON. 'Schwarzkopf sings for the Lord Mayor'
The Times, 19 July 1962, p. 7a-b

ANON. 'Writing music for City Festival'
The Times, 26 January 1962, p. 16d
M COOPER 'Great Britain: A Welter of Music'
Musical America, 82 (September 1962), pp. 96-97
L DUNLOP 'Civic Junketings'
Musical Events, 17 (September 1962), pp. 12ff
N GOODWIN 'London: City Festival and Cheltenham'
Musical Magazine, 164 (September 1962), p. 36
N GOODWIN Sleeve note for L'OISEAU-LYRE SOL 331 (1972)
N KAY 'City of London Festival'
The Musical Times, 103 (September 1962), pp. 615-616
M MARCUS 'Walton and Schwarzkopf'
Music and Musicians, 11 (September 1962), p. 41
E MASON 'Music in Concert: The Lord Mayor's Table'
Choir, 53 (October 1962), p. 176
G MONTAGUE 'Festival of the City of London'
Musical Opinion, 85 (September 1962), pp. 711-712
P J PIRIE 'Broadcasting'
The Musical Times, 104 (April 1963), p. 268

– ORCHESTRAL VERSION (C74a)
E GREENFIELD 'Festivals at Aldeburgh, London, Glyndebourne'
HiFi/Musical America, 20 (October 1970), pp. 27 + 31
E GREENFIELD [A Song for the Lord Mayor's Table]
The Guardian, 8 July 1970, p. 8c-d
C PALMER Sleeve note for CHANDOS CHAN 8824/ ABTD 1449 (1990)
A E PAYNE 'Walton's Lord Mayor's Table transformed'
The Daily Telegraph, 8 July 1970, p. 14a
S SADIE 'City of London'
The Musical Times, 111 (September 1970), p. 912
S SADIE 'Orchestral Songs'
The Times, 8 July 1970, p. 13f
G WIDDICOMBE 'Janet Baker'
The Financial Times, 9 July 1970, p. 3a-b

SYMPHONY NO 1 (C27)
ANON. 'Concerts and *Opera*'
Monthly Musical Record, 65 (1935), p. 13
ANON. [Unfinished Symphony]
Monthly Musical Record, 65 (January 1935), p. 13
ANON. [Walton's completed symphony]
Monthly Musical Record, 65 (December 1935), p. 229
ANON. 'William Walton's Symphony'
The Times, 5 September 1935, p. 10b
ANON. 'William Walton's Symphony: first performance of complete work'

The Times, 7 November 1935, p. 12b

ANON. 'William Walton's Symphony completed: composer hears his last
  movement played'
The Oldham Chronicle, 7 September 1935, p. 7a-b

R CAPELL 'The complete symphony: William Walton's inspiring work'
The Daily Telegraph, 7 November 1935, p. 12e

R CAPELL 'William Walton's First Symphony'
The Listener, XIV, 30 October 1935, p. 781

N CARDUS 'The BBC Concert: William Walton's first symphony'
The Manchester Guardian, 7 November 1935, p. 6d

M COOPER 'William Walton's Symphony'
The London Mercury, 33 (January 1936), p. 325

R CORNFORD-WOOD 'Walton's First Symphony'
Classic CD, no 5 (September 1990), pp. 62-63

T ECKERT 'Neglected delight: Walton's first symphony'
Christian Science Monitor, 11 August 1981, p. 19

E EVANS 'Unique world première for a new symphony'
Radio Times, 49, 1 November 1935, p. 15

W FLANAGAN 'Walton's exuberant first symphony'
HiFi/Stereo Review, 18 (April 1967), pp. 70-71

H J FOSS Sleeve note for GRAMOPHONE CO. ALP 1027 (1953)

H J FOSS and N GOODWIN [Walton's First Symphony] *in* 'London Symphony: portrait of an orchestra' London Naldrett Press, 1954, pp. 145-146

R GUILLAMORE Sleeve note for NIXA NCL 16020 (1957)

H HELM 'Letters to the Editor: Walton I'
The Musical Times, 115 (February 1979), pp. 128-129

R HILL [Walton's First Symphony] *in* 'Music 1951' Harmondsworth, Penguin
  Books Ltd., 1951, pp. 128-133

H HUGHES 'Mr Walton's unfinished symphony'
The Saturday Review, 158, 8 December 1935, p. 508

D HUSSEY 'Mr Walton's First Symphony'
The Spectator, 153, 7 December 1934, p. 877

A J B HUTCHINGS 'The Symphony and William Walton'
The Musical Times, 78 (March 1937), pp. 211-215

C LAMBERT 'Walton's Symphony is really good music'
The Sunday Referee, 10 November 1935, p. 20c

T W LIBBEY 'Dutch Maestro's varied musical vistas'
The New York Times, 22 August 1982, Section 2, p. H21

K McINTYRE 'Waxing Eloquent'
Canon, 4 (June 1951), pp. 549-552

B MAINE 'Historic night for British music'
The Yorkshire Post, 7 November 1935, p. 3d

B MAINE [Walton's First Symphony] *in* 'New Paths in Music' London,
  Nelson, 1940, pp. 39-42, 128-129

E NEWMAN 'William Walton's symphony'

The Sunday Times, 10 November 1935, p. 5b-c
H OTTAWAY 'Walton and the Symphony'
Hallé, no 64 (December 1953), pp. 6-9
H OTTAWAY 'Walton's First and its composition'
The Musical Times, 114 (October 1973), pp. 998-999 + 1001
H OTTAWAY 'Walton's First Symphony: the composition of the finale'
The Musical Times, 113 (March 1972), pp. 254-257
C PALMER Sleeve note for CHANDOS CHAN 8862/ ABTD 1477 (1991)
M PEARTON [Walton's First Symphony] in 'The LSO at 70' London, Gollancz, 1974, pp. 86, 103, 106-107, 153
H RAYNOR 'Some aspects of the 20th century symphony'
The Chesterian, 29 (October 1954), pp. 32-33
S SADIE 'Music Survey: Wilhelm Backhaus'
Musical Events, 16 (June 1961), pp. 27 + 29
B SHORE [Walton's First] in 'Sixteen Symphonies' London, Longman, Green & Co., 1949, pp. 353, 366-387
R SIMPSON [Walton's First] in 'The Symphony: Volume II' Harmondsworth, Penguin Books, 1967, pp. 189-196
P TUROK 'England's modern composers sound a timeless note'
The New York Times, 26 January 1986, Section 2, p. 26
G WIDDICOMBE 'Leningrad concerts'
The Financial Times, 27 April 1971, p. 3c-f
P M YOUNG [Walton's First Symphony] in 'Phoenix Music Guides: 2 - Symphony' London, Phoenix House Ltd., 1957, pp. 58-60

SYMPHONY NO 2 (C68)
ANON. 'New Walton Symphony delayed'
The Times, 25 October 1958, p. 4d
ANON. 'Second Symphony for (1960) Edinburgh Festival'
The Times, 25 August 1959, p. 11a
ANON. 'Sir William Walton's new symphony'
The Times, 15 November 1955, p. 12e
ANON. 'Walton's Second Symphony'
The Times, 3 September 1960, p. 9a
F APRAHAMIAN 'Walton and his New Symphony'
The Listener, LXIV, 25 August 1960, p. 321
J.B. 'Hallé Concerts 1961-1962'
Music Review, 23, no 3 (1962), p. 249
D CAIRNS 'Symphonic Variations'
The Spectator, 9 September 1960, pp. 374 + 376
N CARDUS 'Music in Edinburgh: Walton's Second Symphony'
The Guardian, 3 September 1960, p. 3a-b
J CHARLES 'Sir William's Second Symphony'
Musical Events, 15 (October 1960), pp. 14-15
P.D. 'Szell gives Walton's Second Symphony'

Musical Courier, 163 (March 1961), p. 6
J DIETHER 'After 25 years, Walton's second'
American Record Guide, 28 (April 1962), pp. 658-661
R ELKIN 'Walton's Second Symphony'
The Musical Times, 102 (January 1961), p. 38
A C FRANK Sleeve note for COLUMBIA 33 CX 1816/ SAX 2459 (1962)
S GODDARD 'London Letter'
The Chesterian, 35, no 204 (1960), p. 58
N GOODWIN 'The Edinburgh Festival'
The Musical Times, 101 (October 1960), p. 644
N GOODWIN 'Edinburgh Festival plans new opera house'
Musical Courier, 162 (October 1960), p. 26
G GRIER 'The Edinburgh Festival'
Musical Events, 15 (October 1960), p. 9
C GRIER 'Two new British Symphonies'
Canon, 14 (September-October 1960), pp. 47-48
P HEYWORTH 'Russians in Scotland'
The New York Times, 109, 11 September 1960, Section 2, p. 19
F HRUBY 'New Walton work'
Musical America, 81 (February 1961), p. 20
A J B HUTCHINGS 'Symphony No 2'
Music and Letters, 42, no 2 (1961), pp. 181-183
D JAKSIC 'Contemporary music at Edinburgh'
Zvuk, 41-42 (1960), pp. 72-73
I KOLODIN 'Music to my ears'
The Saturday Review, 44, 18 February 1961, p. 32
D MITCHELL 'Walton's Second Symphony looks back'
The Daily Telegraph, 3 September 1960, p. 8c
R H MYERS 'British Music'
Canon, 14 (January-February 1961), pp. 107ff
C PALMER Sleeve note for CHANDOS CHAN 8772/ ABTD 1410 (1990)
R SABIB 'Annie Fischer heard with Cleveland Orchestra'
Musical America, 81 (March 1961), p. 38
S SADIE 'Music Survey'
Musical Events, 16 (January 1961), p. 16
R WOODHAM 'Walton's Second Symphony'
The Music Review, 22 (August 1961), pp. 251-253
R WIDDER 'Walton and Blackwood works bow in Cleveland'
Musical Courier, 163 (February 1961), pp. 20-21 + 28

THEME FOR CELLO (C85)
ANON. [Music for a Prince]
Performing Right, no 54 (1970), pp. 11-12
PETERBOROUGH [Music for a Prince]
The Daily Telegraph, 20 April 1985, p. 16

THEME FOR ORGAN IMPROVISATIONS (no C number alloted)
D MITCHELL AND P REED (eds) [Theme for Organ Improvisations] *in* 'Letters from a Life: selected letters and diaries of Benjamin Britten' Volume 1. London, Faber and Faber, 1991, p. 441

THREE SISTERS (C83 – no C number allocated to the suite)
C PALMER Sleeve note for CHANDOS CHAN 8870/ ABTD 1485 (1990)

THREE SONGS (1932) (C26)
ANON. 'The Music Society'
The Times, 14 October 1932, p. 10b
N GOODWIN Sleeve note for L'OISEAU-LYRE SOL 331 (1972)
D HUSSEY 'Miss Dora Stevens'
The Musical Times, 73 (November 1932), p. 1036
S NORTHCOTE [Three Songs] *in* 'Byrd to Britten' London, Baker, 1966, p. 110

TOCCATA FOR VIOLIN AND PIANO (C13)
ANON. 'Contemporary Music Centre'
The Times, 15 May 1925, p. 14b

TRITONS (C8)
E BLOM 'Mr Gordon Bryan's Concert'
The Musical Times, 71 (1929), pp. 1124-1125

TROILUS AND CRESSIDA (C62)
ANON. 'Death at the End'
Newsweek, 44, 13 December 1954, p. 90
ANON. 'Editor's Notes (divided opinions)'
The Musical Times, 96 (February 1955), pp. 69-70
ANON. 'Editorial'
London Musical Events, 10 (February 1955), p. 7
ANON. 'Golden Gate Première'
Newsweek, 46, 17 October 1955, p. 102
ANON. 'Inside stuff-concerts'
Variety, 200, 12 October 1955, p. 76
ANON. 'Italian critics on Walton's opera'
The Times, 14 January 1956, p. 8d
ANON. 'Late-Blooming Prodigy'
Time, 62, 17 August 1953, pp. 56 + 58
ANON. 'A new British opera'
The Illustrated London News, 225, 11 December 1954, p. 1047
ANON. 'New opera in Manhattan'
Time, 66, 31 October 1955, p. 40
ANON. 'New Walton opera'

The Times, 29 January 1948, p. 6e
ANON. 'Preview of Walton's new opera'
The Times, 1 December 1954, p. 4d
ANON. 'Proudest Hour?'
Time, 64, 13 December 1954, p. 50
ANON. 'Royal Opera House'
The Times, 4 December 1954, p. 8d
ANON. 'Royal Opera House: Troilus and Cressida'
The Times, 21 December 1955, p. 10d
ANON. 'San Francisco'
Musical Courier, 152, 1 November 1955, p. 29
ANON. 'Sir William Walton's first opera'
The Times, 27 October 1954, p. 9b
ANON. 'Troilus and Cressida'
London Musical Events, 11 (February 1950), p. 52
ANON. 'Troilus and Cressida'
Musical Opinion, 78 (February 1956), p. 285
ANON. [Troilus and Cressida]
The Times, 30 August 1951, p. 8b
ANON. 'Troilus and Cressida as an opera'
The Times, 9 February 1954, p. 8d
ANON. 'Troilus and Cressida: opera by Sir William Walton'
The Times, 28 August 1951, p. 6c
ANON. 'Walton's opera: a parallel with Wagner'
The Times, 10 December 1954, p. 10a
ANON. 'Walton's opera: a personal style'
The Times, 30 December 1955, p. 3a
ANON. 'Walton's Troilus at La Scala'
The Times, 13 January 1956, p. 3f
F G BARKER 'Walton's Troilus and Cressida'
Opera News, 19, 27 December 1954, p. 10
H S BLANKS 'Music in England'
Canon, 8 (March 1955), pp. 332-333
A BLYTH 'Troilus simplified'
The Times, 13 November 1976, p. 9e-g
D BOYDEN 'Current chronicle: England'
Musical Quarterly, 41 (April 1955), pp. 238-241
E BRADBURY 'Troilus and Cressida'
Music and Letters, 37 (July 1956), p. 307
P DRAGADZE 'Troilus and Cressida given cold welcome in Milan'
Musical America, 76 (March 1956), pp. 7-8
R EYER 'Troilus and Cressida – East and West'
Musical America, 75 (November 1955), pp. 3 + 15
C FIELD 'Troilus and Cressida'
Notes, 39, no 1 (September 1982), pp. 222-224

J W FREEMAN 'Walton: Troilus and Cressida'
Opera News, 44, no 20, 19 April 1980, p. 21
P GARVIE 'Walton's Troilus and Cressida'
The Canadian Music Journal, 1 (Winter 1957), pp. 3-9
S GODDARD 'London Letter'
The Chesterian, 29 (January 1955), pp. 88-89
V HAIGH 'Adelaide'
Opera, 15 (July 1964), p. 461
C HASSALL 'And now – Walton's first opera'
Music and Musicians, 3 (December 1954), p. 12
C HASSALL [Troilus and Cressida]
Radio Times, 26 November 1954, p. 5
H W HENZE 'William Walton's new song of Troy'
Center, 2, no 4 (October 1955), pp. 2-6
J HINTON 'Troilus and Cressida in New York'
Opera, 7 (January 1956), pp. 29-33
P HOPE-WALLACE 'A new opera in the old and honoured tradition'
The Manchester Guardian, 4 December 1954, p. 3f-g
F HOWES 'Universal appeal of Sir William Walton's first opera'
Etude, 73 (May 1955), p. 11ff
D HUSSEY 'Walton's Troilus and Cressida'
Music and Letters, XXXVI (April 1955), pp. 139-145
H KELLER 'The half-year's new music'
Music Review, 16 (February 1955), pp. 62-63
J KERMAN 'Troy at the Golden Gate'
Opera News, 20, 30 October 1955, pp. 6-7f
J W KLEIN 'The decade of English opera'
Musical Opinion, 79 (January 1956), pp. 211 + 213
I KOLODIN 'Britten's Eighth, Walton's First'
The Saturday Review, 38, 12 November 1955, p. 36
H W LEVINGER 'The New York Concert and Opera Beat'
Musical Courier, 152, 15 November 1955, pp. 8-9
M MILA 'Reports from Abroad: Walton's Troilus and Cressida in Milan'
Melos, 23 (April 1956), pp. 117-118
D MITCHELL 'Revaluations: IV. William Walton'
Musical Opinion, 78 (June 1955), pp. 539 + 541
D MITCHELL 'Troilus and Cressida: Opera in London'
The Musical Times, 96 (January 1955), pp. 36-37
D MITCHELL 'Troilus and Cressida: two further opinions'
Opera, 6 (February 1955), pp. 88-93
G MONTAGUE 'Walton's Troilus and Cressida at Covent Garden'
London Musical Events, 10 (January 1955), pp. 20-21
A NOTCUTT 'Four new British operas'
Musical Courier, 51 (June 1955), p. 18
A NOTCUTT 'London'

Musical Courier, 51 (January 1955), p. 29

C PALMER Sleeve notes for EMI EL 27 0591 1/ EL 27 0591 4/CDC 7 47944 2 (1987)

M PANTER-DOWNES 'Letter from London'
The New Yorker, 30, 25 December 1954, p. 62

P PARMENTER 'Troilus and Cressida may be heard in New York and Cincinnati'
The New York Times, 104, 26 December 1954, Section 2, p. 9

R PARMENTER 'The World of Music: new opera by Walton'
The New York Times, 103, 1 August 1954, Section 2, p. 7

H RAYNOR 'Tradition and Innovation'
Monthly Musical Record, 85 (October 1955), pp. 207-209

H F REDLICH 'New British operas'
The Chesterian, 29 (April 1955), pp. 111-113

H F REDLICH 'New Music'
Music Review, 17 (August 1956), pp. 259-260

H F REDLICH [Walton's Troilus and Cressida at Covent Garden]
Die Musikleben, 8 (February 1955), pp. 60-61

F REIZENSTEIN 'Walton's Troilus and Cressida'
Tempo, no 34 (Winter 1954-1955), pp. 16-27

H ROSENTHAL 'Covent Garden Opera'
Musical Opinion, 78 (January 1955), p. 203

H ROSENTHAL [Troilus and Cressida] in 'Two Centuries of opera at Covent Garden' London, Putman, 1958, pp. 644-645

C.S. 'Covent Garden'
Opera, 6 (January 1955), pp. 58-59

W SARGEANT 'Near Miss'
The New Yorker, 7 April 1956, p. 140

W SARGEANT 'Troilus and Cressida'
The New Yorker, 29 October 1955, pp. 146-147

D SHAWE-TAYLOR 'Troilus and Cressida'
The New Statesman, 48, 11 December 1954, pp. 782-784

A SKULSKY 'Opera, 1954'
The Juilliard Review, 2 (Winter 1955), pp. 40-41

C SMITH 'Walton's Opera ... '
Musical America, 75 (January 1955), p. 5

W VON EINSIEDEL 'Troilus and Cressida: letter to the Times'
The Times, 17 December 1954, p. 9e

W WALTON and C HASSALL Sleeve notes for COLUMBIA 33 CX 1313 (1955)

J WARRACK 'Walton's Troilus and Cressida'
The Musical Times, 95 (December 1954), pp. 646-649

J WARRACK 'Walton's Troilus and Cressida'
Opera, 5 (December 1954), pp. 724-729

M WEBSTER 'Notes on the Production'

Center, 2, no 4 (October 1955), pp. 6-7
S WILLIAMS 'Walton opera a hit in London'
The New York Times, 104, 19 December 1954, Section II, p. 9

– 1963 Revival
ANON. 'Cressida seen as romantic heroine'
The Times, 24 April 1963, p. 15c-d
F G BARKER 'Troilus Revisited'
Music and Musicians, 11 (June 1963), pp. 37-38
E CHAPMAN 'Walton's Troilus again'
Musical Events, 18 (July 1963), p. 26
D DREW 'Troilus, Diavolo'
The New Statesman, LXV, 3 May 1963, p. 688
F S HOWES 'Walton's opera'
The Listener, LXIX, 25 April 1963, p. 727
A JACOBS 'Covent Garden'
Opera, 14 (June 1963), pp. 419-421
J W KLEIN 'Walton's Troilus and Cressida'
Musical Opinion, 86 (May 1963), p. 467
W WALTON [Troilus and Cressida]
About the House, 1, no 3 (1963), p. 30

– 1976 Revival
J BARKER [Troilus and Cressida]
Opera, 27 (1976), pp. 991-996
A BLYTH [Troilus and Cressida]
Gramophone, 54 (1977), p. 1599
A BLYTH [Troilus and Cressida]
The Times, 13 November 1976, p. 9e-g
E BRADBURY [Troilus and Cressida]
The Yorkshire Post, 15 November 1976, p. 3b-d
R CRIGHTON [Troilus and Cressida]
The Financial Times, 15 November 1976, p. 3e-h
W DEAN [Troilus and Cressida]
The Musical Times, 118 (1977), p. 55
M GREENHALGH [Troilus and Cressida]
Records and Recordings, 20 (1977), pp. 20-22
P HEYWORTH [Troilus and Cressida]
The Observer, 21 November 1976, p. 30b-f
P HOPE-WALLACE [Troilus and Cressida]
The Guardian, 15 November 1976, p. 8f
M KENNEDY [Troilus and Cressida]
About the House, 5 (1976), pp. 38-39 and 41
W MANN [Troilus and Cressida]
The Times, 15 November 1976, p. 12d-f

H OTTAWAY [Troilus and Cressida]
HiFi News and Record Review, 22 (1977), p. 115
H ROSENTHAL [Troilus and Cressida]
Opera, 28 (1977), pp. 101-103
D SHAWE-TAYLOR [Troilus and Cressida]
The Sunday Times, 21 November 1976, p. 39e-g
T SUTCLIFFE [Troilus and Cressida]
Classical Music Weekly, 20 November 1976, p. 12
G WIDDICOMBE Sleeve note for EMI SLS 997 (1977)
G WIDDICOMBE [Troilus and Cressida]
Music and Musicians, 25 (1976), pp. 43-35

– **Symphonic Suite** (C62a)
M BOWEN 'Fire, water and earth'
The Guardian, 5 August 1988, p. 24a-b
B MILLINGTON 'Outline Walton'
The Times, 5 August 1988, p. 19g
G NORRIS 'Mixed delights'
The Daily Telegraph, 5 August 1988, p. 12a-c
C PALMER Sleeve note for CHANDOS CHAN 8772/ ABTD 1410 (1990)
M J WHITE 'An opera in search of singers'
The Independent, 5 August 1988, p. 18c-e

THE TWELVE (C77)
A C FRANK Sleeve note for ARGO ZRG 725 (1972)
A WOOD 'Oxford Anthem'
The Oxford Mail, 15 May 1965, p. 4f

THE TWELVE: ORCHESTRAL VERSION (C77a)
ANON. 'Walton anthem with words by Auden'
The Times, 3 January 1966, p. 5e
E CHAPMAN 'Music Survey: New Walton anthem'
Musical Events, 21 (February 1966), p. 31
M COOPER [The Twelve]
The Daily Telegraph, 3 January 1966, p. 15a
E GREENFIELD [The Twelve]
The Guardian, 3 January 1966, p. 7f
C PALMER Sleeve note for CHANDOS CHAN 8824/ ABTD 1449 (1990)
A PORTER 'Westminster Abbey Celebration'
The Musical Times, 107 (February 1966), p. 134-135
K L THOMPSON 'Radio in Retrospect'
Musical Opinion, 89 (February 1966), p. 285

TWO PIECES FOR VIOLIN AND PIANO (C56)
ANON. 'Two Pieces for Violin and Piano'
Musical Opinion, 74 (May 1951), p. 409

ANON. 'Two Pieces for Violin and Piano'
Music Survey, 3 (June 1951), p. 290
J.S.W. 'Two Pieces for Violin and Piano'
Music Review, 13 (August 1952), p. 248
E.L. 'David Davis ... violinist'
Musical America, 76 (March 1956), p. 27

VARIATION ON SELLINGER'S ROUND (C61)
'DIAPASON' 'Aldeburgh Festival's notable attractions'
The East Anglian Daily Times, 22 June 1953, p. 7a-b
D MITCHELL [Variation on Sellinger's Round]
The Musical Times, 94 (August 1953), p. 376

VARIATIONS ON A THEME BY HINDEMITH (C76)
ANON. 'Walton's new music for a birthday'
The Times, 9 March 1963, p. 4a-b
ANON. 'Walton's Variations on a theme by Hindemith'
Musical Events, 18 (March 1963), p. 21
E CHAPMAN 'Royal Philharmonic Society'
Musical Events, 18 (April 1963), p. 26
M COOPER 'Walton's new ideas from Hindemith'
The Daily Telegraph, 9 March 1963, p. 10e
J H ELLIOT 'Philharmonic Anniversary Concert'
The Guardian, 9 March 1963, p. 5b-d
A C FRANK Sleeve note for COLUMBIA 33 CX 1935/ SAX 2576 (1965)
N GOODWIN 'Walton's Variations on a Theme by Hindemith'
Tempo, no 64 (Spring 1963), pp. 33-34
F HRUBY 'Ohio'
Musical America, 83 (June 1963), p. 12
L HUGHES-JONES 'Sesquicentenary'
Music and Musicians, 11 (March 1963), pp. 41-42
L HUGHES-JONES 'Walton varies Hindemith'
Music and Musicians, 12 (July 1964), p. 39
C MASON 'The Music of Sir William Walton'
Canon, 16 (June 1963), pp. 7-8
D MITCHELL [Hindemith Variations]
The Daily Telegraph, 9 March 1963, p. 10e
A PORTER 'Walton's Variations'
The Musical Times, 104 (April 1963), p. 265
A.W. 'Walton's Night'
Musical Opinion, 86 (May 1963), p. 456

VARII CAPRICCI (C86a)
A BLYTH [Varii Capricci]
The Times, 6 May 1976, p. 14g
M COOPER 'LSO at best with Stravinsky rarity'

The Daily Telegraph, 5 May 1976, p. 13e-f
E GREENFIELD [Varii Capricci]
The Guardian, 5 May 1976, p. 13d-e
P GRIFFITHS [Varii Capricci]
The Financial Times, 6 May 1976, p. 3g-h
P GRIFFITHS [Varii Capricci]
The Musical Times, 117 (June 1976), p. 589
C PALMER Sleeve note for CHANDOS CHAN 8862/ ABTD 1477
D SHAWE-TAYLOR 'Silver Sound'
The Daily Telegraph, 9 May 1976, p. 38g

VARII CAPRICCI: BALLET (C86b)
J ANDERSON [Varii Capricci]
The Dancing Times, 72 (June 1983), pp. 697-698
A CROCE 'Dancing: loyal to the Royal'
The New Yorker, 9 May 1983, p. 102
D DOUGILL [Varii Capricci]
The Sunday Times, 24 July 1983, p. 39c-d
N GOLDNER 'A small-scale, jokey dance from the Royal Ballet's Frederick
  Ashton'
Christian Science Monitor, 28 April 1983, p. 17
D HARRIS [Varii Capricci]
The Guardian, 22 April 1983, p. 11a-h
J KAVANAGH [Varii Capricci]
The Times, 22 April 1983, p. 15a-f
A KESSELGOFF 'Varii Capricci'
About the House, 6 (1983), pp. 36-37
A MACAULEY [Varii Capricci]
The Dancing Times, 72 (September 1983), pp. 935-936
A NUGENT 'Old Friends, New Friends'
Dance and Dancers, no 406, October 1983, pp. 15-16
J PARRY [Varii Capricci]
The Observer, 24 July 1983, p. 26a-c
J PERCIVAL [Varii Capricci]
The Times, 21 July 1983, p. 7a-d
D VAUGHAN [Varii Capricci]
The Financial Times, 26 April 1983, p. 12a-e
M WALSH 'An affair to remember'
Time, 2 May 1983, p. 79

WENT THE DAY WELL? (C47)
ANON. 'The Battle of Bramley End'
The Times, 29 October 1942, p. 6d
ANON. 'Went the day well?
Kinematographic Weekly, 308, 29 October 1942, p. 6

C PALMER Sleeve note for CHANDOS CHAN 8870/ ABTD 1485 (1990)
W WHITEBAIT 'Went the day well?'
The New Stateman, XXIV, 31 October 1942, p. 288

WHAT CHEER? (C73)
A C FRANK Sleeve note for ARGO ZRG 725 (1972)

WHERE DOES THE UTTERED MUSIC GO? (C52)
ANON. 'Our London Correspondence: Henry Wood Memorial'
The Manchester Guardian, 27 April 1946, p. 4d-e
ANON. 'Sir Henry Wood: Memorial Window unveiled'
The Times, 27 April 1946, p. 3a
A C FRANK Sleeve note for ARGO ZRG 725 (1972)
D.G. 'A Henry Wood Window'
The Musical Times, 87 (May 1946), p. 156

THE WINDS (C6)
ANON. [The Winds]
The Times, 1 November 1929, p. 14d
E BLOM 'Mr Gordon Bryan's Concert'
The Musical Times, 71 (December 1929), pp. 1124-1125

THE WISE VIRGINS (C38)
ANON. 'Sadler's Wells Ballet: The Wise Virgins'
The Times, 25 April 1940, p. 4e
ANON. [The Wise Virgins]
The Dancing Times, no 356 (May 1940), p. 464
C W BEAUMONT [The Wise Virgins] *in* 'The Sadler's Wells Ballet' London,
Beaumont, 1946, pp. 161-167
D DREW [The Wise Virgins] *in* 'The Decca Book of Ballet' London, Muller,
1958, pp. 56-57
A C FRANK Sleeve note for COLUMBIA 33 C 1016 (1953)
D HUSSEY 'Ballet: return to Sadler's Wells'
The Spectator, 164, 21 June 1940, p. 837
I KOLODIN Sleeve note for CAPITOL P 8583/ SP 8583 (1962)
W McNAUGHT 'The Wise Virgins'
The Musical Times, 81 (June 1940), pp. 278-279
H OTTAWAY Sleeve note for EMI ASD 3317 (1977)
C PALMER Sleeve note for CHANDOS CHAN 8871/ ABTD 1486 (1990)
D VAUGHAN [The Wise Virgins] *in* 'Frederick Ashton and his Ballets'
London, A & C Black, 1977, pp. 183-186 and 473

General Index

This index contains personal and other names which appear in the chronology and the sections on manuscripts, letters and recordings. Only works mentioned in the bibliography are indexed.